RECONSTRUCTING THE FEDERAL BUDGET

RECONSTRUCTING THE FEDERAL BUDGET

A Trillion Dollar Quandary

Edited by
Albert T. Sommers

PRAEGER

PRAEGER SPECIAL STUDIES • PRAEGER SCIENTIFIC

New York • Philadelphia • Eastbourne, UK
Toronto • Hong Kong • Tokyo • Sydney

Library of Congress Cataloging in Publication Data
Main entry under title:

Reconstructing the federal budget.

Includes index.
1. Budget—United States—Addresses, essays, lec-
tures. I. Sommers, Albert T.
HJ2051.R417 1984   353.0072′2   83-23801
ISBN 0-03-068902-3 (alk. paper)

Published in 1984 by Praeger Publishers
CBS Educational and Professional Publishing,
a Division of CBS Inc.
521 Fifth Avenue, New York, NY 10175 USA

©1984 by Praeger Publishers

456789 052 9876545321

Printed in the United States of America
on acid-free paper

PREFACE

There is no larger challenge facing the U.S. economy in the early 1980s than to reimpose order in its federal budget. The conclusion is widely accepted that the present and prospective condition of the budget, particularly with reference to the prospective course of the budget deficit, has produced reactions in the U.S. capital market, and even in international capital markets, that threaten to compromise the nation's prospects for long-term growth in its investment, for improvement in its efficiency, and for its ability to deal with a range of serious social problems.

In response to this challenge, The Conference Board invited a dozen preeminent economists, representing the academic, business, and governmental wings of the profession, to consider the basic practical and conceptual issues surrounding federal budgeting. Their essays, organized here into four basic themes, comprise the bulk of this volume. They are preceded by a summary essay that explores the areas of agreement and disagreement among them, and seeks to identify the crucial issues on which conclusions must be reached and acted upon if the U.S. budgetary performance is to make its necessary contribution to balanced, vigorous, noninflationary economic growth in the 1980s.

This project was conceived and directed by Albert T. Sommers, the Board's chief economist, who edited the papers and is the author of the summary chapter. He was assisted by Vincent Massaro and Lucie R. Blau. Lillian W. Kay edited the entire manuscript for publication. The Board is also indebted to Elmer B. Staats, former Comptroller General, and Rudolph G. Penner, of the American Enterprise Institute, who served as consultants to the project.

I take this opportunity to express the gratitude of The Conference Board and its trustees to the following organizations, which provided funding for the program:

- American Express Company
- Bank of America National Trust
-   and Saving Association
- Chemical Bank
- The First Boston Corporation
- The Ford Foundation
- Goldman Sachs International Corporation
- The William and Flora Hewlett Foundation
- The Andrew W. Mellon Foundation
- Morgan Stanley & Co., Inc.
- Norton Simon, Inc.
- The John M. Olin Foundation, Inc.
- Salomon Brothers
- The Alfred P. Sloan Foundation

James T. Mills
President
The Conference Board

CONTENTS

RECONSTRUCTING THE FEDERAL BUDGET

CHAPTER ONE

INTRODUCTION

Albert T. Sommers

The title of this book is by no means a journalistic extravagance. Total outlays by our Federal Government are indeed approaching a trillion dollars annually, and the accumulating federal debt is approaching $1.5 trillion. By present projections, the accumulating federal deficits of the next several years will add another trillion dollars to the debt. In economics, numbers are relative matters, of course, and the growth of federal spending, federal deficits, and federal debt should properly be viewed against the growth of the economy as a whole, which now produces goods and services at the awesome rate of $3.5 trillion annually. It is nevertheless true that recent history has carried the ongoing spending and the accumulating debt of the Federal Government to formidable new peaks, evidently to be overshadowed by still vaster peaks in the next several years.

How should we view these immense numbers? And how should we appraise their consequences for an economic and political system that was born in a revolution against the power of government and has carried throughout its history a nearly religious faith in private, individual effort as the source of all progress, spiritual as well as material?

1

The essays in this book are about ways of viewing the federal budget, its related statistics, and its impact on our lives, as seen by distinguished economists on both sides of the political and ideological center. The contributing authors—two of them Nobel laureates and all of them eminent contributors in the field of economic policy—deal valiantly, and readably, with the complexities of federal budgets and the impact of federal deficits. Their technical disagreements—and there are plenty of them—are described in the ensuing summary. But the reader should be forewarned (and is warned again in the closing pages of the summary) that more than technical differences divide the authors. Cutting across the chapters is a deep and crucial philosophical fissure.

Economics is a human science, a social science; it cannot escape its human content, and it cannot, in the end, free itself from values. Nor can economists. The philosophical, political, ideological positions of the authors account for some of their sharpest disagreements over the role of government and the control over its finances. In the early 1980s, a liberal philosophical tradition that took its original energies from the Great Depression of the 1930s has continued to sustain a high rate of growth in federal spending, while a newly restored conservative, individualistic philosophy that constrained the size and role of Federal Government throughout much of our early history has subdued the trend of federal revenues. The deficits, whose conceptual treatment dominates these chapters, have their taproot not in economics itself, but in a historical conjuncture of antithetical value systems. Economists can (and in these pages they do) educate us on the consequences of what we are doing to ourselves. But in the end we must depend upon a high quality of disinterested representation, in the Congress and the Administration, to restore coherence to the financial operations of the Federal Government.

The present state of federal budgeting and its impact on the economy have yielded an abundant crop of paradoxes. In the early 1980s, tax reductions intended to *stimulate* investment produced financial reactions so severe as to result in *declining* investment—in private plant and equipment outlay, in housing, and in the infrastructure outlays at all government levels. The long-standing traditional proposition that a balanced federal budget is the only "fiscally responsible" budgetary outcome has come to coexist with

2

views, recently espoused even by policymakers of a conservative administration, that budget deficits may be anything from a "necessary evil" to a matter of little concern. Throughout the past dozen years, Administration after Administration has dedicated itself to the conventional conservative view and projected budget surpluses a few years out, only to incur deficit after deficit, even in years of relative prosperity in the private sector.

Budgetary outcomes have taken this unorthodox course at a time when monetary policy, in the United States and elsewhere, has accepted the constraining orthodoxy of monetarism. In the early 1980s, the consequences of the violation of budget orthodoxy and strict adherence to monetary orthodoxy were apparent throughout the West. Private-sector investment subsided almost everywhere, and underutilization of both capital and human resources spread almost everywhere, as a reflection of two recessions in only 18 months. The recessions themselves constrained revenue bases, contributing a cyclical component to what now appears to be a secular deficit condition; and the consequent widening of the deficit imposed an interest-rate premium on capital markets that further suppressed both investment and the revenue side of the budget. Paradoxically, the size of the deficit has produced efforts to restrain expenditures and raise taxes, or to forego scheduled further tax reductions—precisely the reverse of the cyclical logic that prevailed throughout the first three decades of the post-World War II period.

All of these paradoxes affecting the budget are paralleled by related paradoxes surrounding the interpretation of the level and growth of federal debt, its implications for inflation, and its bearing on the supply of capital available to the private sector. As with the federal deficit, almost precisely contradictory interpretations of the significance of the federal debt prevail among the public at large, within the Administration and the Congress, and in the business and financial communities.

It is hard to resist the conclusion that theory and practice with respect to the financial operations of the Federal Government have grown plainly incoherent; actual experience has departed violently, perhaps even permanently, from the orthodoxy that was widely accepted (even, with some modifications, by Keynesians themselves) for three decades after the end of World War II. While actual experience has gone far to destroy the old orthodoxy, no body of new theoretical and practical guides to budgetary performance has developed to replace it.

Throughout the disturbing history of a destroyed orthodoxy giving way to a vacuum, the actual accounting structure by which the Federal Government records its operations, sets its program, and appraises its results has reacted little or not at all. The legislative process for the budget was importantly revised by the legislation of 1974, but the accounting practices and concepts have remained largely unchanged. An immense revolution in the relative size and complexity of government still leaves the accounting system in a simple cash-flow condition developed in a bygone era, when the impact of the Federal Government on the economy as a whole was trivial.

The issues raised here are the essential elements in what can fairly be called a trillion-dollar challenge—to restore effective control over the finances of government in an era of unavoidably large governmental impact on the general welfare.

The chapters contained in this volume bear on several facets of our budget dilemma. Together they comprise a stunning portrait of the concerns of economists, and the degrees of confidence, uncertainty, and even exasperation with which they view their profession and its intellectual equipment. While they focus on the federal budget and its implications for monetary policy, inflation, and capital markets, they understandably work their way toward the performance of the economy in the early 1980s. Here and there, they also work backward, even toward the nature and significance of economic science in a democracy: an exhilarating, sometimes encouraging, sometimes disturbing revelation of agreements, disagreements, and simple vacuums of knowledge, all resting on (and drawing from) differing views of the role and limits of government in a system that combines democratic processes with free-market institutions.

The individual pieces stand by themselves and it is hardly necessary to summarize each of them. Instead, this essay is organized by issue. With respect to the chapters appearing in the first three theoretical sections, it attempts to integrate the views of the authors on a number of important questions of theory and concept bearing on the federal budget and its significance to the system as a whole. The fourth section turns to questions of the improvement of the budgetary process, budgetary concepts, and the accounting system; these pieces examine more or less distinct issues in federal accounting, with little overlap, and their treatment here is more nearly a summary of the views expressed in each. The discussion of these sections is followed by more interpretive comment, seeking to distill the principles that seem to underlie the views of the authors, the sources of their differences, the needs for additional information, the opportunities for reconciliation, and the lessons for the makers of economic policy.

THE MEANING AND SIGNIFICANCE OF THE FEDERAL BUDGET

The present condition of the federal budget, and particularly the prospect of budget deficits of record absolute and relative size extending several years into the future, lies at the center of what Paul Samuelson calls "a perceived crisis in fiscal policy." Herbert Stein says the meaning of budget outcomes is now so uncertain, even to economists, that it is no longer "trusted or trustworthy as a guide to fiscal policy." There is no certain guide to the proper position of the budget, no rationale for current and prospective deficits, no conclusive view on whether it is public expenditures or the net budget position that is critical, no absolute assurance that federal borrowing and federal taxing have very different ultimate effects, no certainty *why* deficits matter or what policy should be. Fiscal policy is being conducted in a partial vacuum. This is the weight of the argument in the first three chapters. It is by no means a unanimous view and perhaps not a majority view; but parts of the description are subscribed to by almost all of the authors.

Traditionally, the conceptual guidance to budget making called for a budget balance as an overriding criterion—a balance every year, since any departure from balance was a departure from an inherent and widely accepted, nearly exceptionless rule of conduct—a free-standing rule, requiring no reference to monetary policy or cyclical position.

The rule has long since been buried in a stream of departures. In its place arose the concept of a budget balance over the course of the cycle. That rule disappeared as experience revealed continuous deficits—deep deficits in recession, but deficits even in prosperity. It was modified to the essentially Keynesian position that the budget should be calculated to seek high employment, and that deficits experienced below a level of high prosperity are desirable stimulants to aggregate demand. Unlike its two predecessors, this rule would permit secular growth in outstanding federal debt, a condition that has prevailed for three decades in any event. Stein calls this "functional finance"; the budget deficit should be "large enough to yield full employment." The criterion thus moved from the budgetary position itself to its presumed influence on aggregate economic performance.

Even that rule has been vacated by current and prospective experience, partly because the rule (or the way the rule has been managed) has increasingly been associated with inflationary outcomes, and price stability has become as much a criterion of economic performance as high employment. Torn between two *antithetical* criteria (policies that are good on employment grounds are often bad on inflation grounds and vice versa), fiscal policy seems to have lost its independent guidance system. It is left in a vacuum, without a firm doctrinal position from which departures can be measured and then treated.

While there is no rationale for present deficits and general (although not unanimous) concern over future deficits, there is little support among the contributors for balanced-budget legislation, either statutory or constitutional. Nor, as Stein points out, have any of the proponents of such legislation come forward with a plan that would bring the budget into balance in the foreseeable future. No one sought the deficits that lie ahead; the supply-siders who supported massive tax reduction seem to have expected a surge in output and incomes that would more than restore federal receipts. The economy experiences unintended deficits, with indeterminate consequences; at one agonized point, Stein raises the question whether perhaps the deficit is not itself a "chimera," and all fiscal policy so clouded with uncertainty as to be meaningless.

Samuelson raises even wider questions about the significance of budget outcomes. There are a *dozen* budget outcomes, depending upon the accounting convention employed. Under *any* accounting convention, there is no single right target; each size and sign of budgetary outcomes have different substantive effects. There is no neutral solution. Inextricably involved with our views of the budget is the ultimate question of how large the public sector should be.

The authors are in almost unanimous agreement that budget deficits are not inherently inflationary; different combinations of budgetary outcomes and monetary policy can yield satisfactory levels of employment (implicitly, without unacceptable inflation). But they yield very different results for the public and the private sector and for relative proportions of consumption and investment in the economy as a whole. A high deficit, offset by restrictive monetary policy, tends toward a high-consumption, low-growth economy and a high government share in total activity. Tight budgets and accommodative monetary policy tend toward a low-consumption, high-growth economy and a high private share in output.

Selecting among these alternatives raises large, value-laden issues of choice in a democratic society. Growth may be desirable inherently, but at what cost in current consumption? How can a democratic society weigh consumption by its current citizens against the consumption levels available to future generations? This issue of intergenerational transfer of resources available for consumption comes close to the essence of interpreting budgetary outcomes. A fixed legislative or constitutional constraint will not resolve it; according to Samuelson, "a democracy has to face up to the substantive issue."

Despite the conceptual uncertainties, a variety of proposed working rules for guidance of the budget position appears in all of the theoretical papers. Henry Wallich and Allan Meltzer come close to a conventional, conservative view: Given a budget balance at high employment (and under favorable conditions with regard to tax treatment, regulation, and other factors), the private sector will ordinarily make use of all of the savings available and produce a growth rate that will "maximize consumption over time." Robert Eisner argues that budget outcomes should be set at levels that ensure high employment; this by no means prescribes a budget balance at high employment, and is also neutral with respect to the size of government. James Tobin takes essentially the same position and argues further that reasonable adjustments to the budget to exclude the budgetary reflections of debt incurred in prior accounting periods reduce the foreseeable deficits to manageable and even appropriate proportions. Benjamin Friedman would seek a deficit such that the growth of public debt bears a constant relationship to the growth of aggregate debt. Since aggregate debt has been highly stable relative to total income, this argues for a percentage increase

7

in public debt related to the percentage increase in general income or GNP throughout the economy. This formulation would tolerate (indeed, might even require) continuing deficits. Leonard Santow would extract defense from the budget and seek to balance the remainder, tolerating deficits in the combined accounts that should never exceed 5 percent of GNP and would presumably average substantially less than that.

Several authors raise questions about whether constraints on the budget deficit, offset by easy monetary policy, will produce high investment and growth, if growth requires substantial capital outlay for "infrastructure" by government itself. Is all government outlay to be treated as consumption? The treatment of all public capital outlay as consumption reflects national accounting conventions and the federal budgetary practice of treating the Federal Government's own capital investments no differently from its current outlay. Only a very few of the contributors would advocate formal capital budgeting for the Federal Government. But treating the portion of federal expenditures to be financed by debt as a drain on the saving available for investment imperfectly reflects the true aggregate investment of the system, and may overstate the consumption consequences of deficit financing.

THE POLICY MIX

It is apparent in all of the chapters that fiscal policy cannot be isolated from its monetary environment. The condition that finally disarmed "functional finance" as an effective rule for fiscal policy was the increasing recognition accorded to the role of monetary policy, particularly with respect to the rate of growth of money stock, and its implications for inflation. Functional finance treated monetary policy as a handmaiden, prepared to accommodate the deficits experienced—particularly during recessions and early stages of recovery. Fiscal policy, argues Wallich, was powerful only as long as monetary policy supported it. As monetary theory grew more confident and more widely respected for its explanation of the ascending trend of inflation over the last 15 years, to the point where inflation became a criterion of economic performance as significant as unemployment itself, monetary policy gradually assumed an equal partnership in the policy structure.

In recent years, indeed, monetary policy has become the dominant partner—a major reason for the apparent decay of fiscal orthodoxy and its descent into the vacuum described here. The fiscal stimulus provided by a very large budget deficit can be neutralized and even subverted by monetary restraint. If monetary policy does not monetize the deficits, the stimulus expected by functional finance will be vitiated by high interest rates, the crowding out of private-credit demands, and the subsidence of markets in the private sector.

This formulation of the relationship between budget outcomes and monetary policy does not seem to defy the general assumption, accepted by many of the authors, that there is a broad continuum of fiscal and monetary mixes—all consistent with high employment, although differing markedly in their effects on investment. Monetary policy describes the implications of money growth in excess of the growth of output, *and assuming a high-employment condition*, as decisively inflationary. It is not the deficits that are inflationary; it is the "monetization" of the deficits, should the Federal Reserve accommodate them directly or indirectly, that produce excessive money growth and the inevitable rise in the price level. This is now the conventional *long-term* wisdom supported by the arguments in many of these chapters. Implicit in this view is, conceivably, a guide for budgetary outcomes; *under a monetarist rule*, large deficits inevitably impair the financial saving available to the private sector. Budget deficits are *dissaving*: A monetarist rule will enforce the financing on the private sector, reducing the supply of external funds available for private investment. To do otherwise at high employment would ensure inflation.

This reasoning applies to a steady-state, high-employment, noninflationary condition maintained by a monetary rule. But what about the financing of deficits in the short term, at activity levels below high employment? Enter, dramatically, expectations. Among the principal themes of this book is a profound awareness of the role of expectations in modern economies and their power to alter a current situation in the light of anticipated future developments. The association of high money growth with inflation is widespread

9

throughout the financial community—so widespread that even in the presence of substantial idle resources, rapid growth of money will find its way into the attitudes of lenders and precipitate rising rates of interest long before real strains in resource availability develop. The fiscal stimulus implicit in functional finance can be blocked by interest-rate reactions *at far below high employment*— either elevating nominal rates or maintaining them at levels abnormally above the inflation rate, producing a restrictive "real rate" (the interest rate, less the prevailing rate of inflation). Wallich says, "The game is known." He concludes, in these circumstances, that as the expectational lag shrinks and monetary consequences are more rapidly anticipated, even the Federal Reserve cannot control the real interest rate. Paradoxically, fiscal conditions regain a measure of influence in these circumstances. Wallich states it flatly: The Federal Reserve may influence *nominal* rates, but it is fiscal conditions—the size of the deficit and its latent implications for money growth—that control the *real* rate.

The implications here have a powerful bearing on the dilemma confronting policy in this decade. What is clear is that the simple powers of Keynesian fiscal policy, used with vigor and general success for two decades after the end of World War II, are in eclipse, drained and exhausted by the monetarist description of the causes of inflation, the wide acceptance accorded it among participants in financial markets, and their inevitable anticipations of the future. Almost all of the more conservative authors support these propositions. Understandably, they would all seek a substantial reduction in prospective deficits. The budget deficits that occur in *recession* now seem to ensure real interest rates that are inappropriate for prolonged *recovery*. Substantial deficits seem to leave no alternatives but inflation in the future or deep recession in the present. The time available for monetary policy to mediate between these extremes grows briefer and briefer, as the anticipating antennae of investors telescope the causalities involved, and as the "credibility" of the Federal Reserve in enforcing its monetary rule becomes the central element in expectations of inflation and of *future* interest rates. In a stunning reversal of the Keynesian inference, it can be argued that in the presence of a monetarist rule, large budget deficits are *contractionary* rather than *stimulative*, because of their reflections in real interest rates.

THE DEFICIT AND CAPITAL MARKETS; SAVING FLOWS AND CROWDING OUT

A considerable number of the authors are unsatisfied with this grim appraisal, which rests primarily on two propositions: first, that *under all conditions*, the money growth associated with the financing of deficits becomes self-defeating through its impact on interest rates; and, second, that the financing of the deficit draws dollar-for-dollar on a fixed "pool of saving," shrinking the availability of capital for the private sector, regardless of cyclical conditions.

These issues are partly a matter of evidence. But, conceptually, is the pool of saving indeed fixed, or is it itself affected by the outcome of the budget? On this large question the authors come to no real agreement. Some of the disagreement seems to reflect differences in assumptions concerning the cyclical position of the system—saving in a steady state of high employment versus saving in the course of a business cycle.

In national accounting, any instantaneous increase in the ongoing rate of federal deficit (for example, through instantaneous reduction in tax rates) is an increase in dissaving that will be instantaneously offset by an increase in saving (on the part of beneficiaries of the tax reduction). A portion of the incremental income will then be spent and a portion saved, the portions depending upon the spending propensities of the beneficiaries. This is the simplest case for arguing that the pool of saving responds positively to the deficit; the argument will take different forms, depending upon whether the economy is operating near high employment or under such recession conditions as have prevailed, generally, in the early 1980s.[1] Indeed, the national accounts themselves reveal at least a temporary increase in personal saving at each point in the progressive personal tax reductions of the past three years.

Other, more abstruse reasons for expecting a longer-term response in the saving pool are adduced by some of the authors. Some argue, for example, that the beneficiaries of such a tax reduction consider that the resulting increase in federal debt will have to be paid for in the future in any event, and increase their saving (elevate their propensity to save) as preparation, even over a long term, to carry the incremental burden of taxes that would appear to lie ahead. (This principle need not be restricted to the beneficiaries; all parties may feel obliged to do so.) To the extent this mechanism operates, a budget deficit would appear to generate the saving to finance it; it is also noninflationary and even non-stimulative.

Others argue that the widely expected inflation consequences of an enlargement of the budget deficit induce higher saving to protect the real value of liquid asset accumulations against the effects of the prospective inflation. Stein makes these points, and Tobin reasons that the interest payments by government resulting from the incremental deficit are likely to carry a higher saving coefficient than most other income streams. Wallich argues that tax reduction increases the saving pool but with an effect of no more than about 0.3 of the aggregate reduction. (Increases in government spending are said to be more stimulative than tax reduction, precisely because of this saving effect.) Stein sees some elasticity in the saving pool, but he still argues that the best argument for a balanced budget is the "crowding-out" effect of the deficit. Friedman accepts the conclusion that public deficits carry negative connotations for private investment. Indeed, looking ahead, the deficits he foresees accelerate the growth of public debt and necessitate a falling volume of private-debt formation, given the constancy of the aggregate relationship of total debt to GNP. The decline is so sharp that even virtual elimination of debt incurred in the housing market would not offset the relative rise in government debt. The implications for private investment in plant and equipment are serious. (The differences among the authors on this issue seem to reflect a failure to distinguish cyclical conditions from long-term, steady-state, high-employment conditions.)

Wallich and Friedman focus on still another distinction: that between "gross saving" (including capital-consumption allowances) and "net saving" (excluding such flows). For the capital markets, *gross* saving may be the relevant measure, since capital-consumption allowances are a component of the cash flows available for reinvestment. But from the point of view of growth, the net saving is relevant. The capital-consumption allowance reflects actual exhaustion of capital requiring replacement. It is to the *net* flow of saving that the deficit and its associated borrowing requirements should be related. This produces a higher measure of the deficit's consequences for private investment.[2]

The sophistication of the saving-flow arguments, and perhaps also their lack of closure, reflects considerable departure from the cyclical Keynesian view of saving and investment that prevailed in the first 20 years of the post-World War II period. The Keynesian view (embodied in the structure of the national accounts) treats ex-post saving and investment as identical quantities. From the beginning, an instantaneous enlargement of the public deficit is accompanied by an instantaneous enlargement of saving. In the ensuing accounting period, the excess of saving over that dictated by the existing propensity to save will be spent, increasing economic activity generally, enlarging the revenues to government under the new tax rates, and reducing the government's dissaving and the private sector's saving equally as expansion proceeds. This description assumes an economy experiencing underemployment of resources. It does not seem to involve any crowding out at all, and does not even seem to require exceptional growth in the availability of credit, even though the credit demands of the private sector will rise with expanding activity. Under conditions of high employment, however, tax reduction may produce excessive aggregate demand, accompanied by inflation and rising interest rates. Under these conditions, the private sector, being an interest-rate–sensitive borrower, will depart the capital markets, while the government, which borrows regardless of interest rates, will stay in.

Still further complexities could be added to this simple description of the Keynesian view. But that was fundamentally the description that prevailed for decades, during which actual crowding out was a momentary phenomenon, experienced under conditions of very high employment, rising inflation, and rapidly rising interest rates—in other words, *only at an appropriate point in the business cycle*. The new formulation applies to this structure an activist monetary policy, pursuing its own purposes against inflation *even under conditions of underutilization of resources*, and restricting the supply of money in such wise as to force the financing of the deficit onto the private sector, reaching the saving-investment identity by con-straining credit formation and investment in the private sector rather than through cyclical expansion of the aggregates. What defeated the expectation of the supply-siders responsible for the tax bill of 1981 was not, apparently, the failure to do it all at once, with no hesitations or withdrawals. Instead, the failure resulted from real crowding out (real "pricing out," Santow would say) by Federal

Reserve policies that were directed toward disinflation rather than cyclical recovery. And the Federal Reserve's behavior, in turn, was dictated by its deep awareness, very possibly correct, of the power of anticipations to produce high interest rates in the presence of rapid money growth *regardless of the cyclical position of the system*. As a result, government dissaving continued to grow in 1981 and 1982, and enlarged its share of a saving pool that was *not* being enlarged by cyclical expansion of aggregate incomes flows.

The prospect, as Friedman and others describe it, will worsen over time, because of the deepening deficit forecast for the next several years. To stabilize private investment, future deficits, according to Friedman, must be cut roughly in half, preferably by spending reductions.

THE DEFICIT AND INFLATION

There is general agreement among the authors that deficits themselves are not inherently inflationary. According to Meltzer, inflation results from *persistent* deficits financed by monetization— that is, by sales of government securities to the central bank, which increase the stock of money. Inflation is a money phenomenon, not a budgetary phenomenon. *But the persistent deficits raise the presumption of monetization*. Enough monetization leads to generalized inflation and a flight from money to tangibles. Meltzer holds that an increasing public share in total economic activity may be inflationary altogether apart from the budgetary outcome. He assumes generally lower efficiency in the public sector. Finally, regulatory and other forms of legislation may impose costs on the private sector without any accompanying budget reflection. The implicit reduction in the efficiency of the private sector may also be a source of inflation. Inflation is traceable to rapid money growth, considerably in excess of growth of output; but it may also result from lower output growth, traceable to inefficiencies within government, and government actions imposing inefficiency on the private sector. Lower output in an environment of constant money growth also yields inflation.

Neither of these views of the deficit—the one essentially monetization, and the other essentially efficiency—is held unanimously by the authors. None flatly disagrees with the proposition

14

that there are rates of increase in money stock, presumably produced by monetization, that inevitably result in a rising general price level. But Eisner argues that public deficits are not a cause of inflation any more than increases in private debt. Friedman's arguments on the stability of aggregate credit relative to GNP do not seem to distinguish either public or private debt with respect to its impact on inflation; but the impact on the future growth rate may be substantial.

Eisner disagrees that government expenditures necessarily have a higher inflation potential than private expenditures. In his view, some government *outlays* are actually *antiinflationary*, in the sense that they improve productivity in the private sector and in the economy as a whole. And some *revenue* is inherently *inflationary*; for example, receipts from payroll taxes, which pass directly into the cost of production. Excessive aggregate demand, according to Eisner, is the ultimate source of inflation, and inadequate aggregate demand is the ultimate source of unemployment. Money growth, whether the result of monetization or other causes, can be inflationary only insofar as it drives aggregate demand toward and beyond the limits of supply. He notes that high interest rates add to the cost structure and are themselves inflationary.

The observations of the authors on this subject fall into two classes. One derives its premises from monetary theory and addresses money-stock data directly, and the other, essentially Keynesian, rests on the response of markets to varying levels of demand. The second view takes not money but the degree of resource use as the variable directly related to inflation. (Some of the authors would wish to consider both.) Under the circumstances of high money growth at substantially less than full resource use, the two ways of explaining inflation yield very different guides to policy. To put it differently, the resource-use perspective would see little current or prospective inflation, and would judge the future by the prospects for resource use; the monetarist perspective would see impending inflation, regardless of resource use. Samuelson makes the observation, more in connection with the deficit than with money growth itself, that policy stimulus to an economic system operating well below high employment will divide itself approximately two-thirds to real growth and one-third to price; the percentages would presumably gradually reverse as resource use rises.

HOW BIG IS THE DEFICIT, REALLY?

Budgetary outcomes are the consequences of the accounting conventions employed in their measurement; different accounting concepts would yield very different results. But altogether apart from the accounting, economists reserve the right to apply their own principles in seeking an effective economic measure of the deficit that will reveal its macroeconomic consequences. The authors offer two broad sets of considerations.

In the first place, the budget deficit can be disaggregated into a component that represents the basic position of planned expenditures and tax rates, on the one hand, and a component that reflects the operating level of the economy as a whole and the revenue base it offers up for taxation, on the other. The calculation of a "high-employment budget" represents an effort to make this separation. The high-employment budget, in effect, calculates the spending and the revenues that would be generated under current tax law and under current spending intentions, if the system were operating at a defined level of high employment. The definition of the unemployment rate that would qualify for "high employment" is itself a matter of dispute among economists within these chapters. While the presently available figures use an unemployment rate slightly above 5 percent, a number of the authors would seem to accept 6 percent, and a few of them something more than that, while others, including Tobin and Eisner, would be more hopeful that policy could achieve a rate below 5 percent. Quantitative research on this subject, to which monetarists have made a heavy contribution, identifies a NAIRU—a nonaccelerating inflation rate of unemployment—which is approximately the equivalent of the rate of unemployment that can be achieved without inducing rapid inflation simply for market reasons (that is, for reasons of demand for and supply of labor, given the available quality of the labor force). The figure of 6 percent commonly appears in this research. Some of the past unhappy experience with inflation occurred, according to Stein, because the unemployment target of policy was set too low—that is, below the NAIRU prevailing at the time.

In any event, and granting the difficulties of establishing the assumptions on which it rests, once the high-employment calculation is determined, it permits a division of the total deficit into that portion that is attributable to the economy being below high employment and that portion that would remain even at high employment. These are, respectively, the cyclical and the structural deficits. Those authors that refer to this point seem to accept the fact that each percentage point of unemployment above the high-employment assumption is responsible for between $25 billion and $30 billion of the deficit. As much as three-fourths of the deficit experienced in 1983 currently is thus *cyclical* and about one-fourth is *structural*—that is, the residual deficit that would remain after reaching high employment, under present spending intentions and tax rates, would be only about one-fourth of the total deficit. This distinction underlies many of the unalarmed references to the current deficit by Tobin, Eisner, and, to a lesser degree, Samuelson. Friedman's analysis, working backward from acceptable growth of debt to acceptable deficits, is not incompatible with this way of dividing the total deficit. Wallich's chapter seems also to accept a workable distinction between a strucutral and a cyclical deficit.

A related distinction, referred to particularly by Tobin, divides the deficit into a "passive" and an "active" component. As a static division of an existing deficit, these terms are very nearly identical to the distinction between a cyclical and a structural component; but the passive-active distinction is useful for characterizing changes in the deficit by their causes. A tax reduction (or an increase in spending) creates an active deficit; recession produces a passive deficit, which is more nearly measuring the recession than providing aggressive stimulus for growth. It should be noted that these distinctions rest on a business-cycle view of the system. They relate the deficit to the rate of resource use of the system. The general effect of the distinctions is to reduce the sense of outrage at the size of the deficit, and to increase the outrage at the degree of unemployment being experienced by the system. The authors are divided, along expectable lines, in their expressed concern over one or the other form of outrage. Meltzer and Wallich are writing mainly about inflation; Tobin, Eisner, and Samuelson mainly about unemployment. Stein's exasperation runs impartially to the conceptual uncertainties. Friedman's concern is with the displacement of private investment and lost long-term growth; in a section of his chapter, he seems to be addressing only a high-employment condition.

In addition to the breakdown of the deficit into a secular and cyclical component, some of the authors refer to a provisional revision of the deficit measure, based upon the effects of inflation on the Federal Government's outstanding debt. As in all debtor-creditor relationships, inflation benefits the debtor by reducing the real value of the obligation. The U.S. Treasury being the world's biggest debtor, inflation is of most particular benefit to it. The reduction of the *real* value of the debt existing at the beginning of an accounting period could conceivably be entered into the records of the accounting period as a kind of credit to governmental operations. Moreover, the inflation will reduce even the *market* value of the debt, as interest rates rise and the prices of Treasury securities fall.

Eisner carries out this reasoning, making substantial adjustments in the deficit for the real debt reduction accruing to the Federal Government as a consequence of inflation. He finds, astonishingly, that with this adjustment, the high-employment federal budget was in surplus as recently as fiscal 1981; and he concludes that the cyclical recession of the early 1980s reflected a tight money policy responding inappropriately to a fiscal policy that has been stimulative only in an illusory sense.

Tobin also engages in recalculations of the deficit. He excludes all debt service on existing federal debt from the expenditure side of the federal budget, along with tax receipts received against the interest paid by the Federal Government from the receipt side. He treats the residual as the "primary deficit." While this does not reduce the actual deficit to zero, the adjusted deficits revealed for the present and the next several years in Tobin's calculations are manageable. (Friedman's calculations do not envision Tobins' reconstruction of the accounting of the deficit. Since debtors, private and public, benefit in roughly the same degree from inflation, the process would seem to leave his proportionate debt proposition unaffected.) Wallich and others note that in times of inflation, the inflation premium in interest rates generates payments to holders of the federal debt that might be treated as amortization—a return of capital, and "not part of the deficit." (The figure involved could be very large—perhaps one-quarter of the total deficit!)

These sophisticated reinterpretations of the budget outcome, based on the effects of inflation on the real equivalent of the federal debt, may be subscribed to, as appropriate mechanics, by a considerable number of the authors. But only a few would fully accept the liberalization of the concept of the deficit that is involved.

These explanations should be treated as economists' manipulation of the debt, distinguishable from the actual increase in nominal debt and the associated actual financing requirements that concern the majority of the authors. But it may be significant that a conceptual distinction with such large numerical consequences is still a matter of real debate.

Other recalculations of the debt include Santow's proposal to remove defense and treat it separately, and proposals for installing a capital account in federal budgeting, which would remove capital outlay from the expenditure side of the account, presumably to be replaced by a depreciation flow. Neither of these recalculations is given serious consideration by the authors as a group.

INTERNATIONAL REACTIONS TO THE DEFICIT

The international consequences of budgetary outcomes receive less attention here than many of the authors would give it in other contexts. Wallich and Meltzer describe the international outcomes of deficits at home. The deficit absorbs saving (a statement that raises the "constant pool" questions referred to above) and drives up interest rates (a proposition that reflects their views of Federal Reserve responsibilities in the presence of a deficit). On these assumptions, the international reactions are such as to elevate the value of the dollar, and thereby to attract foreign investment, making the United States an importer of capital. The importing of capital helps to finance the deficit (it enlarges the pool of saving). The high dollar constricts export markets and induces increased imports because of their lower prices. This is a cyclical, real-world, nonexpectational constraint on inflation; the constraint is exercised simply by falling aggregate demand for domestic output. An extension of the argument would be that weakened domestic markets would lower the revenue base (as it did in 1981 and 1982, through reduced taxable incomes and wage payments in automobile and steel manufacture, among others) and enlarge the deficit, perhaps by as much as the inflow of capital enlarges the saving pool. In any event, the portion of the budget deficit financed through capital import can be only a very small fraction of deficits of the size now being run. Moreover, the mechanism raises questions about whether a very highly developed economy should be absorbing

istration and the Congress, in dealing with ever more complicated budgets. The resort to overall appropriations measures—"continuing resolutions"—is a reflection of these pressures, and is itself a source of anxiety and ultimate inefficiency. These considerations lead him to suggest that biennial budgeting is worth experimentation, allowing for off-year adjustment of programs sensitive to economic change.

The chapters by Sidney Jones and by Alice Rivlin and Robert Hartman examine critical dimensions of the budget dilemma. Jones attributes a pronounced renewal of interest in capital budgeting by the Federal Government to the growth of federal spending itself and recognition of "the enormous magnitude of public investments required to rehabilitate and improve the national infrastructure." Along with Staats, Jones is impressed with the need for much greater attention to the investment outlays of government. The issue is whether the fracturing of the unified-budget accounting system by segregation of a capital account is worth the cost of losing the full cash-flow focus provided by the unified budget.

Jones' list of the advantages of capital budgeting, and the disadvantages of failing to segregate a capital account, is exhaustive. A capital account would make budget estimates more logical, understandable, and accurate. It would avoid a serious timing mismatch when current spending for goods and services is simply combined with long-term investments that need not be paid for with current revenues. The absence of a capital budget means ignoring the value of assets required and exaggerating the appearance of current consumption in the budget. Removing capital expenditures from current budgets would provide a different perspective on fiscal responsibility; it would clarify the meaning of a "balanced budget." The budget would require only a balance of current expenses (including depreciation) with current revenues. But a capital budget would suggest continuing government borrowing to finance durable assets. The continuously accumulating debt burden would be viewed against the backdrop of continuing growth in accumulating federal assets.

Jones agrees with Staats that Special Analysis D in the budget provides only retrospective and historical value. Moreover, it is obscure and is not maintained in a condition of current revision. Improved spending control could conceivably result from better control of an operating budget freed from the "lumpy" spending patterns of capital outlay. Advocates of capital budgeting also argue that it would lead to better project evaluation, better asset management, and a more long-term orientation of aggregate outlay. In Jones' words, "advocates of the capital budget believe that long-term planning, project evaluations and controls, property management, and program accountability would all be improved." And they argue, most particularly in the present context, that capital budgeting would invite solutions to the "unfortunate juxtaposition of growing public infrastructure needs and extraordinary levels of unemployment."

Finally, Jones lists the argument that capital-budgeting procedures, by providing an inventory of potential projects preapproved for execution, should provide faster use of public capital spending for counterrecession purposes, which, in turn, would reduce reliance on the acceleration of transfers and other forms of inefficient fine-tuning reactions to the business cycle.

The list of disadvantages associated with capital budgeting is equally long. The separation of capital and current outlay applicable to individual programs reduces the possibility of efficient trade-offs between the two types of spending. The splitting of the aggregate budget into two components and the implied borrowing for the capital component do not alter the fact that all federal outlay must be financed in a capital market in competition with the needs of the private sector. The very separation may reduce resistance to aggregate spending and weaken the "pragmatic value" of "the balanced budget dogma." The increased capital investment that the advocates of capital budgeting argue for may well turn out to be simply incremental spending, resulting from a reduction of "fiscal responsibility." Other objections: The presumed special warrant for capital outlay implicit in the creation of the capital budget might well tilt spending arbitrarily toward long-term projects, simply because the capital outlay would appear to be easier to justify; some of the advantages of capital budgeting are already reflected in the creation of off-budget and credit operations; a capital item in government accounting is very different from its private-sector equivalent, and presents greater difficulty in establishing values and appropriate depreciation rates; defense outlays offer a particularly acute appraisal problem.

Jones concludes that many of the objectives sought by those advocating a capital budget are desirable, even necessary, for a future that seems to require substantial elevation of outlay for infrastructure. Nevertheless, he argues that the increased focus of attention, research, and management required for future federal capital outlay can be achieved without doing violence to the unified budget, and that the disadvantages of partitioning the unified budget are serious. The unified budget provides a "major advantage of comprehensive analysis of the economic and financial results of current budget decision." Separation would "dilute managerial control." The current unified budget, modified "to include increased emphasis on the importance of public investments," satisfies these needs, without losing the advantages of a single comprehensive reflection of Federal Government operations.

The control of federal credit, addressed by Rivlin and Hartman, raises a wholly different set of issues. Unlike the proposal for a capital budget, a credit budget does not invade the unified-budget concept. On the contrary, it produces a series of products that should enrich and clarify the measures of spending incorporated in the unified budget.

The present treatment of credit items in the unified budget leaves a great deal to be desired. Direct loans are reflected in the budget as net outlays—gross loans less repayment of principal on past loans. Prepayments being difficult to control or forecast, the net loan estimates are conditional. Guaranteed loans present even greater difficulties, since the credit advanced does not enter the budget at all. Loan guarantees are "free goods" as far as unified-budget accounting is concerned; an outlay is recorded only when loans default and a federal payment is made.

The off-budget entities, all of which involve credit, further reduce the significance of the unified budget. The Federal Financing Bank serves as an intermediary between off-budget agencies and the Treasury, but it is the Treasury that must do the ultimate borrowing, and this is not reflected in the unified budget. Credit programs have thus become an attractive alternative to programs covered in the unified budget; and as budget controls themselves have tightened, the attractiveness of credit programs has grown—a tendency clearly reflected in the recent history of both direct and guaranteed loans.

The beginning of a credit budget dates to 1980, with inclusion in the budget of estimates of obligations for direct loans, commitments, and plan levels of the Federal Financing Bank. The Congressional Budget Resolution now includes aggregate limits on obligations and loan commitments, classified by budget function. The credit estimates are still forecasts, not targets, and there is no mechanism for reconciliation or for adjusting excessive individual appropriation bills for credit overruns.

Rivlin and Hartman propose two courses for further development of the management of federal credit—develop an independent credit budget and/or integrate credit decisions with spending decisions. The Congress is presently going in the direction of developing a free-standing credit budget, ultimately requiring control through obligations and commitments. In time, this will require better understanding of the "lend-out rates" of different programs and substantial research on the effect of federal credit on capital markets in general and on particular submarkets.

A second approach would focus on the overuse of federal credit. It would encourage trade-offs between noncredit and credit programs. This raises major analytical problems, stated generally, in relating a dollar of credit commitment to a dollar of actual outlay. The conversion ratio may be taken to be the present value of the interest subsidy involved in the credit extension; the conversion would vary from program to program. For guarantee programs, the "shadow cost" might again be measured as the interest rate subsidy—the rate the borrower would have to pay in the absence of a government guarantee less the rate actually paid. The authors conclude that both integration of the cost of credit programs into the unified budget and the establishment of a free-standing credit budget ought to be pursued. Each has its advantages; together they offer the promise, perhaps a little distant, of improving the unified budget, inviting attention to credit programs that would otherwise have escaped it, and, ultimately, curbing abnormal and unnecessary growth in aggregate federal credit.

Rudolph Penner's chapter deals with constitutional and statutory approaches to limiting budget aggregates. Penner is clearly in favor of constraints on spending, and would not even be reluctant to use a constitutional amendment for that purpose. But the practical difficulties are enormous. The proposed legislation (Senate Joint Resolution 58) is more likely to worsen than to ameliorate the situation.

The problem is real. Special-interest groups exert spending pressure with an intensity far greater than the "diffused" resistance to deficits. The old fiscal norm of a balanced budget provided discipline over spending; its disappearance has left a vacuum and a strong bias toward deficits. Beneficiaries of spending programs are now so numerous (Penner uses the social security system as a central illustration) that we are in danger of exploitation of a minority by a majority.

With respect to the great variety of devices proposed for restraining a spending bias, there are tough implementation problems. Budget outcomes depending upon economic conditions—difficult to forecast even within large margins of error. Non-economic variables intrude themselves on the outlook. Multiyear appropriations may distribute the actual spending with large annual errors (as in defense outlay). Perverse incentives are developed by the very knowledge of a rigid limitation on annual spending. A race will be on, early in the game, to pin down and commit outlay in some programs, to put them beyond the reach of cuts that may be necessary later to meet the target. Receipts forecasts may be deliberately overoptimistic. Under plans that involve a requirement for a super majority to exceed budget estimates, assembling the majority may require an even larger overrun. In any event, there are immense problems of enforcement, ultimately reaching the question of whether the courts themselves would become involved.

Moreover, Penner points out, constitutional restraints on the budget are easy to evade. Government regulation may often be "almost a perfect substitute for taxing and spending." Other possible evasions: loan-guarantee programs, government-sponsored corporations, extension of off-budget activities. Penner concludes that constitutional constraints are unlikely to counter "the biases in our current system toward higher spending levels and higher deficits than the typical voter desires." They are likely to do more harm than good. The trouble lies, ultimately, with the information level available to the public: "It is only the public that can eventually constrain the politicians."

Almost all of the other contributors share Penner's skepticism on the subject of a constitutional amendment. Stein points out that among those urging action, nobody has described a path to the desired balance. Santow says that it "makes little sense" to struggle to legislative balance. Samuelson argues that the budget balance, as well as legislation seeking it, is "seeking a religion—an evasion, a shibboleth." Only Meltzer firmly supports an "amendment limiting expenditure and revenue." It would yield "manageable deficits" and would increase the general efficiency of the system as a whole by restraining the government's share. Many others besides Meltzer seem to regret the growth of government, but almost all of the authors seem to accept Penner's exhaustive list of reasons why legislative constraints are unlikely to be effective.

THE TRILLION-DOLLAR CHALLENGE

This work reveals striking differences among the authors in budget definitions and the conceptual structures by which they relate budget outcomes to the real economy. With respect to the mechanics of the budget and the influence of budgetary outcomes, several propositions seem to warrant inclusion in a "consensus," but even for these propositions the consensus must be described as weak and full of qualifications.

• There is a consensus that a budget outcome is not a meaningful concept, taken by itself. A budget "balance" is an excessively rigid conception; efforts to impose it by legislation are conceptually naive and unworkable in any case.

• The size of the deficit nevertheless retains some meaning. While the authors generate a wide variety of alternative budgetary calculations, the cash-flow accounting that reflects (imperfectly) the borrowing requirements of the Federal Government has a bearing on the use of saving in the system. At high employment, large deficits reduce the saving available to finance private investment. There is wide disagreement over the effects under conditions of cyclical recession.

• Granted to the difficulties of making the separation, *a high-employment "structural" deficit carries a significance greater than the total deficit position.* Most of the authors use or accept the distinction. *Of those that do, most are concerned more about future structural deficits than about the present deficit, which is largely cyclical, or passive.*

• Any generally acceptable calculations of the total deficit can be interpreted only in connection with the course of monetary policy. *The principal exogenous variable in the system is not a fiscal condition, but a money rule.*

• Inflation itself is a *money* phenomenon, and not a *budget* phenomenon. The inflation effects of *any* budget condition must be measured by its presumed consequences in a money and capital market, whose size is heavily influenced by monetary policy.

● In the absence of perfect confidence in a monetary rule, large budget deficits support inflationary expectations. The combined monetary and fiscal position is reflected in interest rates. The monetary rule and the degree to which it is conformed exert a powerful influence over nominal rates. The budget deficit, combined with the uncertainty over the Federal Reserve's conformance with its monetary rule, exercises an influence on real interest rates.

The authors subscribe to this skeletal description of consensus in widely different degree. But perhaps more important than the technical distinctions that account for the dispersion around the consensus is the fact that virtually all of the authors reveal immense difficulty in constructing a policy framework that satisfies long-term considerations but retains options for the short term. This is the essence of the *trillion-dollar challenge*.

This project sought to examine the conceptual structure in which the federal budget and its outcomes could be viewed. Given this purpose, the assignments to writers did not specifically demand reference to economic conditions in the early 1980s. But the subject is dealt with at length in many of the chapters. This outcome was surely inevitable. The essays were prepared at a time of the most powerful economic distress of the post-World War II years—a condition of deep cyclical recession, record unemployment, record low utilization of capacity, rapidly falling private investment, and a powerfully subdued rate of inflation, all in the presence of a deficit in the unified budget approaching 6 percent of national output. It would be hard to find, in the record of the early 1980s, much evidence of a deficit's supposed inflationary influence, or even its supposed Keynesian stimulus. The real world inevitably intruded on the authors' conceptual deliberations.

Under such conditions, one might have expected them to draw sharp distinctions between prescriptions directed toward the great recession of the early 1980s and prescriptions for long-term, steady-state economic behavior. In other words, the conditions suggested substantial attention to the business cycle; to the characteristics of the economy's Phillips Curve, defined simply as the relation of resource use to price strength; to conventional period analysis of the consequences of cyclical revival for private investment, saving, and the deficit itself. Comment on the great dilemma posed by the deeply depressed condition of the system appears in many of the essays, but only a few reach prescriptions directed toward economic recovery. There is, in fact, no discernible consensus on a general set of fiscal and monetary rules that would contemplate *both* cyclical recovery and long-term performance.

The theoretical papers accept the premise that there are many offsetting fiscal and monetary mixes consistent with high employment, although yielding different outcomes for individual sectors. But the "weak consensus" described above relates very largely to a noncyclical steady state. What kind of mix is necessary for cyclical recovery? For restoring high employment?

Eisner seeks simply a fiscal policy that pursues high employment. He has no trouble prescribing a monetary accommodation of the present deficit. Wallich accepts the fact that the private sector is so "debilitated" that a high-employment deficit may be necessary now, even though he would ordinarily argue for a balanced budget or a surplus at high employment. Similarly, Samuelson argues against "austere" fiscal policy now, even though he proposes a surplus (in the presence of accommodative monetary policy) at high employment.

Wallich also accepts the conclusion that there are situations in which "both policies should be pulling in the same direction." Tobin points out that just changing the mix in offsetting ways will not provide the net new energy the system seems so desperately to need. In several of the chapters (those of Meltzer and Friedman, among others), substantial cuts are called for in the aggregate spending of government, but generally with no comment on monetary changes that might offset the disinflationary consequences of spending reductions.[3] Tobin argues that tight monetary policy has contributed heavily to the budget deficit as actually calculated; it is predominantly a "passive" deficit. Cuts in government spending in response to the size of the deficit would constitute a contractionary "double whammy." Samuelson states that under present conditions, "increased thriftiness" (that is, policies and reactions that would presumably add to the saving pool) would probably reduce actual achieved investment. Tobin's short run is "unabashedly Keynesian": The economy exhibits Keynesian underemployment. Savings to finance deficits could be generated "from incomes associated with

29

expansion of production and employment." Eisner asserts that the present inhibition to investment is not the public deficit, but the low utilization rate of existing capacity.

All of the writers share common long-term goals of high employment and price stability. Their differences in this respect are technical, philosophical, and subject to compromise in that they concern the kind of composition of output and demand that should be sought at high employment. Nor do most of them seem to doubt the blessings that would flow from strong and continuing economic recovery—benefits even to the budget deficit, which, it is agreed, has consisted very heavily of a cyclical component. What issues forestall consensus on cyclical revival, if all desire it? Why cannot a majority find solutions to a short-term concern that are compatible with widely shared ultimate objectives for the long term?

The answers are not hard to find. They lie in the significance that individual authors attribute to inflation expectations, and in the attitudes of individual authors toward issues of the role and size of government in the system.

THE ROLE OF EXPECTATIONS

The essays are shot through with references to expectations variables—expectations of future tax burdens, expectations of prospective regulation and deregulation, expectations even of macroeconomic policies of the future, expectations for the future of interest rates. And, most spectacularly of all, the reasoning of the authors with respect to short-term recovery focuses almost hypnotically on expectations of inflation; particularly, "rational expectations" about the future of inflation drawn predominantly from policy variables—the prospective size of the deficit and the actual and prospective growth rate of the money stock.

The incorporation of expectational variables in the reasoning of economists represents very nearly a revolution in *applied* economics (expectations *theory* has been around for a very long time), and comes close to paralyzing both arms of policy in their efforts to find a policy structure that is not only consistent with a desired steady state in the long run, but is also conducive to cyclical recovery in the short run. In considerable measure, the differences among the authors rest on differences in views with respect to the significance of expectations.

Wallich argues that interest rates will accelerate long before high employment is reached. If the federal debt is not monetized, interest rates will rise; if it is monetized, interest rates will rise, but later: "Financial markets in the United States need to be convinced by week-to-week adherence to monetary targets" (unlike in West Germany, paradoxically, fears of inflation are so great and so well known that policymakers are not *expected* to behave in inflationary ways!) *Expectations have collapsed the distinction between short run and long run. Policy behavior even momentarily inconsistent with the precepts of monetarism on long-run inflation threaten immediate perverse effects in current interest rates.*

Is the budget deficit a major component in U.S. sensitivity to inflation and its interest-rate consequences? Wallich argues that a deficit can cause inflation just because people believe it will. Stein writes, "or if people think other people think it will." Much the same expectational envelope might be wrapped around the money stock itelf. Growth of money will cause inflation and higher interest rates if people believe it will, or if people believe other people believe it will. Among the results, as both Samuelson and Tobin point out: high real interest rates attributable to these fears are such that the economy got little or none of the antirecession benefits of the 1982 deficit, even though the deficit was itself substantially a reflection of the recession. It could be said that, in many ways, the deficit and the monetary rule are locked in a grim circle, of which expectations are the closing link. Meltzer notes the same effect: *Assuming rational expectations* for rates, a *positive* causal relationship runs from current or prospective inflation to the size of the deficit—an inversion of the usual causality! A deficit that is largely a passive measure of recession produces high real interest rates, which enlarge the passive deficit! Wallich surmises that rational expectations, if widely prevalent, "reduce the effects of government policy to mere changes in the rate of inflation, without lasting impact on the real economy."

This is certainly a major dilemma confronted by the economics profession. Cyclical recovery would shrink the deficit; expectations derived from the deficit itself threaten to forestall or enervate the cyclical recovery. Even the Federal Reserve is immobilized. Failure of the week-to-week "fix" would send up rates and abort the recovery. *The historical opportunity for policy to mediate between current conditions and ultimate objectives has withered away; the time to engage in discretionary variations of policy on the road to high employment has been collapsed by inflation expectations and their prompt discounting into current interest rates.*

The discounting rests on widely publicized correlations between the growth of the money stock and the performance of inflation as much as two years later—a correlation that overflies the entire intermediate course of economic activity. It overflies the Phillips Curve and ignores admonitions (of Eisner and others) that rising prices are a market phenomenon, occurring in conjunction with revival in general business conditions and rising utilization rates. The overarching relationship of money to inflation, with its statistical two-year lead, passes in one step across all of the phases of the business cycle so exhaustively examined in the landmark studies of the National Bureau of Economic Research in the pre- and post-World War II years, and forecloses the opportunities of policy to achieve a progressive and modulated course toward high employment.

Does this overstate the significance of expectations, particularly inflation expectations? One can point to the behavior of interest rates in the second half of 1982. While money growth accelerated, the rates actually fell. The record of rational expectations—its ability to contribute to an explanation of economic developments—has not been notably good. Why, it might be inquired, if *restrictive* monetary policy falls so heavily on *output* on the way down, should *accommodative* policy have so much effect on *inflation* on the way up? It is nevertheless true that market comment continues to describe uneasiness among bondholders in the presence of rapid growth in the money aggregates. While interest rates are sharply below their levels of a year ago, the inflation rate has also subsided, and real interest rates, by most calculations, remain far above their historical norms.

If we were to assume, with many of the authors, that inflation expectations are still alive and well out there, what would it take to terminate them? How much unemployment? How much reduction in inflation itself? How much sense of idle capacity and constrained investment? How much reduction of the deficit through reduced expenditures and/or higher taxes? (Keynesians would doubt that such measures would reduce the deficit at all, since they would tend

32

to shrink the revenue base.) How much of a reduction in the rate of growth of money? (Wallich and others agree that the result of such a reduction would be a rise in rates in the short term.) How do we know that the cyclical energy that would result from a return to lower real interest rates would not promptly reawaken such expectations?

How will we know when inflationary expectations are vanquished and the job finished? Can we assume, reasoning backward from consequence to cause, that a return to a historical real interest rate in the bond market would be conclusive evidence that inflationary expectations are dead?

Do real interest rates reflect *only* inflation expectations? Santow offers a number of other probable causes of the high level of real rates. He comes close to suggesting that the money and capital markets have themselves departed from the competitive paradigm; interest rates, like wages and other prices, are "sticky." Deregulation and recognition of increased credit risks have also tended to support nominal and real rates. Credit-risk conditions begin to close the circle, since the elevation of credit risk is a reflection of recession itself. And Eisner completes the closing of the circle; High interest rates *cause* inflation because they are a cost of doing business and because they are a big contributor to the conventionally measured budget deficit on which inflation expectations rest.

Are economists themselves partly responsible for the sensitized expectational behavior patterns they observe? Have they trained the financial markets to react to deficits (when they cannot agree themselves on how to calculate the deficit or what the consequences of deficits may be)? Have they trained the bond market to react so violently to the weekly data on the money stock? Have they *imposed* the derivative expectations (what other people will think) that influence the judgments of individual participants, as both Wallich and Stein point out? Outside the financial market itself, how widely are inflation expectations now? If economics is to give such overwhelming weight to expectational variables, should it not seek documentation of their presence and ways to measure their intensity over time?

There is also the possibility that the inflation record buried in the minds of bond traders is not attributable exclusively to such mistakes of policy as "excessive" money creation and "excessive" budget deficits, to which rational expectations are attached. If inflation expectations draw their strength from recollections of the soaring price indexes of the 1970s, how much of that record was attributable not to errors of policy (in shooting for excessively high employment, as Stein argues) but to two explosions in the prices of oil and food (as Eisner points out), inevitably spread throughout the system by the indexation so prevalent in today's economic structure? International and meteorological accidents are hard to predict; they are hardly subjects for rational expectations. And it is hard to deal with them with a monetary rule that calls for *general* price stability. Eisner asserts that in reality "we do not get downward adjustment in prices not directly affected by a supply shock." Much of the record of the 1970s was "cost-push" inflation.

Finally, the criteria of "excessive" money creation and budget deficits may change over time with changes in the legislative and institutional structure. Monetary and budgetary experience comparable with our own exists all over the West, which shares with us the history of a developing mixed economy and of markets greatly altered by technology and social legislation. Samuelson notes that the "paradigm" of equilibrium economics is failing; markets—particularly, but not exclusively, the market for labor—are no longer clear in the new institutional structure. He refers to "tremendous differences between actual economic history and the refined theoretical micromodels of economists." Tobin makes the same point: In today's economy, some degree of inflation is necessary to permit relative adjustment in real wages and prices.

Apart from these comments, the record is almost silent with respect to the institutional change that has overcome the system in the last several decades and that is partly reflected in the reversal of the mix of government spending from the dominance of real purchases to the dominance of transfers. Does any given budgetary outcome mean the same thing today as it did in the 1950s, when the bulk of expenditures was for highly stimulative purchases, with a high feedback into the revenue base?

Is it not reasonable to suppose that the Phillips Curve of this system—that is, the relationship of resource use to inflation—has been shifted upward, all along its length, by the institutional developments of the past several decades? If inflation targets and inflation expectations are to dominate economic policy, the new curve may condemn the system to operating at far below the levels of resource use that would have been tolerable 20 years ago.

Conversely, to achieve even a reasonable definition of high employment might require bigger deficits, more money growth, and more inflation than was required 20 years ago.

This range of material is only hinted at in these chapters, since none of the assignments focused upon it, but it is hard to ignore in a summary of where we are. Strikingly, income policies, which are directed specifically to such issues, were not mentioned by any of the authors. With only rare exceptions, the material generated clings to the equilibrium paradigm, although few of the authors might have accepted the paradigm without qualification, if their attention had been directed to it by their assignment. Nor, for the same reason, is there any mention of "industrial policies," which, like incomes policies, take their ultimate rationale from a presumed deterioration in the functioning of competitive markets.

Institutional change is hard to quantify, and "accidents" to the price level are, by definition, hard to predict. The minimal reference to them in these essays suggests that economic science is more at home with "rationality" and "rational expectations" than with the anecdotal confusions and evolving structures of living history. It is, in the main, the rational human who runs through the chapters, and comprises the society to which macroeconomic policy addresses itself. Extended to include rational expectations, this formulation multiplies the opportunities for complex research, but it also very nearly vacates, for those who subscribe fully to it, the power to separate the short term from the long term and to describe a pragmatic course from the present to the ultimate objectives sought by all.

A last uneasy but necessary point—uneasy, because it relates to attitudes and philosophies that lie outside the design of the project, and even outside Samuelson's value-free, "positivist" economics: The overriding dilemma of the U.S. economy in the early 1980s has been underutilization of its human and capital resources. The immense obstacle to the application of fiscal and monetary policies to this dilemma is inflationary expectations, drawn from past Federal Reserve behavior, past behavior of the price level, and the present deficit. This collage of concerns is a prominent part of the "weak consensus." But the willingness not necessarily to question this formulation but to take risks with it varies widely among the authors. This collection of essays seems to disclose an association between the degree of willingness to take a circumspect, risk-taking approach to the consensus, on the one hand, and philosophical attitudes toward the size and role of government, on the other.

At one extreme, Meltzer is least willing to take the risks. He is also the most outspoken in his views that inflation originates exclusively in government, that government is less efficient than the private sector, and that a legislative constraint on government spending would be desirable. Penner paints an almost satiric portrait of the political causes of deficits; he would favor even constitutional constraint, if he thought it would work. Jones finally rejects capital budgeting, despite his own list of its many virtues, for fear that it would relax constraint over total spending. Rivlin and Staats refer repeatedly to the tendencies of federal spending to rise and the need to tighten control. Wallich argues for concern over the deficit because "it imposes some constraint on political spending in a world where little such constraint sometimes seems to be left." Stein puts it that "the chief object of the balanced-budget doctrine was to resist the weakness of the flesh, or of the political process . . . a policy for balancing the budget derives from the need for expenditure discipline."

At the other extreme, Tobin and Eisner are most willing to take risks; they seem to carry a respect for government functions, deny that all government outlay is consumption and that all inflation originates in government, and question even the validity of the "weak consensus" view that present and prospective deficits are clearly too big. Tobin argues for a "once-and-for-all increase in the monetary base" to get out of the present dilemma, taking his chances on the ultimate inflation consequences (although not really denying them) in order to escape from the present. Eisner comes close to denying the consensus itself, and argues for direct, immediate treatment of the present.

In the eyes of its supporters, the consensus mechanism seems to have, as one of its virtues, a constraint on the growth of government—perhaps the only available constraint, given the difficulties of constitutional or statutory control, and given (if one accepts it) the intense self-interest of "politicians" and "bureaucrats" described so vividly by Penner.

In the end, it must be said that the policy issues to which the program was directed are partly derivative and lie partly outside formal economics. A fundamental underlying confusion in economics reflects its lost innocence with respect to the political process and its lost bearings with respect to the place of government in an economic philosophy suitable for this country at this time. Samuelson and Stein come closest to dealing with this most general issue. Samuelson concludes that the "fiscal crisis" represents "frustration on the part of those more critical of government's role in the economy than are the effective majority of the voters and their representatives." The deficits produced by the 1981 tax reduction legislation were a way of "putting pressure on the Congress to cut expenditure programs." That effort has failed thus far. The essence of the "fiscal crisis" is the growing *structural* high-employment deficit that has appeared in the wake of that failure and its implied enlargement of the share of government in the nation's economy and its capital markets.

NOTES

1. The term "saving pool" is a convenient but imperfect metaphor. The quantity to which it applies is not "savings" but "saving." It is not a pool of assets accumulated in the past, not a reservoir, but a flow generated in the course of the economy's operation in any accounting period. The term carries the suggestion of a fixed quantity, uninfluenced by activity in the present. In fact, the saving generated in the system, like all such flows within an accounting period, bears a relatively constant relationship to nominal output. The dollar value of the flow grows with the dollar value of the system itself, and it shrinks with recession.

2. Readers should be reminded that the figures on "gross saving," while they doubtless have their own statistical problems, may be more dependable than the series on "net saving." The difference between them is a calculated deduction representing the "true" exhaustion of capital (not the more measurable tax-based depreciation that can be drawn from data on corporate and personal tax returns). The estimate of capital consumption rests, uneasily, on theoretical schedules of exhaustion of capital, by type. The actual inventory of capital is hardly known, nor is the real exhaustion rate well known. For this reason, the aggregate that has come to dominate national accounting is the "gross national product"—"gross" because it is free of any deduction for capital consumption. The national accounts carry a "net national product" figure, but it is generally considered weak and is rarely referred to in analysis of the national accounts.

3. Presumably they would be automatic; the real interest rate would fall with the deficit.

PART ONE

ECONOMIC SIGNIFICANCE OF BUDGET OUTCOMES

CHAPTER TWO

THE SAD STATE OF FISCAL POLICY

Herbert Stein

Fiscal policy in the United States is in a greater state of uncertainty, disagreement, confusion, and even hypocrisy than at any time in the last 30 years. The clearest evidence is our schizophrenia about budget deficits. No one likes large deficits. Indeed, we compete with each other in the depth of our revulsion at them. But nobody thinks the deficits will be reduced for a long, long time.

The gap between talk and practice is highlighted by the proposed constitutional amendment requiring that the budget be balanced. The President strongly supports such an amendment; over two-thirds of the Senate and one-half of the House of Representatives voted for it in the last Congress. More than 30 states enacted prompt calls for a constitutional convention to adopt such an amendment. But no supporter of this amendment has suggested a combination of tax and expenditure measures that would bring about a balanced budget by the time such an amendment might go into effect—or even at a later date. No supporters of the amendment, as far as I know, have offered any explanation for their inability or unwillingness to describe a policy path that would bring the budget into balance by 1987—except the obvious one that if such a path were described, support for the amendment would evaporate.

That practice should deviate from the conventional descriptions of policy is not unusual in the United States. But in the present case, the deviation is exceptionally great. Moreover, even where practice deviates from conventional or official descriptions of policy, there is usually someone who rationalizes the practice. No one has come forward to rationalize the deficits. (The *1982 Annual Report of the Council of Economic Advisers* took a half-step in that direction and then retreated.)

Sometimes it seems to economists that there is a consensus on proper policy that is shared by all informed or expert people, but from which actual policy deviates because of public ignorance or political venality. If that is ever the case, it is not the case with fiscal policy. Professional economic thinking on that subject is characterized by disagreement and uncertainty.

THE RISE AND FALL OF FUNCTIONAL FINANCE

Fifteen or twenty years ago, there was a national consensus on fiscal policy by which we tried to live, and more or less did live. The consensus was for a moderated or domesticated version of functional finance. My book, *The Fiscal Revolution in America*, is the story of the evolution of policy from Hoover's 1932 tax increase to the Kennedy-Johnson tax cut of 1964, which was taken as a sign of the arrival of that consensus. The book was published in 1969, which was too early to report the decline of that consensus. The country has since discarded this functional-finance principle, and for good reason. But it has not been replaced by any new policy that we are willing to accept as a guide and a limitation to action. Instead, there are a number of slogans to which all pay obeisance, but that are not compelling.

Simply stated, functional finance is the belief that the proper and dominant test of the size of the budget surplus or deficit is that it be large enough to yield full employment, and that the deficit or surplus be changed from time to time as required by the changing state of the private economy. By saying that this idea, which originated in the 1930s, had been moderated or domesticated by the early 1960s, several things are meant. There had been some recognition that it was not practical to keep fiscal policy in constant flux in response to every wiggle of the private economy—despite the implications of the term "fine tuning." There was more awareness than there had been earlier of the danger of inflation. Greater weight was given to monetary policy as a partner with fiscal policy in economic stabilization. But still the dominant lesson of functional finance was that the deficit should be big enough to yield full employment; these qualifications were only footnotes to that lesson.

The consensus that existed on functional finance, even as so modified, has broken down and been left behind. There were several reasons for this. The most important was that the policy—which was no longer purely fiscal policy but monetary-fiscal, with monetary as the senior partner—turned out to be inflationary as practiced. That was not logically necessary. In principle, the rate of unemployment consistent with stability of the price level could have been known, and the combination of fiscal and monetary policies could have been aimed at achieving it. But they were not. Policies were regularly aimed at unemployment targets that were too low and that caused inflation. This was probably inevitable for political reasons. Once the government assumes responsibility for the rate of unemployment, politicians will compete for votes by promising a low rate of unemployment, which will lead to an inflationary target. This has happened over enough time and to enough Administrations and Federal Reserve Board chairpersons to suggest that it is extremely likely, if not inevitable.

The development of thinking among economists has tended to diminish confidence in the functional-finance prescription. There was increasing doubt that fiscal policy had any significant role to play in the fiscal-monetary partnership for the management of aggregate demand. Fiscal policy seemed only a less efficient way of doing what monetary policy could do alone with less costly or diverting side effects. Moreover, there was doubt about whether the management of nominal demand could make any lasting contribution to the maintenance of full employment or would affect only the rate of inflation.

These were good reasons for abandoning—or at least more radically limiting—the role of functional finance as a guide to fiscal policy. They may not, however, have been the decisive reasons for what happened. Functional finance may have reached its apogee in December 1965 when *Time* ran a picture of Keynes on its cover. This popular and official acceptance of functional finance came just as the economy was entering a prolonged period of accelerating inflation to which a number of other ailments, notably slow economic growth, were added in time. No one ever proved that functional finance was the only, or main, cause of these economic miseries, any more than it had been proved to be responsible for the economic miracle of the previous generation. But functional finance, usually called Keynesian economics, was on the scene of the crime or accident, and was assumed to be guilty.

Despite the general demotion of functional finance, certain aspects or reflections of it have remained, although in rather ironic forms. Conservatives, anti-Keynesians or monetarists, have repudiated the notion that deficits could stimulate the economy. Their argument is epitomized in Milton Friedman's question: "Where do they think the money comes from to finance the deficit—the tooth fairy?" But they have been reluctant to abandon the belief that deficits are inflationary. This superficial inconsistency has been resolved by the proposition that deficits by themselves are not inflationary, but that deficits cause monetary expansion, which *is* inflationary.

The connection between government deficits and monetary expansion has been the subject of several econometric studies. The studies have not led to a firm conclusion about whether deficits have caused an increase of monetary expansion in the past. There seems to be no economic reason why a deficit should cause or require more monetary expansion than a surplus. This leaves politics aside— which is a big thing to leave aside. But it is important to try to distinguish between what is economically necessary and what is politically necessary, especially because what economists say is economically necessary affects what is politically necessary. The Federal Reserve has been sticking to its preferred monetary course in spite of large federal deficits. The experience of the last several years may be convincing evidence that a Federal Reserve that cares seriously about doing so can follow a disinflationary course despite large deficits.

There is now also a curious reversal of the standard Keynesian doctrine that budget deficits are expansive and stimulating. This has reached the point where an experienced economist recently said that we know the size of the deficit multiplier but do not know whether it is positive or negative.

There are three routes by which people are reaching the conclusion that big deficits are depressing the economy, that is, depressing it in the short-run sense of holding down aggregate demand and creating a gap between actual and potential output, not in the longer-run sense of slowing down productive investment and thus decreasing the rate of growth of potential output. Sometimes people proceed directly from the common proposition that high interest rates depress the economy through the proposition that big budget deficits depress the economy. That, of course, is a slovenly argument. It is like saying that high prices of sugar depress the sales of sugar, an increase in the demand for sugar raises the price of sugar, and, therefore, an increase in the demand for sugar will depress sales of sugar. The proposition about interest rates depressing the economy is a proposition about what would happen *if* interest rates rose and all other things were constant. But, obviously, if interest rates rise because the deficit has increased, all other things are not constant. There is an increase of demand arising from the government sector, and interest rates rise to "crowd out" some demand originating in the private sector. But the demand crowded out will not be larger than the additional demand arising from the deficit. It is the fact that the combined demands have increased that makes the interest rates rise.

The second kind of argument relies on psychological factors, or confidence. Deficits, it is acknowledged, are not depressing in an objective sense. The mere act of borrowing to finance government expenditures would not depress the economy if people did not know that it was happening. But people do know that it is happening and are accustomed to thinking that deficits are bad for the economy. Therefore, the sight of deficits causes the private sector to pull in its horns—to cut investment and consumption— and *that* depresses the economy. This line of thinking first struck me when writing the aforementioned book on fiscal history: Why did Herbert Hoover, who was not a stupid man, take what later seemed the bizarre step of raising taxes in 1932, at the depth of the depression? The explanation was that he wanted to restore confidence by reducing the budget deficit. He was concerned about the confidence of U.S. investors. He was concerned about the confidence of foreigners who, if suspicious of our finances, would withdraw gold and squeeze our money supply. He was concerned about the confidence of the Federal Reserve Board because it had indicated extreme reluctance to increase the money supply while the budget was in deficit. Even some sophisticated economists believed that with this psychological background, a tax increase was desirable; however, that conflicted with what was already conventional economics.

This line of thinking seems to have returned. People who do not themselves believe that deficits are a threat to the recovery think that other people think so, and, because other people think so and react adversely to deficits, the deficits really are a threat to the recovery. This is a hard kind of argument to deal with because so little is known about what makes people think what they do. That is precisely why many people find it convenient to make the appeal to confidence: They can be quite free in deciding what creates confidence. But the best assumption is probably that people's beliefs conform to the objective facts, and that deficits will not be depressing unless there are objective reasons why they should be. Herbert Hoover had more reason to think what he did than there is to think the same thing 50 years later.

The third argument, that deficits are depressing and that reduction of the deficits would help to promote recovery, comes from an unexpected source—the economists whom we are accustomed to call liberal, or Keynesian. Their proposal involves a change in the fiscal-monetary mix. They think that recovery would be assisted if monetary policy were more expansive and fiscal policy less so—that is, if the budget deficit were smaller. This proposal does not appear to specify in what proportions the monetary easing and fiscal tightening are to be combined, or even in what dimensions the two instruments are to be measured. One way of looking at the mix proposal is to suggest that the two instruments be recombined in such a way that the rate of growth of total spending, as measured by the rate of growth of dollar GNP, is unaffected. If that is meant by a change in the policy mix, it is unclear why this should raise the level of total output or its rate of growth. One would expect the change in the policy mix to affect the output mix. With a smaller deficit, one would anticipate lower real interest rates and more housing, private investment, and durable goods sales, but also less defense production, or less production of nondurable consumer goods, or less of something else, depending on the way in which the

budget deficit was reduced. But unless there are special circumstances not now apparent, there is nothing in this process to make
total output higher. On the other hand, if the mix is to be changed in
a way that will make total spending rise more rapidly, reducing the
deficit is not needed. That could be accomplished by increased
monetary expansion alone. The proposal to cut the deficit as part of
the package serves one or more political or psychological purposes.
It blunts the complaint that the objective is simply monetary
expansion, which would be inflationary. It places blame for
unemployment on the Administration, which created the deficit by
its tax cut and expenditure increase. And possibly, if the mix change
were effectuated, it might lull the private sector into thinking it was
not inflationary and so help to raise output with less inflationary
consequences.

One can imagine that even though today's budget deficits are
not depressing, the prospect of large future deficits is depressing.
This is an ironic adaptation of Keynes' argument about the liquidity
trap. Keynes said that there could be a condition in which monetary
expansion would not stimulate the economy: everyone would
expect higher interest rates in the future, so they would hold any
additions to the money supply rather than risk the capital loss
involved in buying long-term bonds. Therefore, interest rates would
not fall, and the monetary expansion would not succeed in
stimulating the economy. The current counterpart of that argument
is that the expectation of large future deficits leads to the expectation
of high future interest rates, which keeps present long-term interest
rates from falling and so obstructs the present recovery. But there is
a critical difference between the condition Keynes described and
today's parallel. In Keynes' case, people expected high interest rates
in the future because they had experienced high interest rates in the
past and had not learned any better. That is, they were not expecting
high interest rates in the future because they were expecting the
demand for capital to be strong in the future. More recently, a
situation has been visualized in which interest rates will be high
because the demand for capital—combining private and government demands—will be strong. Such a condition should strengthen
the present demand for capital and make investors willing to pay the
high interest rates.

Another aspect of this argument may be especially relevant to
recent circumstances. A decline of interest rates is believed to be

essential to keep many businesses and financial institutions from bankruptcy. This is said to rule out a recovery with high interest rates, as would be implied by a policy of large budget deficits. There is something to this. But what is important from this standpoint is nominal short-term interest rates, and the main determinant of these will be a policy that reduces the expected inflation rate. The size of the deficit affects real interest rates, and the range within which even large changes in the deficit can affect interest rates is probably small, so that the contribution that reducing the deficit can make to the financial problems of businesses and financial institutions caught in the swings of the inflation rate is probably also small.

This is not meant to imply that the size of budget deficits has no effect on the overall level of economic activity or on the rate of unemployment. If one believes that everything affects everything else, and if one is ingenious and determined, one can find—or at least imagine—what those effects are. But, in fact, the relationship between the budget deficit or surplus and unemployment or total output in the short run has become so uncertain, even to economists, that it is no longer trusted, or trustworthy, as a guide to fiscal policy.

THE BALANCED-BUDGET DOCTRINE

It might have been thought that the decline of the functional-finance doctrine would be matched by the elevation of the balanced-budget doctrine. Ever since the notion that the budget should be managed so as to achieve full employment came into prominence, the rule that the budget should be balanced has been its chief opposition and alternative. The rise (or rebirth) of the budget-balancing doctrine as disillusionment with functional finance mounted was symbolized by resolutions in more than 30 states calling for a constitutional convention to adopt an amendment requiring that the budget be balanced. And a President was elected who seemed more devoted to budget balancing than any since Coolidge. (Hoover's approach to that issue was more pragmatic.)

Despite this apparent rise of the budget-balancing doctrine, the country is now confronted by the largest deficit in history, and very large deficits are expected for as far into the future as the eye can see.

This is a great irony. It is as great an irony as the current claim of many devout Keynesians that the budget deficts are depressing output and employment.

Why are there such large deficits in the land and regime of the budget balancers? One might say that the flesh is weak and we all are sinners, so it is not surprising that people do not do what they think is right. It might also be said that conditions have been unusually difficult; efforts to balance the budget have been made but were unsuccessful in these circumstances.

But these explanations are not sufficient. The chief object of the balanced-budget doctrine was to resist the weakness of the flesh, or of the political process. And the doctrine did not say that the budget should be balanced unless it was inconvenient to do so. It said that there should be strenuous efforts to balance the budget and that few grounds for failure should be recognized.

The fact is that there has not been a strenuous effort. No one has been willing to sacrifice anything considered very valuable in order to balance the budget. The basic reason for this appears to be that although everyone is now a budget balancer, for different reasons, no one considers the reasons—even the most appealing ones—overwhelming.

For a long time, the basic argument made against budget deficits was that they were inflationary. This was, for example, the argument commonly used by Ronald Reagan before he became President. It has already been noted that this had a certain Keynesian flavor, because it implied that total spending could be increased by increasing the deficit. This argument became more and more questionable as more weight was given to the role of money. The Federal Reserve has been demonstrating the possibility of conducting a noninflationary monetary policy in the presence of large budget deficits. The President has not been referring to deficits as a cause of inflation, but has been referring to spending increases, which are quite different. Balancing the budget is still frequently said to be necessary in order to avoid inflation, but the statement is coming to be more and more ritualistic. It does not move or inhibit anyone very much.

A more substantial case for a policy of balancing the budget derives from the need for expenditure discipline. The basic point is that government expenditures grow too rapidly or are too high, and that, given the public dislike for raising taxes, expenditures will be smaller or grow more slowly if the budget *has to be* balanced, so that increasing expenditures requires raising taxes.

This is what underlies a great deal of the talk about the importance of balancing the budget and much of the complaint about the budget deficits of the last 50 years. The complaint was not that the deficits were too big, but that the expenditures were too high. This is clear in the record of many of the business organizations that were the strongest champions of balancing the budget, such as the U.S. Chamber of Commerce. Although they regularly resisted almost all expenditure increases on the grounds that they would cause or increase deficits, they also supported all proposals for tax reduction and resisted all proposals for tax increases.

A large part of the motivation behind the proposed constitutional amendment is also the desire to hold expenditures down. An essential part of the amendment, in the minds of many of its supporters, is the requirement that revenue as a percentage of GNP not rise without an affirmative vote of more than 50 percent of all the members—not just the members present—of both houses of Congress. The objective is not just to get the budget balanced, which in the thinking of some sponsors is secondary, if not absolutely irrelevant, but to ensure that expenditures do not rise as a percentage of GNP.

Some people who rely on the expenditure-discipline argument for a balanced-budget rule are sufficiently logical to realize that what they want is not a balanced budget, but a rule requiring a balanced budget. Maximum downward pressure is put on expenditures by the combination of a large actual deficit and a strong devotion to the principle that the budget be balanced. People who think like that, for example, want a big tax cut, even though they know it will unbalance the budget, because they believe that the sight of the deficit will put pressure on people who fear deficits to cut expenditures. Whether this can be a viable position for long is a question to be discussed below.

The use of the budget-balancing rule as a discipline on expenditures can be justified, and frequently is justified, as being something more than an expression of a private preference for smaller expenditures. It is said to be justified by an inherent bias in the decision-making process that leads governments to spend too

50

much, mainly because the beneficiaries of expenditure programs have intense interests in them that tend to override the objections of the rest of the community that may not appreciate the costs being imposed on them. To counter this bias and arrive at proper expenditure decisions, it is necessary to impose a rule that requires the expenditure decision to be matched by a tax decision, since the tax decision will mobilize the opposition of the part of the community that is not the direct beneficiary of the proposed expenditures.

There are several difficulties with this argument. For one thing, it implies that expenditures must be financed by taxes, even when, by criteria other than expenditure discipline, that is not the best way to finance them. If taxation were the superior means of finance, it would not be necessary to invoke the expenditure-discipline argument. One could say that budgets should be balanced because it is the better way to finance expenditures. But that is not what the discipline argument implies. It implies that the only superiority of taxing over borrowing is that taxing is more painful to the voter. Thus it suggests acceptance of a potentially inferior method of finance in order to make the expenditure decision more painful than it would otherwise be.

Moreover, the case for the existence of bias that makes expenditures in general too large is incomplete. One can certainly think of elements in the decision-making process that tend in that direction, but the net result may differ. One can also imagine elements in the process that work in the other direction. Anyone who has ever thought that any government expenditure was too low is aware of that. For example, the military-industry complex may tend to create a bias for excessive military expenditures. But there may also be a tendency for the public to underestimate a threat that is distant in time and comes from a source that is not well understood; this creates a bias in the direction of inadequate military spending. The net of these biases may be that too little has been spent for defense. In that case, making the expenditure decision more difficult by requiring that it be accompanied by a decision to tax would result in a worse, not a better, expenditure decision. A person who thinks that could not deny the possibility that expenditures for research, or education, or bridges, or welare are inadequate simply by asserting that there are some biases in the political process that would tend in that direction. One cannot be sure of tipping the balance in the right direction by putting another weight in the scale on the side of less spending.

In any case, the force of the budget-balancing rule derived from the argument that balancing the budget is needed to restrain expenditures is not strong now and will probably grow weaker. People's belief that budget balancing is a good thing, for good or bad reasons, will tend to restrain expenditures. But they will not be restrained by a rule whose only purpose and justification are to restrain them. The argument for abiding by such a rule adds nothing to the argument for restraining expenditures. If individuals are told that $1 million spent for something they favor will unbalance the budget, they will not be persuaded unless shown that other bad consequences will result. But they will not want a balanced budget if its only purpose is to keep them from doing something they want to do.

There may be justification for an overall rule limiting expenditures, and conceivably all the claimants for government expenditures would agree to be bound by such a rule. They would agree because they would decide that the costs to them of unconstrained expenditures for the benefit of others would outweigh the gains to them of the expenditures they want. But that would not be a reason for subscribing to a rule in the particular form that requires a balanced budget *unless* people believed that expenditures financed by borrowing do more damage than expenditures financed by taxes. There would have to be some reason for opposing deficits in addition to the reason for opposing expenditures; otherwise there would be no reason to distinguish between tax-financed and deficit-financed expenditures.

The most sophisticated supporters of the balanced-budget amendment, as has already been noted, do not care much about balancing the budget. They would have preferred a limit on spending directly, perhaps in the form of a limit on expenditures as a percentage of GNP. They became supporters of the balanced-budget amendment when it was altered to include the limitation on revenues, which, of course, transformed the amendment into one limiting expenditures. They hoped in this way to harness their objective of limiting expenditures to the strong popular sentiment that they believed to exist in favor of a balanced budget.

I followed this line of reasoning 35 years ago, when I was at the Committee for Economic Develoment. The CED wanted a rule of fiscal policy that would serve, among other things, as a restraint on government expenditures. It chose a variant of the budget-balancing rule; it did so partly, although not entirely, because it believed that there was a strong traditional allegiance among the public to the idea that the budget should be balanced and therefore a rule relying upon that allegiance would have a good chance to be observed.

After the experience of the last 35 years, it appears that the traditional allegiance we counted on really is not there. Despite the public opinion polls, which consistently show that people want the budget to be balanced, people regularly elect government officials who have never balanced it and never will. In the 1969 study (which has been cited several times), the balanced-budget doctrine is called a flag that is more often saluted than followed. It seems that most of the people now supporting the balanced-budget amendment are saluting a passing flag that they have no intention of following. To get people seriously interested in following it, some reason more compelling than that following it will keep people from doing what they want to do will have to be determined.

The classical and, in this author's opinion, most important argument for balancing the budget—or at least limiting deficits—is the crowding-out argument. Government borrowing to finance a deficit absorbs saving that would otherwise be available for, and probably used for, private investment that would promote future economic growth. But to proceed from this proposition to any specific rule of fiscal policy involves a number of uncertain steps.

In the first place, the argument assumes that private saving does not increase enough as a result of the increase of the deficit to leave undiminished the amount of saving available to finance private investment. There are three reasons why this assumption might be wrong. Taxpayers may increase their saving to keep their net-asset position intact in the face of the liabilities for future taxes implicit in the deficit. This seems a plausible description of rational behavior, and it is a hypothesis that needs further examination. But neither introspection nor available observation of the savings rate in the United States indicates that people do indeed behave in this way. A second possibility is that a deficit may be created by measures that do, in fact, stimulate saving, such as tax reliefs designed to increase the after-tax return to saving. This is a possibility in particular cases, but it does not seem to be a qualification of very general importance, given present estimates of the elasticity of supply of saving.

There has been a good deal of attention lately to a third way in which a deficit may stimulate private saving. In a time of inflation, the government pays an inflation premium in the interest on its debt to compensate the debt holders for the decline in the real value of their assets. To the extent that the debt holders save more than they ordinarily would in order to keep the real value of their assets intact, the government's deficit is offset by private saving. Whether debt holders actually behave in this way is an empirical question. William Fellner of the American Enterprise Institute has made some investigation of this question and concludes tentatively that there is a tendency in this direction but that it is not very strong. That is, the additional saving generated by the inflation premium in interest is a small fraction of the additional interest.

A more serious qualification to the crowding-out argument arises on the other side of the equation—what happens to investment rather than what happens to saving. If policy is concerned with the crowding out of private investment, it is mainly, although not entirely, because of the implications for the future rate of economic growth. Not only private investment but also many other current uses of resources contribute to growth, and some of them are government uses of resources. More government spending on roads and bridges, on research, on education, and so on increases growth. If financing such expenditures by a budget deficit crowds out some private investment, the net result may not be a reduction in growth. One might say that such government expenditures produce less growth per dollar than private investment. This might provide an argument for financing government investment in part, but not entirely, by taxes.

This line of thinking leads to capital budgeting, with a presumption for balancing the current accounts but not the capital accounts. This thinking also leads to a morass of accounting and definitional problems. If there is no test of pecuniary return, it is hard to decide what is a capital asset and at what rate the asset depreciates. An especially large and difficult case is defense expenditures. These expenditures defend the national income and much else for this generation. They simultaneously defend the national income and much else for future generations. How are today's defense expenditures to be divided between the current and the capital account?

There is an even more baffling puzzle in all this. By what standard should the country decide on the proper net effect of the budget on future growth? It seems to be assumed that more growth is better than less, but that is not really true unless the growth is free, which it rarely is. If increasing growth entails the sacrifice of something else valuable, like current consumption, people recognize that there is a point beyond which further sacrifice is not worthwhile. At least they recognize that in their private decisions. If the government is making a decision about growth involving the allocation of the national output between consumption and investment, it should recognize that point also. But how to pinpoint it?

Suppose it is known that if the budget were balanced, the economy would grow by 3 percent per annum, but that the growth rate would be 2 percent if there were a deficit of $100 billion, and 4 percent if there were a surplus of $100 billion. Which is the right budget policy? What is the obligation to future generations? Is it to leave them present real per capita incomes? Is it to give them the same increase over us as we had over our parents? One may have feelings about such questions, but there are no objective answers. One can say that such questions are none of the government's business. The government should only be neutral with respect to the supply of savings available for private investment or with respect to the rate of growth. But given a large government sector that affects savings and growth negatively and positively in a great many ways, neutrality bears no easy relation to a balanced budget.[1]

The purpose of these nihilistic comments is not to suggest that deficits do not matter. They do matter, probably less than one might judge from our talk but more than one might judge from our actions. The point is that there is no certainty or agreement about why deficits matter and how much, or about what national policy should be. Therefore, policy is highly unpredictable. No one knows what credence to place in government pronouncements of its intentions. The inability to predict what policy will be and to estimate what difference it makes is a great uncertainty overhanging the economy and must impair economic efficiency and progress. And that effect is apart from the consequence of making wrong decisions as a result of ignorance.

Fiscal policy has been discussed as if it were identical to policy for the size of the deficit or surplus. Although this has been conventional, it is not necessarily valid. The government's budget is the product of hundreds or thousands of individual decisions. What is meant by fiscal policy is a limited set of decisions that are made prior to the others and to which the others are made to conform. The decision about the size of the deficit or surplus is commonly thought of as the first of these prior decisions. It may be that it does not deserve this role. Some people would say that the decision about total expenditures is the first of all decisions, and the division between taxes and borrowing secondary.

But no greater certainty or agreement is found when the question is how large expenditures should be. The universal answer is "smaller," but that cannot be taken seriously as an answer without limit. Moreover, "total expenditures" is an extremely heterogeneous variable about which to make any significant statement. Probably the two main goals that lead to the idea of limiting total expenditures are freedom and efficiency. Different kinds of expenditures must differ enormously in both of these dimensions. If large government expenditures are a threat to freedom, that threat is much less per dollar for outlays that are made according to an objective, mechanical formula, such as old-age benefits, than for outlays where there is discretion to choose purposes and recipients, like research grants to universities. And defense expenditures may safeguard freedom rather than threaten it. If large government expenditures sap the efficiency of the national economy, that must be more true of expenditures that use resources than of expenditures that only transfer income around, and more true of expenditures that produce services that the private sector can also produce—like medical care—than of expenditures that produce uniquely governmental services—like the judicial system.

Perhaps the whole notion of a fiscal policy is a chimera. There are several hundred or thousand decisions to be made in the budget on both the income and output sides, and each of these decisions must be balanced against all the others at the margin in terms of all their consequences. There are no prior limiting decisions to be made. If everything were known absolutely and objectively, that would be the basis on which to proceed. But, of course, not everything is known. If an attempt is made to build a budget entirely from the ground up without any prior constraints, important considerations will be neglected. That is why there is a budget and a budgetary process.

A few big decisions must be selected that will be made by high-level authorities—the President and the Congressional Budget Committees—and to which lower-level authorities will make the smaller decisions conform. However, there are no well-understood and agreed-upon principles by which these big decisions will be guided—or even knowledge of what the big decisions are. The decline of both functional finance and budget balancing has left a vacuum in fiscal policy that needs to be filled.

This essay does not offer a prescription for filling that vacuum. Its purpose is to alert people to the fact that the vacuum exists and to try to get them to take seriously the need to fill it, rather than continuing to repeat old nostrums while following totally undisciplined ad hoc practice.

A mobilization of thinking on this subject is necessary. There is an impressive contrast between the state of the national discussion of macroeconomic policy today and that of the period around the end of World War II. That was also a time of great uncertainty and disagreement. But the nation went through a process of extraordinarily constructive public consideration of economic policy that led to a consensus that worked well for some time. There were exceptionally thoughtful and fruitful congressional hearings, first in the drafting of the Employment Act of 1946 and later in the work on fiscal and monetary policy done by a subcommittee chaired by the late Senator Paul Douglas. A number of private organizations made contributions: the Committee for Economic Development, the National Planning Association, and the Twentieth Century Fund among them. The American Economic Association appointed two committees to draft plans for fiscal and monetary policy.

What characterized these efforts, in retrospect, was the degree to which they were open minded, nonpartisan, and addressed to finding solutions that recognized the existing diversity of views. The depression and the war had left people with the strong feelings that the nation's future was on the line and that narrow parochial considerations had to be subordinated. The war had left a clear policy slate to write on. Keynesianism provided a new stimulant, or irritant, for thought.

It will not be easy to recapture the spirit and intensity of that discussion. The intellectual problems are probably more difficult and the political environment less congenial. But we should try.

NOTE

1. In 1967, commenting on a paper by James Tobin at the American Economic Association meetings, I said that although the government could not be neutral, it could be indifferent to the effect of its deficit or surplus on economic growth. At that time I thought there was an expenditure-discipline case for sticking to "conventional" standards of budget balancing. Fifteen years later, the discipline and the convention seem weaker.

CHAPTER THREE

BUDGET OUTCOMES, DEBT, AND MONETARY POLICY

Henry C. Wallich

Relations between monetary and fiscal policy have run through a series of stages. The present situation stage is one in which considerable economic effectiveness is generally ascribed to monetary policy, while fiscal policy seems to be more a part of the problem than of the solution. It is helpful to review earlier phases of this relationship, beginning with the 1920s when the Federal Reserve first had an opportunity to play a peacetime role as a central bank.

During those halcyon years, the concept of a flexible fiscal policy had not even been formulated. The budget was generally in surplus, and the large debt accumulated during World War I was being reduced at a good rate. Income taxes were cut repeatedly. The Federal Government was a net supplier of savings, and the long-term interest rate was sometimes below the short-term rate as generally high economic activity called for some degree of monetary restraint.

Monetary policy was oriented primarily toward interest rates, with considerable attention given to the balance of payments. Nevertheless, considerations that today would be called monetarist were not absent. Irving Fisher's quantity theory of money was the dominant analytical approach. The Federal Reserve's chief statistician, Carl Snyder, argued for a stable rate of money growth of 4 percent. Price-level stability was regarded as the principal objective of monetary policy, combined with a mild anticyclical orientation to deal with the moderate fluctuations of the period following 1921. Monetary policy generally was regarded as a powerful economic tool.

The 1930s brought the great depression and the advent of fiscal policy as a major policy tool. Monetary policy increasingly was downgraded. It had failed to stem the depression, and it seemed unable to bring the economy back to full employment. Banks were choked with excess reserves; the money supply (M1) was growing at 11 percent over the years 1933 to 1940. Short-term interest rates were close to zero, long-term rates were dropping, with interruptions, to—and even below—the 2.5 percent level at which World War II was financed. Finally, monetary policy had no other function than to peg this interest-rate structure in order to facilitate Treasury financing.

It is difficult now to visualize the low opinion then held by most economists of the capabilities of monetary policy. Congressional hearings in 1952 again and again brought out the view that monetary policy could do very little to curb inflationary pressures. Business and consumers were very liquid and thus protected against monetary restraint. Severe restraint, on the other hand, would cause serious difficulties in managing the public debt, perhaps causing the bond market to fall into a "bottomless pit." It was against broad-based resistance that the Federal Reserve finally broke loose from the obligation to support federal debt to restore a monetary policy oriented toward price and cyclical stability.

This development marked the end of an important phase in the subordination of monetary to fiscal and debt policy. Even then, monetary policy for many years continued to be regarded as the junior partner in the fiscal-monetary team. This clearly was so during the vogue of the "new economics" of the 1960s. Nevertheless, with each succeeding business cycle, there was increasing evidence of the power of monetary policy both to restrain and to stimulate.

The fiscal policies pursued during the 1960s were supported by a monetary policy oriented mainly toward interest rates, a combination that brought strong inflationary pressures. Inflation turned attention to the money supply. In the course of the 1970s, monetary policy shifted toward money-supply targeting. This powerful device significantly altered the balance of power between fiscal and monetary policy. It soon became apparent that fiscal policy was a powerful instrument only so long as monetary policy supported it by allowing the money supply to accelerate. Once it became the goal of monetary policy to avoid undue acceleration, the potential of fiscal policy was much reduced.

At the analytical level, this change has been symbolized by the ascendancy of monetarism. Beyond that, the frustrations encountered by both monetary and fiscal policy have given rise to a new line of economic theorizing that says that neither fiscal nor monetary policy, as it has been pursued in the past, is likely to have any effect. If people have rational expectations, that is, if they understand that the government faced with unemployment will inflate and faced with inflation will allow unemployment, they will act to protect themselves. Their protective action reduces the effect of government policy to mere changes in the rate of inflation without lasting impact on the real economy.

THE STRUCTURE OF THE FEDERAL BUDGET

To examine the relation between monetary policy, the budget, and the debt, a look at the general contours of budget and debt is first needed. Other contributors to this volume examine the numbers of the budget in greater detail and with more authority. The purpose here is to indicate a general configuration by which to assess the environment for monetary policy. The economy is now looking at a budget deficit of about 5 percent of GNP, of which something like 2 percent is structural, the rest cyclical. That is to say, at high employment, calibrated at about 6 percent unemployment, there would remain a deficit, making allowance for the 1983 midyear tax cut, of 2 percent, or $55 to $65 billion. If nothing is done, these already excessive numbers will rise substantially in subsequent years. In other words, the structural deficit is much too large both in terms of long-run growth needs and of the smooth functioning of the economy in the intermediate future. This essay is not addressed to very short-run problems.

Long-run growth needs begin, at least at a theoretical level, with an assessment of the desirable level of the capital stock. A capital stock that is too small will not, over time, give the maximum of consumption, because total output will not be large enough. A capital stock that is larger than optimal, on the other hand, will also hold down consumption, because of the higher investment and, therefore, saving required to keep the stock growing and to replace its wear and tear.

A study by the staff of the Federal Reserve Board suggests that the present capital stock is not seriously inadequate, and that a higher rate of saving and investment than has prevailed on average in the past would not yield large benefits. I have some difficulty with this finding because I think of the pace of technical change as being influenced by investment, so that more investment would also accelerate growth through that channel, which, in turn, would call for and justify a larger capital stock. In any event, the Federal Reserve study provides no justification for large structural budget deficits. At high employment, a balanced budget, or a better surplus, seems appropriate in terms of long-run growth needs. Given a cyclical economy, balance on average may mean surpluses at high employment.

It is instructive to digress and look at Japan in order to illustrate the situation of the U.S. economy. Japan has a very high saving rate, quite possibly in excess of what its optimal capital stock requirements and indeed in excess of what the Japanese economy can absorb, at least under present conditions. In a closed economy in the short run, this condition could mean unemployment, with the excess savings going uninvested despite low interest rates, whereas in the long run it would imply a wasteful level of investment. Actually, Japan is able to export its savings by investing abroad. In doing so, it depresses the yen, which generates an export surplus that effectuates the capital transfer and maintains high employment. The United States is likely to find itself in the opposite position. High absorption of savings by the government is making the supply of capital for the private sector inadequate. The result is a high level of interest rates that drives up the dollar and generates a current-account deficit. In that way, the United States becomes a capital importer.

To say that optimal growth of the U.S. economy requires investment and, therefore, savings of some particular fraction of GNP does not, of course, necessarily imply that this level of investment would be forthcoming even if the savings were available. This is a question of investment opportunities, of the responsiveness of investment to interest rates, of the tax system, of regulation, and of other aspects of the investment climate. A great deal is heard about all of these factors. In particular, there has been a continuing, very adverse interaction between business investment and deficit spending. Government has run deficits, and on an increasingly large scale, in order to reduce cyclical and, perhaps, secular unemployment. But its policies seem to have been of a sort to discourage—not to elicit—complementary private investment. As a result, deficits have expanded and business investment has retreated from what it would have been. If deficits were to be eliminated, would business investment fill the void? Or would, perhaps, interest rates and, therefore, the dollar fall to a level at which the United States became a large capital exporter with a large export surplus? That would maintain full employment, although it might not be optimal for growth of the capital stock. Or would the savings go to waste, with attendant unemployment?

These are questions concerning the basic resiliency of the U.S. economy on which people have "gut feelings" but no statistics. My gut feeling is simple: Under favorable conditions as to tax treatment, regulatory treatment, appropriate monetary policy, and general investment climate, the private sector of the U.S. economy should be able to absorb the full-employment savings of the economy with the federal budget in balance and even in moderate surplus. Given a more realistic set of conditions, I fear that the private sector of the economy has been so debilitated that it may not, in the short run at least, be able to absorb full-employment savings. That would imply the need for either a sizable export surplus or else a structural government deficit. Given the need of the developing world for more capital, it is obvious which way the choice should go. However, there is the question, which cannot be addressed at this point, of how to finance a larger flow of public or private funds to developing countries. There remains a concern that the United States may have put itself in a situation where some structural high-employment budget deficit may be needed, although obviously much smaller than that at present.

It will be helpful to set forth some of the magnitudes relevant to evaluating the kind of structural deficits that have been sketched. The gross saving of the economy (as conventionally measured to include personal and business saving, including corporate and noncorporate capital-consumption allowances, and all government saving, including the negative saving of the federal sector) is of the order of 17 percent of GNP. After capital-consumption allowances in the neighborhood of 10 percent, there is left some 6 to 8 percent net saving to finance private, domestic, and foreign investment. (These data come from the National Income and Product Accounts; the corresponding federal deficit measures do not exactly match the Office of Management and Budget numbers.)

To appraise the absorption of saving by the Federal Government and resultant crowding-out, the difference between gross and net saving is important. From the point of view of the financial markets, gross flows are significant, at least in the short run, since at least part of capital-consumption allowances accrues in liquid form and can enter the capital markets. But, ultimately, net saving is a more significant concept. It is the size of the capital stock that ultimately determines the return on capital, and the real interest rate that must, on average, be equated to it. Increases in the capital stock can only come out of net saving, after wear and tear have been made up. In the aggregate, making up wear and tear absorbs the capital-consumption allowances, even though in terms of particular firms and households, there is no precise replacement of worn-out equipment.

Thus, present total deficits of about 5 percent of GNP and high-employment deficits, now about 2 percent of GNP (and likely to grow), must be weighed against gross saving several times larger but net saving not very much larger. Crowding-out is, therefore, a very real possibility under the present budget structure. On the other hand, a balanced budget, if it were possible, would leave us with a need to increase investment by a very large factor. Hence, the probable need for a full-employment deficit of some, hopefully modest, magnitude.

In addition to the size of the federal deficit, both structural and cyclical, it makes a difference at what overall level of federal spending a given deficit occurs. The Federal Government would absorb fewer resources and leave more for the private sector if it were to reduce its share in GNP by cutting both expenditures and taxes. The resources released by the Federal Government can be used by the private sector for both investment and consumption. In all probability, only a small proportion of resources released will be saved, the larger part going to consumption. Nevertheless, as we look at the absorption of resources by the budget, we should be aware that things can be improved not only by cutting the deficit, but by cutting the budget on both sides without reducing the deficit.

THE FISCAL-MONETARY MIX

The concept of the fiscal-monetary mix goes back to the period of the 1950s and 1960s when monetary policy was thought of primarily in terms of interest rates and when inflation was analyzed principally in terms of excess demand. The quantity of money played a secondary role in either connection. It then seemed plausible that a combination of a budget surplus and low interest rates would be favorable to investment, with fiscal policy supplying additional savings and monetary policy facilitating their investment. This mix seemed to have a desirable orientation toward faster economic growth. Alternatively, a combination of budget deficits and high interest rates could be designed that would produce the same degree of overall stimulation or restraint. It would do so, however, with less investment and a stronger balance of payments, since foreign capital would be attracted. This mix commended itself when there was a need to strengthen the dollar, even though at the expense of growth.

The analysis was not carried to the point of asking what would happen to the money supply under regimes of low or high interest rates, respectively. It seemed sufficient to conclude that either mix could be made noninflationary by aiming at a nonexcessive level of aggregate demand. However, at low interest rates the money supply may be expected, other things being equal, to be higher relative to GNP than at high interest rates. Thus, the relationship between the money stock and nominal GNP would develop differently under different mixes. Those who believe that, in the long run, this relation matters would have to conclude that the neutrality of alternative mixes with respect to inflation could hold only in the short run. In the long run, the easy money-tight budget mix would be more inflationary than its opposite. That also would mean that initially low interest rates would eventually be pushed up by inflation.

Given the view that the stock of money matters in the long run, and that excess money must lead to inflation, it follows that monetary policy has lasting power only over nominal rates, not over real rates. Monetary policy can influence nominal rates by influencing the rate of inflation. Specifically, the sequence of events following an "easing" of monetary policy would be an initial drop in short- and long-term interest rates, then, as inflation began to accelerate, a rise at least in long rates while the central bank was holding down short rates. Eventually, the whole rate structure would be forced up. In the opposite case of a tightening monetary policy, interest rates first would rise; subsequently they would come down as inflation was reduced. Moreover, once the market had come to understand this mechanism, it might telescope the process via expectations. Knowledge that a policy of low interest rates with an attendant acceleration of the money supply was under way, long-term interest rates, which the central bank cannot easily control, would move up immediately, before higher inflation actually set in. Even more, the inflation would be anticipated by the market, and prices and wages would move up before pressures on capacity began to be felt.

Under such circumstances, the central bank has lost control over real interest rates. It can influence only nominal rates, which, however, will move, with a lag, in the direction opposite to that that it had intended. The only influence that can be exerted over real interest rates is that of fiscal policy. A budget surplus increases savings; a deficit absorbs them. Interest rates, other things being equal, will move accordingly. Instead of a fiscal-monetary mix, fiscal policy becomes the sole control over real interest rates, with monetary policy determining nominal rates via the rate of inflation.

These are hypotheses about the behavior of markets. For the Federal Reserve, the critical question is how quickly the assumed processes work. If one is talking about a decade before a change in the relation of money stock to GNP makes itself felt in prices, there is plenty of time for temporary changes in the fiscal-monetary mix, provided they are reversed soon and are not allowed to affect the money stock permanently. This may have been the situation during the 1950s, and may be the most appropriate interpretation given to then-emerging theories of the fiscal-monetary mix. Alternatively, if the effect of money on prices comes quickly, or—worse yet—if expectations cause this effect to be anticipated, there is little room for mix manipulation.

If the market is sophisticated, however, it should be possible for the central bank to enlist expectational effects on its side. In some countries, such as Germany and Switzerland, the market seems to believe that the central bank, or more plausibly the entire government, or still more plausibly the entire population, will not allow much inflation to occur. The market then will not interpret every change in the mix designed for a temporary problem as a decision to go for higher or lower inflation for all time. In a country where the market seemingly needs to be convinced by week-to-week and month-to-month adherence to a rigid money-supply target, temporary departures from target must remain much more limited.

Finally, in a cyclical framework, the optimal combination of fiscal and monetary policy is not necessarily a "mix" aiming at a constant degree of overall stimulation or restraint. Instead, there may be a need for simultaneous tightening or easing of both fiscal and monetary policy. The history of anticyclical policy has not been particularly creditable since the middle 1960s. Previously, however, so long as adequate efforts were made to prevent expansive phases from far outweighing contractive phases, there was a degree of success. The possibility of future situations in which both policies should be pulling in the same direction deserves to be borne in mind.

This form of interaction of fiscal and monetary policy also provides an explanation of historical circumstances conveying the impression that monetary policy was being dictated by the Administration. Two policymakers looking at the same set of facts may well arrive at similar conclusions as to the need for stimulative or restraining action. It is a measure of the degree to which we have become accustomed to wide differences in the thrust of fiscal and monetary policy that this obvious interpretation is sometimes overlooked.

MONETARY POLICY AND THE STRUCTURE OF THE PUBLIC DEBT

Long gone are the days when the structure of the public debt was regarded as a major determinant of the effectiveness of monetary policy. In the late 1940s and early 1950s, banks, corporations, and the general public held large amounts of short-term debt that provided a liquidity cushion. It was not obvious that a rise in short-term rates from 1 to 1.25 percent would greatly reduce that liquidity. Neither was it very apparent why exchanging a 90-day Treasury bill for a bank deposit, with an attendant increase in the money supply, would significantly increase liquidity. These questions have now disappeared. Few transactors hold demand deposits of any size. Most forms of money yield high interest rates. Short-term Treasury securities, although they constitute 7 percent of the Federal Reserve's broadest money-supply measure (L), do not seem to influence the behavior of that variable much. Under these conditions, the structure of the public debt, and especially the proportion of short-term debt, seems to matter a great deal less for monetary policy than it did at one time.

Gone also is the influence that "even keeling" of Treasury issues had on the volume of money and bank reserves. In days of smaller deficits and little inflation, the Treasury was in the market perhaps once a quarter trying to sell a mixed bag of securities at a fixed price. The Fed helped to the extent of not making major changes in monetary policy before and shortly after the issue; under a regime of interest rate targeting, that meant pretty much keeping rates stable. The danger of unintended debt monetization from that source has passed now that the Treasury, while it is in the market almost constantly, operates on an auction basis.

The heavy short-term component in the government's debt, which the Treasury has valiantly tried to hold down, has implied wide swings in interest costs for the Treasury. This can lead to unhappiness on the part of the Secretary of the Treasury and the Director of the Budget. By and large, however, it has been seen as a necessary cost of a firmly restraining monetary policy.

On the other hand, wide swings in interest rates have shown themselves to be a serious burden for the private sector, both for business and for financial institutions. Corporations today are acutely aware of the need to increase the liquidity of their balance sheets by funding short-term obligations. Thrift institutions and even banks have suffered from a mismatch of the maturities of their assets and liabilities. Accordingly, another mismatch appears to exist in the form of the allocation of relatively scarce long-term funds to the users that need them least. Given that the Treasury seems better able to bear the uncertainties inherent in short-term debt, something would seem to be gained by reducing its competition with the private sector for long-term funds. The danger that the private sector might lock itself into high-coupon issues with long maturities to an undue extent would be minimized by the fact that corporate issues typically provide only five- to ten-year call protection, in contrast to the almost complete call protection of Treasury issues. The task of monetary policy would be eased if the impact of tightly restraining money-supply targets on business interest costs could be softened.

The role of the public debt and the impact of debt creation on the economy and on monetary policy are obscured and complicated by inflation. At a high rate of inflation, part of the debt is inflated away each year. If one were to ignore other inflation-related adjustments, such as the indexing of unfunded social security liabilities, one could arrive at the conclusion that, on an inflation-adjusted basis, the deficit is much smaller than it appears to be—or possibly nonexistent. Alternatively, one could say that the inflation premium contained in the interest on the public debt was a form of debt amortization. In this view, a considerable part of the $90 billion of net interest payments on the federal debt really would represent debt repayment; that is, it is not part of the deficit. Analogous statements could be made about corporate and other private debt. On the other hand, the inflation premium is taxed. Furthermore, it is not clear whether the recipients of high-interest payments correctly separate out the inflation premium and add it back to principle, in which case their real interest rate after tax would be negative in many cases. Taxability and tax deductibility of the inflation premium tend to push up interest rates. Among the victims are interest payers who cannot deduct interest and the central bank, which must count on wider interest-rate swings than a money-supply target would otherwise imply.

DEBT MONETIZATION

It has already been noted that the importance of debt monetization depends on how significant the distinction between monetary and nonmonetary assets is under prevailing conditions. Under present-day conditions, the evidence seems to show that it is substantial. Historically, debt monetization has often been a cyclical phenomenon. Banks bought Treasury securities in recessions to replace business loans that were being paid off. Given adequate control over the money supply, this has not been an inflationary development.

Finally, the absence of monetization of public debt is no assurance against excessive money creation if other financial assets are acquired by the banking system. The reason why there is concern about monetization of public debt in the presence of the large deficit is the fear that the debt could not be placed outside the banking system. In many countries other than the United Staes, this fear is well founded, owing to limitations of national capital markets. Where nonbanks do not possess a highly elastic demand for government paper, especially short-term, this paper necessarily gravitates into the banks. In the United States, an extensive nonbank market exists for short-term government paper, making the monetization of this debt a good deal less than inevitable. On the other hand, the accumulation of short-term paper in nonbank hands can represent an increase in liquidity that, in circumstances less liquidity constrained than the present, could quickly become inflationary.

Under these circumstances, monetization or nonmonetization of public debt remains a decision for Federal Reserve policy. Adequate control over the growth of the money supply prevents or limits monetization. Refusal to monetize debt, to be sure, raises interest rates. But so does monetization, although with some lag until the inflationary consequences are perceived. The difference between monetization and nonmonetization of a large deficit is that if debt is not monetized, interest rates will rise, and if it is monetized, they will rise, too, but a little later, and possibly much higher.

DEFICITS AND INFLATION

Do deficits cause inflation? It is a fairly safe bet that a simple correlation between inflation and deficits would show them to be negatively related. Deficits, after all, mount during recessions, when inflation tends to go down. This says little about their causal relationship. But it makes suspect econometric evidence that claims not to find a positive relation, because it is not easy to control for the joint effect of the business cycle on both variables.

It is widely believed that deficits cause inflation. This view receives suport from the basic Keynesian analysis, which identifies deficits with an increase in aggregate demand and takes for granted that monetary policy will finance the deficit. The popular view also reflects frequently repeated assertions by business executives and bankers (including central bankers) and some politicians, many of whom find this a convenient alibi. The popular view is helpful to the Federal Reserve, because it imposes some constraint on political spending in a world where sometimes little such constraint seems to be left.

Analytically, it is just as wrong to say that deficits are necessarily inflationary as to say that deficits have no adverse consequences of any kind. Deficits are expansionary, those resulting from expenditure increases more so than those resulting from tax cuts. Their expansionary effect can be contained by a restraining monetary policy, as is happening now in the United States. Deficits raise interest rates, other things being equal, owing to the government's increased demands on the financial markets. Higher interest rates increase monetary velocity and so can cause inflation with a given money-supply growth, unless the Fed counteracts this by appropriately slowing the money supply. Deficits can also cause inflation simply because people believe they do. In that case, expectations engender actions that cause prices and wages to go up even when there is no immediate pressure.

DEFICITS AND INTEREST RATES

Much the same can be said of the relation between deficits and interest rates. The simple correlation probably is negative, because deficits rise in recessions when interest rates tend to fall. Ergo . . . Obviously it does not follow that deficits reduce interest rates. The question is by how much they raise them.

As pointed out earlier, the federal deficits projected for 1983 and succeeding years will absorb a significant portion of the economy's gross savings and a very large part of its net savings. It has also been noted that gross savings may be more relevant in evaluating the effect of deficits on interest rates, because at least part of the amortization allowances that differentiate gross from net savings is likely to reach the financial markets in one form or another. However, the very high absorption of net savings makes the prospect more ominous still.

Real interest rates are more at issue than nominal. The government's demands on the financial markets are likely to raise both by the same number of basis points, except as the deficit also raises the rate of inflation. A given number of basis points means more with respect to the real rate than the nominal rate.

Since present and prospective deficits are the results mainly of tax cuts rather than of expenditure increases, their impact on interest rates may be somewhat mitigated. From the income restored to the taxpayer, some fraction will be saved. It would be highly optimistic, however, to expect this fraction to be very large. In the absence of wealth effects, the marginal saving out of incremental income is of the order of 0.3 for most income brackets. If higher interest rates depress the price of assets, the resulting negative wealth effect may encourage some additional saving because people want to restore their wealth.

For the Fed, the deficit creates a problem not only in terms of higher interest rates in and of themselves, but also in terms of the crowding-out effect to which they give rise. Crowding out is the nature of the market; somebody will be crowded out. It occurs even at low interest rates. However, the supply of funds becomes more inelastic the higher rates go. Crowding out then becomes more severe. The conflicting claims of different borrowers generate both financial and political pressures. The Fed does not allocate credit, but it does have to be concerned about the way the markets operate and what consequences ensue for the allocation of credit. It also needs to be concerned about the safety and soundness of financial and nonfinancial institutions—all of which are affected by interest rates. The absorption of so large a part of the available saving flow in a country where both gross and net saving already are very low in international comparisons constitutes a serious problem.

THE DEFICIT AND THE DOLLAR

The deficit impinges upon the exchange value of the dollar through a complex sequence of reactions, the final outcome of which is not fully discernible at this time. To begin with, higher interest rates attract foreign capital and, in a floating exchange-rate system, tend to raise the value of the dollar. The proper measure of interest rates for this purpose, in the United States as well as abroad, is real interest rates. An increase in nominal U.S. interest rates accompanied by an even greater increase in the rate of inflation, implying a decline in U.S. real interest rates, would not make the dollar attractive to foreigners. The rise in the dollar by itself helps to reduce the rate of inflation, which is a significant advantage. This, in turn, helps to make the dollar still more attractive internationally.

But a high dollar, as can be observed every day, hurts exports, encourages imports, and pushes the current account of the balance of payments toward deficit. To the extent that such a deficit emerges, which seems very likely for 1983, the United States becomes a net importer of capital. Imports of capital, in real terms, are possible only through a net transfer of goods and services. The rise in the dollar and the creation of a current-account deficit form the mechanism that generates the real transfer.

To the extent that the budget deficit in this manner is financed abroad, some of its domestic repercussions diminish. It is tempting to think that the United States might lay off a good part of its budget deficit on other countries by running a balance-of-payments deficit. The magnitudes of the two deficits, however, at least in historical terms, are very different. U.S. current-account deficits have never exceeded $15 billion. It would take an implausibly large payments deficit to make much of a dent in the financing of the budget deficit. This is quite aside from the question of whether it is economically and politically appropriate, or even feasible, for the richest country in a capital-short world to expect others to so finance its budget deficit.

There is the further question, however, of what large payments deficits would do to the dollar. Theory and experience indicate that currency values are depressed by large payments deficits, probably because the market believes that the continued financing of such a deficit would be difficult. To be sure, when the payments deficit has arisen in the first place out of a strong desire of foreign investors for dollars, it is not immediately clear why the deficit should discourage further capital inflows. The good inflation performance of the dollar (a synonym, in this case, for high real interest rates) may lend further support to this currency.

At the same time, a current-account deficit works against

economic recovery. Net exports, as a component of GNP, can swing from positive to negative, and seem to be in the process of doing so. Having part of the deficit financed abroad, therefore, is costly in terms of domestic output and employment as long as the economy operates at low levels anyway.

The Fed, even though it does not target on exchange rates any more than on interest rates, cannot ignore exchange-rate effects. Wide swings in exchange rates are damaging to the U.S. economy as well as to those of other countries. Insofar as the budget deficit contributes to them, it involves an additional cost.

CONCLUDING REMARKS

The attempt has been made show that while monetary policy can cope with the consequence of a large budget deficit, it can do so only at considerable costs. These costs in the aggregate are likely far to exceed any benefits derivable from a deficit, at least in the foreseeable future. A lower level of investment, lower economic growth, greater difficulty in bringing down inflation, and international disturbances are the main consequences. This does not mean that an instant reduction of the deficit, in the face of a deep recession, would bring an immediate improvement. It is the forward-looking character of the deficit—the difficulty, under present conditions, to anticipate a significant reduction—that creates the most serious difficulties for monetary policy and for the economy as a whole.

CHAPTER FOUR

THE U.S. FISCAL CRISIS OF THE 1980s

Paul A. Samuelson

The U.S. electorate cannot resolve its internal debate on how large the public sector's share of the GNP shall be. The impasse has led to sizable deficits, not only in recession times, and also to questions about the prospect for high employment in the mid-1980s. To try to resolve the ethical debate by finding the right one of the dozen definitions of the budget to balance, and declaring that it must be balanced by constitutional or self-imposed decree, is both naive and an evasion of the democratic decision that needs to be made.

Each fiscal policy leads to a different total of current thriftiness and capital formation, having different effects on consumption of future and present generations. It is an illusion to think that there is one "neutral" solution that lets private family and corporate decisions optimally adjudicate between present and future generations. Even rabid individualists cannot defend letting those now alive and commanding a bare majority of voters do whatever they wish when their actions must have profound effects upon those still to come. Most of what is perceived as a present fiscal crisis dissolves on analysis into understandable frustration on the part of those more critical of government's role in the economy than the effective majority of the voters and their representatives has been since 1980.

In time of trouble, people look for a religion. Often it is for a new religion, since one would not be in trouble had the current religion not proved wanting. But a reversion to an older religion may be grabbed at for a solution.

CRISIS IN FISCAL POLICY

The U.S. economy is now in trouble. After a decade of floundering, we found ourselves in the early 1980s mired in a recession. Whatever the index numbers say, the person in the street does not perceive that inflation is on its way to being cured. The steady rise in living standards that U.S. citizens could always take for granted has been thwarted by OPEC oil scarcity and by Club of Rome's problems with irreplaceable natural resources and the law of diminishing returns. Affluence has brought anomie: The decay of the work ethic has undermined the affluence—leaving the anomie. While Athens degenerates in spirit and substance, the feared Sparta grows in military power—to parity at best, and at worst to superiority.

The choice of the topic of these essays is testimony that the general unease about economic policy narrows down in focus to a perceived crisis in fiscal policy. By conventional definition, the U.S. federal deficit is seen to be at a record high. Looking ahead to the middle of the decade, the informed eye sees continued record deficits. If all of this were the work of the left-of-center Democratic administration, there would be less mystery in the process. But, ironically, the agitation about departure from fiscal grace occurs during the term of office of a conservative Republican and following an apparent election landslide against New Deal programs.

What worries those who seek a balanced budget is not that Ronald Reagan is a big spender. Only in the area of national defense has the Administration promoted new expansionary expenditure programs.

Sophisticated advocates of budget balance can shrug off that part of the current deficit attributable to the loss in tax receipts engendered by the 1981 recession. What they cannot shrug off is the deficit envisaged still to be with us long after recovery has brought the United States back to the low levels of unemployment characteristic of good phases of the business cycle.

TAX REDUCTION TO FORCE
EXPENDITURE REDUCTION

In 1980, the Laffer-Kemp wing of the Republicans professed to believe that the massive reductions in tax rates would actually lead to a great upsurge in tax revenues, implying no deficit at all, but rather a surplus available to permit interest rates to fall and to permit further tax-rate reductions. That did not happen, but it was the intention.

The monetarists, regarding the level of the budget and of its algebraic surplus or deficit as pretty much irrelevant to the strength of total GNP spending, had reason to be concerned by deficits (as against high-expenditure levels), only to the degree that a deficit in being would generate effective political pressures on the Federal Reserve to depart from steady constraints on the rate of money-supply growth. A large deficit, being equivalent to a large element of public dissaving, might be expected to put some upward pressure on nominal and real interest rates; and to the degree that the Fed was still subject to nonmonetarist hankerings to resist a rise in interest rates, any such crowding-out effect of deficits would put in jeopardy the Fed's successful achievement of its monetarist targets.

Many rational expectationists could agree with the above considerations. But the purists in this camp were inclined to doubt that a so-called deficit would itself have any substantial effects upon anything. So long as people foresee that they and their heirs must incur the tax obligation to pay for current expenditures not covered by current taxes, they will behave in much the same way as they would if there were no tax reductions and, hence, no deficit. (The too-large spending of 1981 to 1982 would, of course, have some substantive effects in comparison with a lower level of federal expenditures; but so long as people plan, in effect, as if they and their heirs will live forever and have to pay their taxes in the future, if not in the present, they will act in the end in the same way—whatever the level of current taxes and the implied so-called deficit. So the argument goes.) The record of rational expectationists in illuminating the probabilities of short-term economic developments has been almost as bad as that of the most imaginative supply-side theorists. But the logic of the paradigm plays down even the crowding-out effects upon investment of deficits.

All the separate wings of the Reagan teams could agree on the desirability of reducing the *total* of government expenditures. The weight of the private market in the GNP was to be increased, so to speak; the weight of the public sector to be decreased. An increase in efficiency would result from deregulation and from reducing the wedge between pretax and posttax returns. Quite aside from efficiency gains, the philosophical virtue of *freedom* would be promoted by such a successful reduction in the total of federal spending (or at least a lowering of the trend of such spending in comparison with previous implied paths). Presidential leadership and threats were deemed desirable to ensure that Congress cut entitlement and other federal programs in order to realize the desired goal.

Many, but not all, Republican economists favored tax reductions as a way of putting pressure on Congress to cut expenditures. What the rascals do not have they cannot spend, was the argument. Inasmuch as a sovereign government has the power to run deficits, those who favored the tax reduction as a ploy to bring down spending must have been implicitly relying on a propensity of Congress to be unwilling to countenance an unlimitedly high deficit. Some conservatives, and also some nonconservatives, warned Congress in early 1981 that this tax-reduction ploy could degenerate into a form of Russian roulette. If it worked, well and good from the standpoint of those conservative in ideology. But what if it failed to bring down spending commensurate with the reduction in tax revenues? Then it would create the kinds of deficits that the United States actually faces.

Anyone who monitors Wall Street and investor brokerage opinions will learn that some of the highness of the real rate of interest during the first year of the Reagan recession must be attributed to the boomeranging of the Reagan tax-reduction program (a program that was gleefully supported by many Democrats who had tax-reduction items of their own to add onto those advocated by the Administration). The depressing effects of high real rates of interest on housing and other durable-goods spending meant that the U.S. economy got little or none of the antirecession benefit of the deficit; and, indeed, every dollar of tax reduction might well have led to a reduction in total spending, employment, and production. Such an induced reduction in the velocity of circulation of money was not desired by anybody; of course, any attempt by the Federal Reserve to try to offset by upward revisions of M targets would have had to be rejected by monetarists as "no-no" fine tuning.

DISTRUST OF DEMOCRACY

If the ordinary workings of representative legislatures lead to such continued levels of public expenditure and deficits, it is natural that there be resort to referenda and constitutional amendments to achieve once and for all what is not achieved by congressional procedures. Economists are asked to specify which of the many competing definitions of the balanced budget is the best one. Once economists identify it for the people, the people are asked to freeze into successful practice the appropriate level of tax-rate structure and to constrain total spending by the total of such available tax receipts.

This is not the place to examine the problems and advantages that might inhere in a system of constitutionally imposed fiscal totals. My primary task is to point out why it is arbitrary to select *any* one definition of budget as the right and neutral one to be balanced.

There is a value-free part of economics that constitutes its scientific core. And, not less important when it comes to any policy applications, there are the values and ethical goals that democracies wish to realize, to argue about, and to compromise over. Positive economic science cannot pronounce that it is desirable for any of the budget concepts to be balanced. What inescapably belongs in the nonscientific realm of value-welfare judgments is the decision on how positive or how negative the deficits ought to be (as defined in each of the dozens of relevant ways). For, according to the positivistic macroeconomics characterizing the real world, each different size and sign of deficit has different substantive effects on the present and future generations of the citizenry. (This is an understatement. There are even discernible trade-offs between present consumption by people who are now alive and their consumption when they are older. The citizenry, recognizing vaguely its own myopias and private-saving idiosyncracies, may rationally choose one size of surplus or deficit over another in order to achieve the optimum feasible compromise.)

There are some present-day models in which the size of the deficit is so subject to being offset by private reactions as to make that size of no substantive importance. As already indicated, such models are not realistic.

HOW FISCAL POLICY MATTERS

In 1933, one of every four workers was unemployed. The system was producing less than two-thirds of what it would have been capable of producing if the years 1929 to 1932 had been years of average productivity growth and employment.

Few economists would expect that the U.S. system could be brought back to a normal employment and production level by a 1933 program that would have tried to balance the budget by a normal 1929 tax structure, and that called for a 1933 to 1940 monetary commitment to a steady 4 percent growth in some measure(s) of the total money supply.

What could be expected to be the outcome of such a program by well-informed macroeconomists? First, they would expect that the normal tax structure would fail to balance the budget. Second, the main reason for this actual deficit would be their confident expectation that the system would remain stuck for years at abnormally high levels of excess capacity and unemployed labor. Third, for how long output might continue *not* to grow would be a question hard to forecast. How fast it might grow once the corner was turned would also be a question that no jury of eclectic economists could be expected to agree on.

This bit of history is not resurrected as an experiment because we are in times as parlous as those of 1933. Nor because I believe we are about to go into an economic tailspin. The reason is to remind us that the economic system cannot always be usefully understood by the tools of market-clearing microparadigms.

WHERE FISCAL POLICY DOES NOT MATTER

A mathematical theoretical Walras-Debreu system would find a full-employment equilibrium path even if it started out from initial conditions like those of 1933.[1] It would not need a crash program of bank expansion to bring it back toward full employment. Indeed, such a program would merely raise its various price levels pretty much in balance. A Walras-Debreu system would not benefit in its real magnitudes of output, consumption, and employment from a program of massive deficit spending, involving tax reductions, expanded transfer payments, and enlarged public purchases of real goods and services. Preparation for war by a 1936 Adolf Hitler might raise prices in a Walras-Debreu system, but it could not achieve most of its effects in the form of higher levels of job activity and consumption satisfactions.

Thus, there are the tremendous differences between actual economic history and the refined theoretical micromodels of economists. Those same differences occur between actual business-cycle developments and the pure models of rational expectationists.

To see this, consider the 1923 stabilizations of hyperinflation in Germany, Hungary, Austria, and Poland. As Thomas Sargent has recently pointed out, quick termination of these hyperinflations—with rather little unemployment and stagnation—would be how a rational-expectationist model might be expected to operate.[2] But Robert Gordon's examination of 14 attempts to fight inflation in the United States and abroad—and report that all but a very few of them seemed to involve considerable sacrifices in real output, employment, consumption, and capital formation—indicate how a rational expectationist's model is supposed not to work.[3]

A REALISTIC FISCAL PARADIGM

The art of political economy is to know when and how to modify abstract models to take account of the discrepancies between them and the real world. My reading of how the real world works suggests the following:

- Usually higher public expenditure, lower tax rates and collections, and greater (algebraic) deficits in short and intermediate runs add to output and employment. They also add something to the algebraic rate of price-level growth. A breakdown of nominal GNP change into about two-thirds output and one-third price change applies until the system reaches abnormally low levels of unemployment and excess plant capacity; then most of the GNP change is dissipated in mere price-tag changes.
- Speeding up the growth of the M (money) aggregates has similar effects, quantitatively and qualitatively. When the growth in M is itself occasioned by a so-called "need to finance the deficit," any partially offsetting reduction in V (velocity) induced by the increases in M, will be weaker. So, normally, simultaneous increases in M and fiscal variables are especially potent.
- Overbalancing the budget (as conventionally defined) by increasing tax revenues relative to public outlays is compatible with high-level employment and vigorous output growth if (and only if) suitably compensating easiness of credit and of real interest rates is achieved. The short- and intermediate-run M target that is required for just-adequate total spending is not the same when a deficit is crowding out capital formation and thereby speeding up V in $MV = PQ$ (money times velocity equals price times quantity). A higher dM/dt growth is tolerable, and may sometimes be mandatory, when public thriftiness via the budget is reinforcing private propensities to save on the part of families and corporations.

These propositions are based on the assumption that some tolerable or desirable behavior of the price level is specified as a constraint for the short or intermediate run under contemplation. Thus, with a whopping deficit, an M growth rate of 3 percent might be much more inflationary than one of 5 percent would be with an overbalanced budget.

- It would be misleading to believe that people in 1982 react as slowly as they used to in 1933. Therein lies the saving germ of truth in the rational expectationists' emphasis. Their explicit and implicit forecasts have so often gone astray since the late 1970s because rational expectationists extrapolated into the short run of a year or two many of the effects that will be correct in the long run of several years or more. But their larger squared errors of estimation should not blind us to the truth that the participants in the economic scenario today are quicker to act than they used to be.

What used to take one or two decades might be compressed into little more than half a decade.

RECENT AMBIGUITIES

Concretely, there are possibly special times when an increment of M contrived by the Federal Reserve could so trigger off inflationary expectations as to lead to higher, rather than lower, nominal and real rates of interest. The weight of the evidence still suggests that in most times a short-run rise in dM/dt will increase capital formation and real GNP, and do this via the mechanism of lower costs of credit and its greater availability, and also via the mechanism of higher wealth capitalizations in corporate- and family-spending functions. However, since expectations are so volatile, and indeed irrational, I am prepared to believe that there have been recent times in which M effects have been opposite in sign to their normal reactions.

Similar "perversities" in fiscal-policy reactions can occur. To explain the puzzle of over-high real interest rates in the year before July 1982, it was useful to put the dummy variable of the size of the deficit into the function of income and the money stock that determines the level of the structure of interest rates. This is an ad hoc procedure, whose main defense was that it worked to predict what was happening and was consistent with what was heard on Wall Street.

But notice what this tinkering with standard macroanalysis does to the system's comparative statics. If a rise in public spending and reduction in tax rates swell the deficit and thereby raise real interest rates, the induced reduction in housing and other durable-goods spending could more than offset the expansionary effects of the fiscal deficit on real GNP. (In technical terms, the positive signs that normally hold for ∂ output/∂ deficit and ∂ output/∂ (−Taxes) could well be reversed!)

Does all this sound academic? It is anything but. The debate between Chairperson Martin Feldstein and Secretary of Treasury Regan on whether the 1983 cut in personal taxes should be advanced from July to January hinges on precisely this question.

How to resolve the puzzle? If the economy stays very weak and the fiscal stimulus contemplated is a large enough one, one would have to bet that the normal positive sign would hold for the partial derivatives. But given the small magnitude of the tax cut and the uncertainty about the sign of the partial derivative, I cannot generate much enthusiasm for either side of the quarrel.

WHICH BUDGET BALANCE?

Once you understand the paradigm that I consider to be realistically applicable in the modern age, my denial that there can be found a unique definition of the budget that we ought to aim to balance as a condition of optimality or of neutrality is understandable. Overbalancing the budget, while at the same time ensuring by Federal Reserve policy that the enhanced overall social thriftiness will not be aborted by induced unemployment, implies a higher capital stock in the future achieved by lower current consumption now. Is that mix a good thing? A bad thing?

There is no way to give a definite answer to these questions within the realm of positivistic economics. If you think future generations ought to enjoy more and the present generation less, you will answer the question affirmatively. If you think the present generation deserves more consumption, you will answer negatively.

Why should the citizenry not decide the matter? A naive approach is to say: "People in their private capacities as family spenders or voters of corporation proxies favoring high or low dividend payments should solely decide. If the right one of the dozen or so alternative definitions of the budget is balanced, public thriftiness will be kept "neutral and optimal capital formation will result."

Such a contention is gratuitous, and has no basis in any system of philosophy or welfare economics. Certainly, in a democracy, the citizenry must decide on everything: on what weight must be given to the needs, merits, and desires of present and later generations; on what social compacts are to prevail, involving what compromises between the "rights" of individual persons and lawful limitations of their behavior. But to conclude without argument that the citizenry must decide to endure that amount of thriftiness implied by the balanced budget is to beg the question at issue.

For more than a quarter of a century, I have been urging the merits of budget surpluses offset by enough credit easiness to keep employment as full as it ought to be. This is for the purpose of encouraging a higher investment-consumption mix at high employment. Such a long-run goal ought to be rejected (or accepted) on its merits and not by the happenstance of constitutional amendments and referenda.

I must guard against being misinterpreted. A rise in taxes and an expenditure cut in early 1983 may well undermine—not enhance—actual investment. The Fed could react to fiscal austerity—or, what is the same thing, less fiscal looseness—by letting it depress the economy further, thereby stepping up the fight against inflation.

Until a recovery is ensured, until the tax-incentive reforms of the 1981 act have some scope for coaxing out capital formation, the economy will operate within the paradox of thrift—with increased thriftiness probably reducing actual achieved investment. It is here that I want not to be misinterpreted in the espousal of a long-range program of fiscal austerity. True, we are not all dead in the long run; but that long run is distinguishable from the present short run that is relevant for immediate U.S. policy. So long as the economy is still in our present short run, I warn against an austere fiscal program appropriate for the long-term future.

CONCLUSION

Public spending out of control is a calamity. Public spending that is inefficient and not responsive to democracy's desires and needs is a pity. Discipline is needed at all times. But to try to fabricate a religion that will impose discipline by creating new shibboleths or trying to resurrect the old makes little sense and, in any case, will not work. When people no longer believe in hell fire, threatening them with the heat of perdition serves little purpose. Pretending to believe, in order to frighten ourselves into doing that that we cannot make ourselves do on its merits, is a charade. For better or worse, a democracy has to face up to the substantive issues.

NOTES

1. Leon Walras, *Elements of Pure Economics*. Homewood: Richard D. Irwin, 1954, translations of 1874–1926 editions by W. Jaffe; Gerard Debreu, *Theory of Value*. New York: John Wiley and Sons, 1959.

2. Thomas J. Sargent, "The Ends of Four Big Inflations." Paper presented at the October 1980 Conference on Inflation, Washington, D.C.

3. Robert J. Gordon, "Why Stopping Inflation May Be Costly: Evidence from Fourteen Historical Episodes." National Bureau of Economic Research, Working Paper 682, March 1, 1981.

PART TWO

BUDGET
OUTCOMES AND
CAPITAL MARKETS

CHAPTER FIVE

A CREDIT-MARKET PERSPECTIVE, 1982 TO 1987

Benjamin M. Friedman

The widespread realization that the United States faces a major government budget problem developed with surprising suddenness. This revolution in attitudes reflected changing economic realities as well as fresh political developments. In 1980, the U.S. Government's deficit was $60 billion, equal to approximately 2 percent of GNP, and it was reasonable to expect that it would shrink over time. At that time, it was still possible to view any lingering deficit problem as the consequence of liberal political preferences, which conservative electoral success could readily stem. By contrast, the federal deficit in the 1982 fiscal year was a record $111 billion, equal to nearly 4 percent of GNP, and current prospects are for further increases even in relation to a growing economy. By now it is clear that elected conservatives seem as willing as anyone else to place other priorities ahead of steps to shrink the deficit.

This paper draws on several of the author's research papers, including especially "Debt and Economic Activity in the United States," in B.M. Friedman, ed., *The Changing Roles of Debt and Equity in Financing U.S. Capital Formation.* Chicago: University of Chicago Press, 1982.

From the perspective of the credit market, the most worrisome aspect of the recent deterioration in the government budget outlook is its negative implication for the broadly accepted goal of stimulating the U.S. economy's net capital-formation rate. Ironically, at least the rhetoric—if not the actual motivation—underlying some key fiscal measures now contributing to the deficit problem was that they would make the economic environment more conducive to saving and investment. With corporate capital spending sharply down and showing little sign of recovery, the question is whether these measures will prove counterproductive even on their own terms. This issue is especially relevant for the credit markets because financial conditions, including both a higher real cost and reduced availability of funds to potential business and individual borrowers, provide one of the principal channels by which government deficits can "crowd out" private capital formation. The crowding-out phenomenon is not a problem during depressed conditions like those of the 1981 to 1982 recession, to be sure, but the fiscal policies now in place imply that large deficits will continue even after a significant economic recovery.

The object of this essay is to assess the likely severity of the U.S. Government's deficit problem over the medium run of the next five years from the perspective of credit markets and capital formation. The intended focus is the economy's performance after it achieves a reasonable measure of recovery. The essay applies an unfamiliar, but potentially quite useful, conceptual framework for evaluating the likely implications for private financing owing to any specific government deficit path by examining the required change in Federal Government securities outstanding in comparison with the economy's growth. To anticipate: The conclusions suggested by an application of this framework to the federal budget outlook for 1982 to 1987 are highly negative for the prospects for private financing and, therefore, for private capital formation as well, if fiscal policy holds for long to its present course.

THE DEFICIT IN HISTORICAL PERSPECTIVE

The U.S. Government's budget deficit is large and growing larger. The September 1982 analysis by the Congressional Budget Office projected a likely deficit of $155 billion, or nearly 5 percent of

GNP, for the 1983 fiscal year, and subsequent evidence suggests an even larger deficit. This magnitude would set a post-World War II record not just in dollar terms, either nominal or adjusted for price inflation, but also in relation to the size of the economy. Moreover, the Congressional Budget Office analysis indicated that the deficit is likely to remain at this magnitude at least through 1985, even with economic recovery. The consensus among budget analysts in the private sector apparently concurs with this outlook, foreseeing a most likely deficit under current tax and spending policies in the range of 5 percent of GNP throughout the medium-run future of about five years. During this period, the deficit will gradually evolve from a passive, recession-induced deficit—which in itself is not an impediment to private financing and capital formation—to an active deficit, owing to the excess of spending over revenues in a fully employed economy.

Table 5-1 places these magnitudes in historical perspective by showing the relationship among the main elements of saving and investment in the United States, stated as percentages of GNP, since the middle 1950s. Four features stand out in these data: First, gross *private* saving has risen, not declined, as a share of economic activity over these years. Second, however, more than all of this relative increase in gross private saving has represented the faster depreciation associated with a more equipment-intensive capital stock. *Net* private saving has declined in relative terms. Third, *state and local* governments have consistently added to the economy's available saving, and by growing relative amounts, since the early 1960s.

Fourth—and most importantly for the purposes of this essay— the *Federal Government* has consistently absorbed the economy's available saving, and by growing relative amounts, in this period. The pattern of U.S. Government deficits shown in Table 5-1 readily indicates the limited validity of the now frequently expressed view that a federal budget deficit equal to approximately 2 percent of GNP, as occurred in both 1980 and 1981, is "about average." A deficit of that size has been average in the United States—but only since 1970. During the 1960s, the federal deficit averaged only 0.5 percent of GNP; and during the 1950s, on average, the federal budget was approximately in balance.

The experience of the first half of 1982, shown in the final column of Table 5-1, highlights the implications of a ballooning U.S. Government deficit in the context of the economy's overall saving-

TABLE 5-1. U.S. Gross Saving and Investment

	1956–1960	1961–1965	1966–1970	1971–1975	1976–1980	1981	1982
Total gross saving	16.2	15.9	15.9	15.7	16.3	16.3	13.5
Gross private saving	16.4	16.3	16.4	16.9	17.0	17.2	17.4
Personal saving	4.7	4.3	5.0	5.6	4.2	4.4	4.6
Net corporate saving	2.4	3.5	3.1	2.0	2.3	1.5	1.1
Depreciation allowances	9.3	8.5	8.4	9.3	10.5	11.2	11.6
U.S. Government surplus	–0.0	–0.4	–0.6	–1.8	–2.0	–2.0	–4.9
State and local government surplus	–0.2	0.0	0.1	0.6	1.2	1.1	1.0
Total gross investment	15.9	16.0	15.8	16.0	16.3	16.2	13.6
Net foreign investment	0.5	0.8	.0.2	0.3	–0.2	0.1	–0.2
Gross private domestic investment	15.4	15.3	15.5	15.7	16.5	16.0	13.7

Note: Data are averages (except for 1981 and 1982) of annual flows, as percentages of annual GNP. Total gross saving and total gross investment differ by statistical discrepancy. Detail may not add to total because of rounding.

Source: U.S. Department of Commerce.

investment structure. The near doubling of the deficit to almost 4 percent of GNP in early 1982 overwhelmed the slight increase in private saving, resulting a sharp decline in total gross saving—and also in total gross investment (as well as its domestic component).

The likely further increase in the U.S. Government deficit to 5 percent of GNP for a sustained period will only exacerbate the recent unfavorable experience. Its prospect, therefore, calls into question the economy's ability to achieve significant progress in raising the capital-formation rate. Although the 1981 tax legislation included several measures intended to stimulate private saving, the data shown in Table 5-1 immediately suggest the apparently limited responsiveness of the share of private saving in the U.S. economy. More sophisticated statistical investigations typically confirm this impression. Moreover, even if these tax measures succeeded in increasing personal saving by fully one-half in relative terms—that is, from the historical average of about 4.75 percent of GNP to an unprecedented 7.25 percent—this would not be sufficient to fund the entire federal deficit and still support private investment even at the historical average level. Especially for those (including this writer) who regard the U.S. economy's historical average capital-formation rate as inadequate for the 1980s, the implications of a federal deficit averaging 5 percent of GNP, even as the economy recovers from recession, are bleak indeed.

FINANCING THE GOVERNMENT AND THE PRIVATE SECTOR

In an economy like that of the United States, both businesses and individuals can finance their activities in a rich variety of ways. Businesses investing in new plants and equipment can rely on internally generated funds, or they can raise external funds from the financial markets. When they do turn to external sources of funds, they can issue either debt obligations or new equity shares in the enterprise. Individuals can likewise use their own or borrowed funds to make major purchases like automobiles, and many individuals can also borrow to finance ordinary consumer spending as well as other hard goods. Even in arranging home purchases (transactions that are almost always partly debt financed), individuals usually can choose what fraction of the purchase price initially represents their own equity. In principle, businesses and individuals are continually making these and other financing choices on the basis of yield comparisons, credit availability, and other considerations, so that the total amount of debt financing does not necessarily have to bear any close relationship to the underlying economic activity.

In fact, however, the relationship between outstanding debt and economic activity in the United States is remarkably steady—indeed, just as steady as the more widely recognized and better understood relationship between economic activity and money. The aggregate outstanding indebtedness of all nonfinancial borrowers in the United States has been approximately $1.40 for each $1.00 of the economy's GNP ever since World War II. Throughout the postwar period, the overall debt-to-income ratio has displayed neither trend nor cyclical variation.

Moreover, the stability of the U.S. economy's outstanding debt in relation to its income has not merely represented the stability of a sum of stable parts, as is apparently the case (apart from trend) among the familiar monetary aggregates. Neither private-sector debt nor government debt has borne a stable relationship to economic activity, but their total has. In particular, the secular rise and procyclical fluctuation in the private-sector's debt have approximately offset the corresponding secular decline (relative to income) and countercyclical fluctuation in the Federal Government's debt.

Figure 5-1 shows the year-end indebtedness of U.S. non-financial borrowers, as a percentage of fourth-quarter GNP, for each year since the end of the Korean War. The top line in the figure shows the total credit-market indebtedness of *all* U.S. nonfinancial borrowers. The lines below divide this total into the respective indebtedness of each of five specific borrowing sectors. The debt totals shown here are "net" in the sense that they net out financial intermediation. In other words, the data include such items as a household's mortgage issues to a bank or a corporation's bonds sold to an insurance company, but they exclude any liability issued by the bank or the insurance company in order to finance that lending activity. The data also exclude debt issued by separate financial subsidiaries of nonfinancial corporations as well as by federally sponsored credit agencies and mortgage pools. The data are "gross," however, in the sense that they include all of an individual household or firm's outstanding credit-market liabilities, not just any excess of liabilities over either financial or total assets, and also

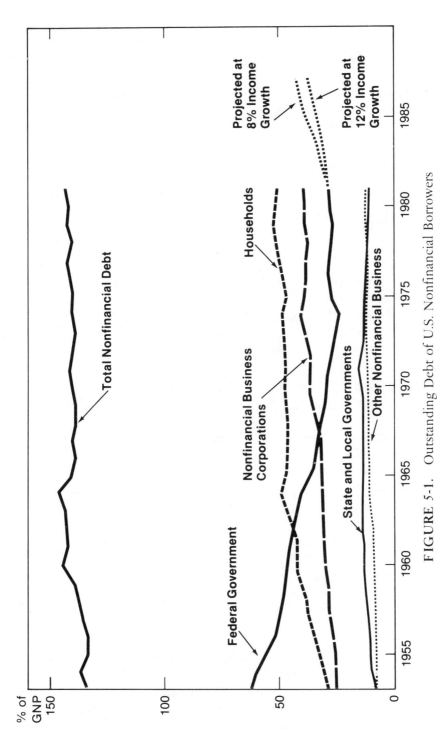

FIGURE 5-1. Outstanding Debt of U.S. Nonfinancial Borrowers

in the sense that they include one household's borrowing from another or one firm's borrowing from another.

The strong stability of the *total* nonfinancial debt ratio shown in the top line in Figure 5-1 stands out in stark contrast to the variation of the individual sector components shown below. The nonfinancial economy's reliance on debt, scaled in relation to economic activity, shows almost no trend and but little variation. The total non-financial debt ratio has trended slightly upward, with a low of 133.4 percent in 1956 and a high of 145.5 percent in 1964. Not surprisingly, the ratio has also exhibited a slight cyclicality, typically rising a point or two in recession years (when GNP, in the denominator, is weak). At 142.8 percent, the most recent annual observation was only slightly above the post-1960 mean of 141.7 percent. Although the severity of the recent business recession suggests that the ratio will probably rise (perhaps even to a record high) before the economy recovers, there is no sign of any interruption of the basic long-run stability.

The individual components of the total, however, have varied in sharply different directions, both secularly and cyclically: The secular postwar rise in private debt has largely mirrored a substantial decline (relative to economic activity) in public debt, while cyclical bulges in public-debt issuance have had their counterpart mostly in the abatement of private borrowing. Households have almost continually increased their reliance on debt in relation to their nonfinancial activity throughout the period covered. Both corporations and unincorporated businesses have also steadily issued more debt, on a relative basis, except for temporary retrenchments during recession years. State and local governments steadily increased their relative debt-issuing activity during the 1950s and 1960s, but just as steadily reduced it during the 1970s. Except only for 1975 to 1976, 1980 to 1981, and 1982, the Federal Government has reduced its debt ratio in every year since 1953, although this relative debt reduction has been slower in years when recession has temporarily inflated the government's deficit (and, again, depressed GNP in the denominator).

This pattern of debt-issuing activity, by the Federal Government in particular, helps to place in additional perspective the magnitude and import of the federal deficit. During the post-World War II period as a whole, the federal debt ratio has declined not just from 62.9 percent in 1953 but from 103.4 percent in 1946.

At 27.7 percent as of year-end 1981, the ratio of interest-bearing federal indebtedness to GNP once again stood at almost precisely its value in 1918. At the same time, the past decade marked a departure from prior experience in an important way. The years 1975 and 1976 were the first since 1953 in which the Federal Government's debt ratio actually rose, and the renewed decline during 1977 to 1979, now largely offset by the recession years 1980 and 1981, was not sufficient to reduce the ratio to its 1974 low.

It is also useful to consider briefly the history of the economy's aggregate debt ratio in a longer time frame. Apart from a one-time adjustment associated with the fall of prices after World War I, the U.S. nonfinancial economy's reliance on debt relative to economic activity has shown essentially no trend over the last six decades. At 142.8 percent as of year-end 1981, the total net credit ratio was virtually unchanged from 141.9 percent in 1921. Nonfinancial borrowers' outstanding debt rose significantly in relation to GNP only during the depression years 1930 to 1933, when the economy was deteriorating rapidly and many recorded debts had defaulted de facto anyway. Otherwise, the economy's total net credit ratio has remained roughly steady throughout this period, and the post-Korean stability appears to be in large part a continuation of a pattern that dates back at least to the 1920s.

IMPLICATIONS FOR PRIVATE CAPITAL FORMATION

The stability of the economy's aggregate credit-to-income ratio—if it is indeed a regularity that will persist—bears significant implications for the current stance of U.S. fiscal policy, especially with respect to the widely accepted goal of stimulating capital formation. An increased rate of capital formation has emerged as a nearly undisputed objective of U.S. economic policy for the remainder of the 1980s. Dissatisfaction with the economy's poor productivity performance in the 1970s, as well as with the erosion of international competitiveness that began much earlier but also became more evident in the 1970s as the international exchange value of the dollar declined dramatically, has elevated what was once largely a business interest into a much more widely shared goal. In today's environment, groups representing labor and consumers also recognize the need for capital investment to create jobs and to raise productivity and, hence, the population's overall standard of living. Even observers who point to other factors as the source of much of the productivity slowdown in the 1970s typically recognize the potential ability of an increased capital-formation rate to offset those adverse developments in the future. On the whole, public discussion has moved from whether more capital formation is desirable to what policies can best achieve it.

An important aspect of capital formation that this discussion has often overlooked, however, is its explicitly financial side. As the saving-investment balance summarized in Table 5-1 clearly shows, in a economy like that of the United States, each decision to create more physical capital necessarily has a financial counterpart. Moreover, the financial transactions associated with capital formation are not merely a reflection of real-resource allocations that would necessarily come about in any case. The setting in which the financing of capital formation takes place can also be a key determinant of real-resource allocations, including not only the total amount of capital formation undertaken, but also its composition. The financial and nonfinancial elements of the process jointly determine one another, and public policy can affect the ultimate outcome by influencing either.

Businesses and individuals in the U.S. economy have, in fact, been undertaking more capital formation rather than less, at least in the usual sense of gross investment in plant and equipment. Table 5-2 shows a breakdown into several major components, again as percentages of GNP, of the gross private domestic investment experience shown in Table 5-1. Over the period covered, gross U.S. expenditures on plant and equipment have increased as a share of the nation's GNP. More importantly, however, while *gross* capital formation has represented a progressively larger share of total output, the corresponding "net" capital formation underwent a sharp reversal within this period. *Net* U.S. investment in plant and equipment (that is, net of the true economic depression) rose rapidly as a share of total output between the late 1950s and the late 1960s, but then fell back almost as rapidly by the late 1970s and thus far in the 1980s.

Still, it is gross capital outlays that the businesses and individuals investing in plant and equipment need to finance. Corporations engaged in nonfinancial lines of business have consistently accounted for nearly three-fourths of all U.S. investment in plant

TABLE 5-2. U.S. Gross and Net Investment

	1956–1960	1961–1965	1966–1970	1971–1975	1976–1980	1981	1982
Gross private domestic investment	15.4	15.3	15.5	15.7	16.5	16.0	13.7
Plant and equipment	9.9	9.5	10.6	10.4	11.2	11.8	11.4
depreciation	7.3	6.6	6.6	7.3	8.3	9.0	9.4
Net investment	2.6	2.9	4.0	3.1	2.9	2.8	2.0
Residential construction	5.0	4.8	3.8	4.6	4.6	3.6	3.1
Inventory accumulation	0.6	1.0	1.1	0.7	0.7	0.7	-0.8

Note: Data are averages (except for 1981 and 1982) of annual flows, as percentages of annual GNP. Total gross saving and total gross investment differ by statistical discrepancy. Detail may not add to total because of rounding.

Source: U.S. Department of Commerce.

and equipment since World War II. Table 5-3 shows the main outlines of the U.S. nonfinancial corporate-business sector's financing, in percentages of total sources of funds. Except for brief intervals of recession, nonfinancial corporate businesses have increasingly relied on external—as opposed to internal—funds, including depreciation allowances, in financing their capital outlays. Moreover, as Table 5-3 also shows, these corporations have consistently raised almost all of their external funds by issuing debt.

As Figure 5-1 makes clear, the chief counterpart to this increasing corporate indebtedness relative to income has been declining Federal Government indebtedness (again, relative to income). As of the 1970s, however, with the growth of the U.S. Government budget deficit, the decline in government indebtedness and the corresponding increases in corporate indebtedness ceased—and with them the trend toward a higher net capital-formation rate. In part, this reversal has reflected the frequency and severity of business recessions since 1970; but the federal budget has also moved more consistently into deficit, even on a high-employment basis.

Under a restrictive monetary policy that prevents a renewed surge of inflation from invalidating the resulting debt, the prospect of deficits averaging 5 percent of even a growing GNP means that in the 1980s, government indebtedness relative to income will be not just flat (as in the 1970s, on balance) but persistently rising. Figure 5-1 illustrates two specific examples: A deficit averaging 5 percent of GNP for the next five years will raise outstanding Federal Government debt from 29 percent of income at year-end 1982 to over 37 percent at year-end 1987 if nominal income growth averages 12 percent per annum; or 42 percent if nominal income growth averages only 8 percent per annum. These deficits will, therefore, return the federal debt-to-total-income ratio to levels last seen 20 years ago. Given the stability of the economy's total net credit ratio, therefore, these deficits will also require that some other borrowers' indebtedness relative to income decline. Although continued depression of homebuilding would be sufficient to reduce household mortgage financing by enough to make up almost all of the required shortfall, even that extreme outcome would not permit any growth at all in the relative indebtedness of the business sector. More probably, business debt relative to income will also have to

TABLE 5-3. Financing Of U.S. Nonfinancial Corporate Businesses

	1956–1960	1961–1965	1966–1970	1971–1975	1976–1980	1981	1982
Internal sources of funds	69.8	67.8	61.5	57.5	60.7	69.8	76.2
External sources of funds	30.2	32.1	38.5	42.5	39.3	30.2	23.8
Equity	4.4	1.1	2.5	5.8	1.6	-3.5	3.7
Debt	25.8	31.0	36.1	36.7	37.7	33.6	20.1

Note: Data are averages (except for 1981 and 1982) of annual flows, as percentages of annual total sources of funds to the nonfinancial corporate-business sector. Negative-equity source indicates excess of retirements over gross new issues. Detail may not add to total because of rounding.

Source: Board of Governors of the Federal Reserve System.

decline in order to make room for the ballooning Federal Government debt. During a recession, some relative contraction of business indebtedness ordinarily occurs anyway; but during and after a recovery, it will represent an entirely new phenomenon.

Without the ability to raise external funds in the credit market, the business sector will largely have to forego taking advantage of the newly legislated investment incentives unless it turns massively to equity financing—an unlikely prospect in light of the history shown in Table 5-3. Put in terms of the factors confronting business decision making, the problem will be that the increased real cost of financing (and, for some companies, reduced availability) will outweigh the added attractiveness of new investment owing to the large favorable tax changes. Hence, business will invest not more but less, and the U.S. economy's net capital-formation rate will decline still further. The chief implication, therefore, is that as the economy recovers, the current stance of U.S. fiscal policy is likely to prove counterproductive even in terms of its own goal of encouraging, rather than further depressing, productive capital investment.

ALTERNATIVE FISCAL POLICIES

Based on this analysis, a specific *minimum* proposal for changing the current fiscal policy in the postrecession period is to reduce government spending, or raise taxes, or do both, at least to the point at which the resulting budget deficit is small enough that the implied increase in Federal Government indebtedness merely keeps pace with nominal income. In terms of averages for the next five years, such a revised fiscal-policy stance would imply deficits averaging no more than about 3 percent of income, if income is growing at 12 percent annually, or about 2 percent of income if income is growing at only 8 percent—in short, deficits no larger than about half the size of those now in prospect. In terms of the familiar trio of frequently suggested ways to reduce the federal deficit between 1982 and 1987—cutting entitlement program benefits (especially under social security), slowing the scheduled increase in defense spending, and deferring (or eliminating) the legislated 1983 reduction in individual income taxes—this minimum proposal approximately amounts to choosing any one-and-a-half of the three options. Budget changes of this magnitude would at least keep the

Federal Government's relative indebtedness from rising beyond today's level, and hence would avert the further squeeze on private indebtedness implied by the current policy stance.

The minimum character of this proposal is clear, however, in that the situation it produces would be merely a continuation of the 1970s—hardly an enviable era for federal budgets, capital formation, or corporate finance. If the U.S. economy is to achieve an increased capital-formation rate in the 1980s, the credit-market perspective explored here suggests that the postrecession revision of the current stance of fiscal policy will have to go significantly further. To achieve a more capital-intensive economic technology overall—that is, a greater ratio of physical capital to output—will almost certainly require a rising business debt-to-income ratio. That, in turn, will require federal budget deficits small enough to allow the government's debt-to-income ratio to begin to decline once again.

CHAPTER SIX

BUDGET OUTCOMES AND CAPITAL MARKETS

Leonard J. Santow

The questions addressed in these essays indicate the frustrations encountered by many analysts over the years in deciding where to start to improve budgetary policy. If analysts cannot even agree upon budgetary definitions, accounting, and goals, it should be little wonder that they cannot agree upon solutions.

To avoid having this essay be mainly a series of personal observations on the effect of public-sector actions on private-sector participants, it starts with a series of suggestions that would improve fiscal policy, then moves to a new approach with respect to government expenditures, and finishes with an analysis of Treasury capital-market borrowings and whether they "crowd out" potential private capital-market borrowers. On this last topic, all one can do is make inferences and arrive at suggested conclusions.

The first two matters relate to the crowding out issue more than initially apparent. If a series of budget improvements can be implemented with respect to targets, controls, and procedures, then the size of the budget deficit can be limited. If the size of the deficit can be limited, then the amount of Treasury financing can be limited; and if the amount of Treasury financing can be reduced, then whatever the degree of crowding out, it can also be reduced. Improvements with respect to crowding out can be meaningful even if one is unable to measure the exact degree of what has been accomplished, or even if the problem is not as severe as some analysts suggest. Finally, basic improvements in the budget should do more to help any crowding-out problem than changes in debt-management techniques.

POSSIBLE BUDGET IMPROVEMENTS

The suggestions that follow are not fully developed here. The brevity of the comments should not be viewed, however, as indicative of their importance.

● Government officials should admit that while there are fiscal policies, there is no one "fiscal policy." The budget process can be as long as two years from beginning to end, and the final results often bear no resemblance to those originally projected. Moreover, no one individual, or even group of individuals, alone has the ability to fine-tune fiscal policy, let alone change its direction.

● Since there is no single fiscal policy, trying to use fiscal policy for countercyclical purposes (except for the automatic stabilizers) is an exercise in futility. A series of fiscal policies designed for current needs are often out of date by the time they are actually implemented. Therefore, given the lack of development of a single and controllable fiscal policy, primary responsibility for cyclical and fine-tuning needs should lie with monetary policy.

● Both the Administration and Congress should set budgetary goals or guidelines that are realistic. In any goals or guidelines, the readily available cash budget—using both "on" and "off" budget items as published in the monthly Treasury statement—should be used. While full-employment and national income-accounts budgets can be useful concepts, they both lack timeliness in reported data. Moreover, the seasonal adjustments in the quarterly national income-accounts budget data are often questionable, while there is always the question of what is "full employment" in the full-employment budget.

● Using the cash-budget basis, the guideline could be a budget that is roughly in balance at the peak of a business cycle, while the guideline at the trough of a business cycle could be a maximum budget deficit of, say, 5 percent of nominal GNP. Moreover, once a deficit reaches 5 percent of nominal GNP, receipts and expenditure changes must be implemented to bring down that percentage.

● In order to help control the growth of government spending, an "expenditure-subject-to-limitation" ceiling should be adopted, using either a quarterly or semiannual period as a basis. This ceiling would replace the anachronistic "debt-subject-to-limitation" ceiling, which is nothing more than locking the barn door after the horse has been stolen. Moreover, all congressional restrictions on types of Treasury financing, such as the restriction on bond financing, should be removed.

● The proposed balanced-budget amendment to the Constitution should be dropped. It makes little sense, since the government cannot control the level of tax receipts, and expenditure policies under the amendment that would be procyclical rather than countercyclical might have to be adopted. There surely is a better way to vent the understandable frustration of many well-intentioned fiscal conservatives.

● The Congressional Budget Committees should be given substantially more power. These committees can never have the influence needed to make Congress a real player in the fiscal-policy process unless such power is forthcoming, especially with respect to other congressional committees.

● The politicizing of budget estimates by the Executive Branch should be limited. Congress should create a small committee of nongovernment budget experts whose task would be to report to Congress and the U.S. citizenry on whether or not the assumptions that underlie the Administration's budget estimates are realistic.

RETHINKING THE DEFENSE BUDGET

If a replica of the Hunt Commission were established for the budget, it would probably find that the most fruitful changes would come in the area of expenditures, since that is where the greatest problems are created with respect to both size and control. If one looks at the components of Federal Government spending, disparities among the various expenditure components become apparent very quickly. In this regard, the one category that stands out is the defense area—both because it is so large and because it is so different.

Defense is something that cannot be placed in the private sector or given to state and local governments in determining priorities of spending; and it has problems entirely different from other areas of government spending. Defense has long lead times with respect to many of its outlays. This makes it very difficult to change drastically over the short run. Its growth pattern has little relationship to business cycles and, therefore, cannot be viewed as a countercyclical or procyclical device. It also requires substantial amounts of long-term planning, but must be flexible enough to respond quickly to unexpected military needs. Finally, defense may be the most politically sensitive and controversial of all of the major areas in the budget—because of its size and also because of the strong personal feelings that it engenders.

With this background in mind, a strong case can be made to assemble a blue-ribbon panel of budget experts to study the feasibility of removing the defense budget from the regular budget and from the regular budget process. The following are some specific suggestions with respect to this separation:

● The defense budget would be removed from the annual budget and the annual budget process. Then, defense would be placed on a two-year budget basis, with a separate defense budget published every other year. This document would be published at the same time of the year as the regular budget (early February). If it were to be published by the Administration at the beginning of odd-numbered years, it would roughly coincide with the beginning of a newly elected Congress.

● The Administration would determine what it believes the proper percentage of GNP military spending should comprise for this two-year period. The primary basis for this decision would be national-defense needs, although national affordability would be a consideration.

● The defense budget would be broken out into a capital budget and an operating budget. Of all of the major areas of the federal budget, it may well be that defense is the easiest area for such treatment. The overall defense-spending target as a proportion of GNP would also be broken out on a capital- and operating-budget basis.

● Authorization, appropriations, and actual outlays would have different timetables than they now have as they conform to the needs of the new two-year budget process. Moreover, while the congressional committees that are involved in the military area would continue to have their same involvement, their timetable would also change.

● Several revenue-raising and financing techniques could be used, with the proceeds going entirely to help meet defense outlays. For example, when filling their income-tax returns, individuals could designate up to a certain amount to be used entirely for the defense establishment, and they would receive a partial tax credit for income-tax purposes. On the financing side, the Treasury could issue "Defense Savings Bonds," possibly with some tax credits given for the interest earned. The Treasury could also auction perpetual maturity obligations on a regular basis, with the proceeds used entirely to finance defense outlays. The logic of these two financing suggestions is that long-term ongoing needs should be matched as well as possible with long-run ongoing financings.

● The defense budget would not be an integral part of any balanced-budget concept or constitutional amendment. The reasons are that the primary factors in determining defense spending should be defense needs and what the U.S. economy and its people can afford to spend. Defense affordability should be based upon the strength of the U.S. economy, as measured by GNP, and not viewed or measured in terms of its percentage of total government outlays.

● Once the defense budget is a separate and distinct process, and the document has a two-year time horizon, both the Administration and Congress may find it easier to improve target and control procedures for the nondefense budget. Moreover, the nondefense budget could be tailored to countercyclical needs much more easily than before.

● The nondefense budget should always run a surplus, with the surplus goals related to nominal GNP. For example, an acceptable range of nondefense surpluses could be 5 to 10 percent of nominal GNP.

● A defense budget determined and presented in this new way would add more openness to the whole defense process. Public attention could then focus on defense issues in a more fundamental and unencumbered manner. Moreover, there would be a reasonable chance that large shifts in the amount and direction of defense spending could be reduced, thus making plans and spending techniques more cost efficient. This improvement in cost efficiency, when combined with the previously mentioned ways of helping to raise funds for defense spending, could help limit the burden of overall government debt financing.

CROWDING OUT PRIVATE BORROWERS

One of the most talked about budget issues in recent times has been whether large amounts of Treasury financing, especially in the bond market, have been a major disruptive force for potential private borrowers. Possibly the best way to attack the validity of this crowding-out issue is to take two hypothetical economic situations that are at opposite extremes.

For example, when the economy is in the third or fourth year of a major business recovery, inflation and inflationary expectations are rising, the Federal Reserve is using a monetarist approach that is erring on the tight side, and corporations want and need to spend money on plant and equipment, then the financings of a large budget deficit will crowd—and probably crowd out—some potential private borrowers. Much of the crowding out, however, could well come in the money market—where the needs of individuals and corporations could be very large at a time when the banks and investors are squeezed for short-term funds—rather than in the capital market. Moreover, one can argue that this type of crowding out is not that bad, because it would tend to limit further financial excesses and imbalances by the private sector.

The hypothetical situation at the other extreme is when the economy is in the third or fourth year of something bordering on a recession, inflation and inflationary expectations have declined, the Federal Reserve is using an approach to policy that does not err on the tight side, interest rates are a major policy consideration, and corporations have little need or desire to build additional plant and equipment because of low utilization of capacity and high uncertainty. Under such circumstances, it would be very difficult to make any argument of crowding out caused by large amounts of Treasury financing. If it is difficult to make this argument, then it would be even more difficult to make the argument that Treasury capital-market financing is severely and adversely affecting private capital-market financing.

While the two previous examples are hypothetical, it should be obvious that recent times are much closer to the second example than to the first, and, therefore, crowding out has not been a problem in either the money or capital markets in several years. Moreover, even in the first example where crowding out is a problem, it appears to be more of a money-market than a capital-market problem. These examples should make it quite clear that crowding out of the private capital market owing to long-term Treasury financing has been overstated in the last few years, both in terms of degree and importance. The explosive rally in all the capital markets in recent months, despite the Treasury's return to the bond market with even larger supplies of new bonds to come, should further help to convince any doubters about the overstatement of the crowding-out issue.

While crowding out may be an overblown issue, it does appear that there have been definite impediments to private borrowers' willingness or capability to raise long-term funds. There is a capital-market problem for many potential private borrowers, but many analysts have been looking in the wrong place for the source of the difficulty. If one thinks in terms of borrowers being priced out rather than crowded out of the market, and the causes of the pricing out, some of the answers should become clear.

The distinction between crowding out and pricing out should not be viewed as one of mere semantics, or opposite sides of the same coin. In order to distinguish between the two, it is important to determine how pricing out can occur. One should first realize that the rates at which many potential private borrowers can raise funds have not declined by anywhere near as much as the more publicized rates on federal funds or Treasury bills. Moreover, not only have rates on corporate bonds, the prime loan rate, and London Interbank Offer Rate stayed relatively high on a nominal basis, but they have stayed very high in real terms, considering the decline in inflation. In other words, the rates that are important to many potential private borrowers have not declined anywhere near the degree that past history or theory would suggest should have been the case.

The key question then becomes: What have been the impediments to a decline in rates for private borrowers, especially in capital markets? It appears that the impediments can be put into four classifications—the unwillingness or inability of investors to "lock up" long-term debt yields; the stickiness of pricing by financing institutions that lend money; the fears of the financial community with respect to large budget deficits; and a monetary policy that, until very recently, has joined a monetarist approach with erring on the tight side. These four areas are frequently interrelated. Adverse changes in one can enhance adversities in the others:

● On the investment side, many firms (especially financial institutions) have had liquidity problems; have had adverse experience investing long term on a fixed-rate basis; have consistently misestimated future inflation and interest rate levels; and have been quite unsure of what the future holds for their own businesses, especially in a rapidly changing deregulation climate. Therefore, they have not been very aggressive in investing in the intermediate- and long-term debt markets, especially when their behavior is compared with similar periods in past business cycles. Up to quite recently, moreover, a downsloping yield curve has dovetailed with all of the other reasons to invest short term. Individual investors also have acted quite conservatively in committing funds to long-term, fixed-rate investment. The main reasons for their reluctance are little growth in personal income during an extended recession-type period, considerable job market uncertainty, an attempt to rebuild liquidity balances, and a desire to pay off excessive debt. In addition, there has been a growing variety of short-term investment outlets for individuals who, until recently, have taken advantage of higher short rates compared with long rates—a combination that can make near-term investments quite attractive when viewed against a backdrop of past investment mistakes and the growing multiplicity of uncertainties.

● On the lending side, many financial institutions have decided that when demand drops off and profits decline, the best way to enhance profits has been to hold up interest-rate changes. This approach has been especially notable with respect to loans to less-than-prime borrowers, to small businesses, and to individuals who want funds to purchase houses or other durable goods. At the same time that lenders have tried to maintain high levels of interest rates, the sellers of the goods and services that are being financed appear to have taken the same philosophy with respect to their prices. Therefore, what seems to have happened is that many businesses have been trying to keep up the price of their products and services in order to improve profits, and many of these businesses are borrowing from financial institutions that are also attempting to achieve the same objective.

This attitude with respect to pricing products, services, and funds has apparently been decided upon by people whose experience is dominated by past inflation and inflationary psychology. In that situation, the answer to profit problems has generally seemed to be to raise prices or rates, even in the face of weak demand.

Unfortunately, many of the people on the other side—the buyers of the product, the service, and the funds—take a different attitude. They have to become much more price selective and price sensitive, and many lenders and sellers of products and services do not seem to realize this change.

● The majority of participants in the financial markets believe that large and persistent budget deficits will ultimately lead to increases in inflation and to tighter monetary policy. They also believe that such budget performances are symptomatic of inappropriate government economic policies. In this regard, investors may well fear that recent improvements in inflation could prove to be transitory, and that, if they are not careful, they could be among those who invest in long-term bonds and are locked into near-the-bottom yields for the next interest-rate cycle.

● The financial community has never been comfortable with a monetarist approach to policy, especially when it is combined with the Fed erring on the tight side, which, in turn, contributes to downsloping yield curves. Financial-market participants do not fully understand monetarism, nor do they like the wild swings it can create in interest rates. They blame much of the thinness in the capital markets on monetarism, and they have lost any feeling for value in a capital-market security. While some theoreticians may strongly argue against such claims, it is the financial-market participants who do the buying and selling—not the theoreticians. Attractive investment opportunities slipped by, not only because many investors did not know where monetary policy was heading, but because they were not even sure where policy is, was, or had been.

These four factors strongly suggest that potential purchasers of any type of long-term, fixed-rate security have been dissuaded, not so much by the actual and potential supply of new issues, but rather by a financial and economic atmosphere that has not been conducive to bringing down *and keeping down* long-term interest rates. For those who have doubts or second thoughts about this analysis, a concrete example helps to prove the point. The Treasury, for a number of years, has regularly sold bonds with a 20-year maturity, but not with the greatest of success. These issues, which have been sold quarterly, have had a history of quick declines in price to a discount, with dealers having a difficult time finding more permanent holders. The argument has been made that these issues have frequently been too large (usually around 1.5 billion), or that the maturity has been too long, for traditional buyers of government securities or too short for such long-term investors as pension funds. In late September 1982, however, the Treasury (after not being able to sell bonds for over a half year) came to market with a huge (2.75 billion) offering of 20-year bonds. The bidding for the bonds proved to be spirited; the issue was much better placed than usual; and both the public and private markets actually took heart from the fact that such a large amount of a previously difficult-to-sell maturity could be placed so easily. The difference between this 20-year offering and previous similar offerings was that a growing number of potential investors believed that some of the previously mentioned bond-market problems were behind us and that long rates had a good chance of staying down for an extended period. Thus, the supply of 20-year maturities proved to be a problem only when demand was missing. Demand, and more specifically the reasons for the demand, were more active ingredients than the amount of supply. Needless to say, the same reasons that caused investors not to buy long-term Treasury maturities were the same reasons for investors not to buy long-term corporate bonds.

CONCLUSION

In the last several years, the private capital markets suffered from pricing out rather than crowding out. These two concepts would be the same in a perfect world that had perfect markets with perfect knowledge, but imperfections are a fact of life. In the case of pricing out, the reduction or elimination of Treasury-bond financing would be of only limited value because they do not get to the source of the problems, many of which have been festering for a decade or more. These problems cover a wide variety of ills and defy a simple solution. Yet, if one were to look for a starting point from which to attack these problems, that place could well be a change from many fiscal policies to one fiscal policy that is more directly related to national objectives.

PART THREE

BUDGET OUTCOMES AND INFLATION

CHAPTER SEVEN

DEFICITS AND INFLATION

Allan H. Meltzer

Few ideas in economics are as widely accepted as the belief that budget deficits are inflationary. Practical persons, professional speculators and traders, Congress members, and other noneconomists are almost uniformly quoted on one side of the issue. Public-opinion polls suggest that their view is the majority view. One can only guess at the qualifications and conditions in the minds of the practical person and the polls' respondents. It seems unlikely, however, that the qualifications would do more than state some conditions under which the positive association may be present, but not always apparent to the naked eye. For example, some may qualify their claim by asserting that deficits keep prices from falling, or inflation from declining, during recessions. Qualifications of this kind change the type of relation from simple to multivariate, but they do not change the alleged positive relation between deficits and inflation. And they change the positive effect from a total to a partial effect that can be observed only if a proper set of "other things" is taken into account.

Recent experience is instructive. It is not an overstatement to say that in 1981 and 1982, we heard monthly and, at times, daily warnings from Wall Street and Capitol Hill about the inflationary effects of budget deficits and their dominant effect on market interest rates. Yet, just at the time when a large part of the 1982 to 1983 deficit was to be financed, interest rates fell and the average rate of inflation resumed its decline.

Wall Street's "doom and gloom" scenario for interest rates and inflation in 1982 to 1983 proved incorrect. Open-market interest rates reached their peaks in 1981 or early 1982. Most broad measures of inflation also reached a peak by 1981. The entrenched belief that deficits would produce high inflation and therefore keep interest rates from falling was as wrong in 1982 as it was in 1975 to 1976, the last time it surfaced above the din created by alternative forecasts.

A year or more after the most recent peaks in interest rates and inflation, the prophets of doom and gloom shuffled their papers and shifted their grounds. Prime rates of 20 to 25 percent are no longer in sight. The new forecast is for interest rates to keep falling, on average, as the economy stagnates or declines. To this reader, the new forecasts seem much more cautious about the inflationary effect of deficits. Very little has happened to the projected deficits; "other things" must have changed.

What are those "other things"? A short list must include actual and expected income, the exchange rate and the balance of payments, the effects of tax laws and anticipations on saving, and the current and anticipated rates of money growth. Serious attempts to study the effects of deficits on prices or inflation that have taken account of these and other comovements in the economy have found no reliable effect of deficits on inflation in the United States. Neither the last 30 years nor earlier periods provide evidence to support the popular belief in a close or reliable positive association between deficits and inflation. Before deciding that this evidence is, or is not, a proper basis for concluding that deficits are *not* inflationary, one should consider some qualifications.

FOUR NECESSARY QUALIFICATIONS

There is nothing new about budget deficits. The fiscal history of the United States, from 1791 to 1983, shows 101 years of budget surpluses and 92 years of deficits. Before 1901, the distribution was

75 to 35, but that distribution is skewed by an uninterrupted sequence of 28 years of budget surpluses from 1866 to 1893. In the years prior to the Civil War, budget deficits were not uncommon. For example, there was only one reported budget surplus between 1837 and 1843. The Warren and Pearson index of wholesale prices fell by 50 percent from 1837 to 1843, rising only in 1939, the year of the budget surplus. The post-Civil War budget surpluses occurred during a period in which prices fell, on average. The two experiences have opposite outcomes, so they do not support any firm conclusion.

Problems of comparability reduce the weight that can be placed on comparisons across the centuries. The distribution of spending between levels of government changed markedly. The definition of deficits also changed. More state and local spending was paid for by transfers from the Federal Government. Difficulties of this kind emphasize the importance of qualifications in any discussion of the effect of deficits in inflation. Simple comparisons tell very little.

Methods of Finance

The first qualification distinguishes between deficits financed by increasing the stock of money and deficits financed by selling bonds to private investors or their agents—pension funds, insurance companies, banks, and other financial institutions. Inflation is often defined as a persistent or sustained rate of increase in a broad-based measure of prices. Few now dispute that a sustained rate of growth of money in excess of the sustained rate of growth of output causes inflation. Persistent deficits financed by selling government bonds, either directly or indirectly, to the central bank increase the stock of money and its measured rate of growth. The same increase in money and inflation would occur, however, if the central bank bought an equal amount of private debt and private investors bought the government debt issued to finance the deficits.

All deficits are financed, initially, by selling debt to foreign investors, domestic investors, and foreign and domestic central banks. If one puts aside the sales to foreigners, for the present, the question is simplified: Are sales of government debt to private investors inflationary?

Domestic private investors make net purchases of government debt from current saving. Government spending and financing decisions affect the level and distribution of private spending and saving, and therefore affect output and interest rates. The response of the price level to such changes is difficult to separate from other transitory disturbances. At most, there is a bit of fluctuation in the price level. There is no reason for a one-time deficit to produce sustained inflation.

Of course, increased government spending and deficits may persist for several years. During the four years of 1977 to 1980, all the leading industrialized countries reported deficits. The Organization for Economic Cooperation and Development (OECD) has attempted to produce a common measure of the deficit for each country. This measure, known as the public-sector borrowing requirement (PSBR), ranged from 2.0 percent of national product in France to 12.4 percent in Italy, on average, for the four years. The average inflation rate covered as wide a range. After allowing for the effect of average money growth, however, average rates of inflation and the PSBR ratio are negatively related. Countries with relatively large debt issues had *lower* rates of inflation during these years, on average, after allowing for differences in their maintained average rate of money growth.

There are several possible explanations of the observed negative relation between debt finance and inflation. First, the appearance of deficits during a period of slow growth or recession reflects, in part, the lower rate of expenditure growth and reduced tax collections caused by the recession. The decline in the rate of inflation may also reflect the effect of recession. The negative association is, in this interpretation, the reflection of a common cause—the recession. Second, the increase in the deficit and in the demand for money may be the result of increased uncertainty about the future. For example, heightened uncertainty about future output growth can cause an increase in the demand for money and short-term assets, a decline in output and tax receipts, higher transfer payments, and a larger deficit. The effect would not be the same in all countries for a number of reasons, including the policy reaction to the effect of heightened uncertainty, but the size of the government's borrowing and the increase in the demand for money may be largest where uncertainty is greatest.

The finding that inflation during 1977 to 1980 was lower where government borrowing was larger does not imply that persistent government borrowing reduces inflation. Yet, like the evidence from the post-Civil War period in the United States, it gives no support to the widely held view that deficits, financed by debt, are inflationary. This leads to the second qualification.

Expected Persistence

Neither one-time increases in money nor one-time increases in government debt produce inflation. Any effect of budget deficits on inflation occurs only if deficits are expected to persist. A large deficit that maintains aggregate demand during a recession may cause a rise, or delay a decline, in the price level. Unless the spending persists, the price level does not continue to rise. There is no sustained increase in prices, so there is no inflation.

In Chile and Argentina, consolidated budget deficits rose to 10 or 15 percent of total output during the fiscal crises of the 1970s. Deficits of this size were large relative to private saving or other sources of nonmonetary finance, so the dominant belief was that money growth must increase. This belief was strengthened by the fall in tax collections. By delaying tax payments, people reduced the real cost of taxes with fixed nominal value. This increased the deficit. Further, the governments of Allende and Isabel Peron did not have programs to close the deficit by tax collection or expenditure reduction. One should not be surprised if, under the prevailing circumstances, money growth and inflation were expected to rise without apparent limit.

Evidence of the effect on expectations is not hard to find. There was a flight from money during the period of high, persistent deficits. Chilean inflation was much higher than the rate of money growth. Once the budget shifted to surplus and money growth declined, the demand for money increased; inflation fell more rapidly than money growth and remained below its rate. In Argentina, deficits were reduced but not eliminated. After a short-lived decline, inflation returned to triple digits. Inflation, currency devaluation, and deficits were expected to persist and, perhaps, to increase.

There is a considerable difference between the effects of temporary deficits and large, persistent deficits. There is no evidence that temporary deficits are inflationary unless they are financed, directly or indirectly, by faster money growth. There is considerable evidence that large, persistent deficits cannot be financed without inflation. In between, there must be a point or, more likely, a range in which deficits are expected to persist and to be followed by higher money growth and higher inflation. Persistent, large deficits that generate expectations of inflation are often followed by inflation.

What is regarded as temporary or persistent depends on expectations about future policies. If taxes on nominal income are progressive, taxes rise with inflation, so nominal deficits may rise or fall. A sequence of deficits that increase faster than private saving raises the prospect of increased money growth and inflation. If the nominal deficit is expected to rise persistently—spending, transfers, and interest payments are expected to rise faster than tax collections—it is not unreasonable to believe that rising deficits will be financed, sooner or later, by increasing money growth. This belief, if firmly held, raises interest rates and reduces tax collections, increasing conventional measures of the current deficit and, possibly, the current rate of money growth.

Real and Nominal Debt

A third qualification concerns the amount of debt that people hold, and the effect of inflation on real indebtedness. An inflation that occurs after debt has been issued reduces the real value of fixed-price obligations. The outstanding nominal debt may rise rapidly during a period of rising inflation and rising deficits, but the real value of the debt typically falls.

The fall in the real value of the debt in a period of sustained inflation contributes, at least for a time, to the rise in the amount of nominal debt issued. The reason is that people anticipate continued inflation and a fall in the real value of all debts fixed in nominal value. Interest rates rise with anticipations of inflation and the anticipated decline in the real value of the debt.

Higher interest rates require higher interest payments. Higher interest payments increase conventional measures of government spending. The rise in interest payments compensates the owners of bonds for the anticipated decline in the real value of the debt that they own.

The change in net interest payments during recent years is not very different from the change in the deficit reported in the national income accounts. Between fiscal 1968 and fiscal 1981, the U.S. deficit increased from $12 billion to $58 billion; net interest payments increased from $10 billion to $67 billion. Similar computations for Britain yield similar results.

Comparisons of this kind imply that there is a positive relation running from inflation to the size of the deficit as conventionally measured. This line of causation goes from inflation to interest rates, to interest payments, spending, and the deficit. The relation is partial, of course. Inflation also increases tax collections (in a system like ours) and components of spending other than interest payments, so there is no necessary connection making the deficit larger as inflation increases.

Exchange Rates

The fourth and final qualification concerns exchange-rate policy. The process by which deficits affect prices in the United States is different now than it was under the Bretton Woods system as it functioned prior to August 1971.

Under that system, exchange rates for most currencies were defined in terms of dollars. Governments and central banks agreed, and were obligated, to buy and sell dollars at a fixed price. When the United States had a budget deficit and a balance-of-payment deficit—as it did in most years of the 1960s—foreigners and foreign central banks acquired claims on the United States. Central banks of other countries held many of the claims in the form of U.S. government securities. For a time, others demanded payment, or partial payment, in gold. Purchases of gold and securities by foreigners contributed to faster money growth and higher inflation abroad. The financing of the U.S. budget deficit produced higher money growth at home, and the sales of debt raised money growth abroad.

Large or persistent differences in rates of inflation cannot be maintained under a fixed exchange-rate system. The inflation at home and abroad was, eventually, reflected in import prices, in world commodity prices, and in the world inflation rate. As long as foreigners continued to buy and hold U.S. securities, they financed part of the U.S. budget deficit. They exchanged goods and services and real assets for claims on the U.S. Treasury. When some of these countries became less willing to acquire additional U.S. securities, the Bretton Woods system ended. President Nixon further restricted gold sales and allowed the dollar to float.

Under floating exchange rates, central banks are not obligated to buy or sell foreign exchange or to finance deficits in other countries' budgets. Foreign central banks and monetary authorities as a group have continued to purchase U.S. government securities, however. This is particularly true of some countries in OPEC, but not only of OPEC countries. Germany and Japan continued to acquire U.S. securities during the 1970s. Many of these purchases contributed to money growth abroad and to fluctuations in exchange rates, prices, and measured rates of inflation.

If foreign central banks insist on strict control of domestic money growth, large U.S. and foreign budget deficits are financed mainly from domestic private saving. Countries in which public-sector borrowing is large, relative to the sum of domestic private saving and noninflationary money growth, must borrow from the rest of the world. All countries cannot borrow simultaneously; some must lend. With very large deficits relative to output or saving in many countries, and relatively low response of saving rates to interest rates in individual countries, exchange rates and interest rates must change over a wide range to finance public-sector borrowing.

Changes in exchange rates change the relative prices of domestic and imported goods, and some of these changes are reflected in broad-based price levels. Fluctuations of this kind are one-time events, distinct from inflation (defined as a persistent increase in a broad-based index of prices).

To discuss the inflationary effects of budget deficits, a number of qualifying phrases and conditions have been introduced. The qualifying phrases are: real, persistent, sustained, in excess of expectations, relative to output, and relative to saving. The qualifying conditions are no less important. The method by which the deficits are financed matters. Deficits have often been financed by central banks. The appearance of large, persistent deficits, or the expectation that deficits will persist and grow relative to output, strengthens the belief that money growth will rise. This belief is not always borne out, but it has been correct too often to be dismissed.

The qualifying phrases and conditions help to explain why the views of practical persons about the inflationary effects of budget deficits are not always borne out. Governments can prevent inflation from accelerating by fiscal reform, spending reduction, or higher taxes. This lowers the deficit, the expected rates of money growth, and inflation.

THE "COST" OF GOVERNMENT

As the deficit grows, some analysts increase the size of "the deficit" by adding off-budget activities to government spending. These are an attempt to compute some measure of total government borrowing, based on the apparent belief that every dollar of government borrowing adds to the government "deficit." Other activities include government loan guarantees as a measure of the borrowing sponsored by government.

Many of the off-budget activites financed by government loans have positive productivity. This remains true even where the activity would not occur unless government subsidized borrowers by relending at a rate below the open-market rate. The subsidy increases the amount the public borrows from the government credit agencies or under the government's guarantee. Some of the borrowing is a substitute for private borrowing. Adding the entire off-budget borrowing to the deficit overstates the net addition to borrowing and has no clear relation to any meaningful definition of the budget deficit.

One reason for the measurement problem is that as government activity expands, some formerly private activities are taken over by government. Activities are encouraged or deterred by taxation, regulation, or subsidies. The burden the economy bears, or the benefit it receives, from government activity is a neglected item in the discussion of government deficits.

Suppose a private utility decides to build a power plant and, after careful planning, elects to finance most of the expenditure by issuing bonds. The sale of the bonds is an ordinary business event, in no way remarkable. What changes if the utility is a public enterprise? Many may say "nothing," but in my opinion that is incorrect. Public enterprises in many countries, including the United States, frequently operate under different restrictions and often pursue different goals: They may not pay taxes. Often they do not pay dividends or a rental price for capital. They may issue more debt per unit of physical capital than is found in the private sector. In many countries, public enterprises have higher employment per unit of output and lower efficiency. Pricing below cost of production is not uncommon.

The example brings out that differences in efficiency are likely to be important when comparing public and private enterprises. The social cost of public enterprises in many countries is more a reflection of the inefficiency with which these enterprises use labor, capital, and other resources than of their contribution to the public-sector budget deficit.

The government's ability to borrow and subsidize is not unimportant. The subsidies delay or prevent adjustments, including plant closings, that a private firm would make. Concentration on the budget deficit, or the borrowing requirement, neglects the more important difference between public and private ownership.

The principal differences between the private and public sector arise from the way in which resources are used. Governments produce services that the market does not provide—for example, defense and police protection. And governments redistribute income and wealth directly and by charging prices below cost of production—as in education—or, often, in nationalized industries. Further, they regulate and prohibit numerous activities under interpretations of the police power.

Government activities both create and remove distortions that arise in the market economy. Since the time of John Locke, careful arguments have been set out showing that defense and police protection are produced most efficiently if they are produced collectively. Other collective goods include administration of the judicial system and pollution control. The efficiency with which governments provide these services and the extent to which efficiency and centralization are related remain open issues. There is a presumption, however, that welfare and efficiency are increased where defense and police protection are adequate.

Governments do not limit their activities to the provision of collective goods. Taxes and deficits finance programs to redistribute income among and within generations, income classes, and social groups. These decisions may conform to voters' decisions and respond to voters' demands, yet distort decisions to work, save, invest, produce, innovate, or hire.

The real cost or benefit of government is the difference between the distortions that government imposes and distortions that government removes. This measure of the cost of government, although difficult to compute, is a better measure of the burden than conventional measures of the budget deficit. There is no reason for the two measures to be related. Governments impose regulations that raise costs but do not increase the budget or the deficit. Government spending may increase the efficiency of the private sector by reducing crime, for example.

If government regulation, taxation, and spending impose a net burden, output, efficiency, and welfare are reduced. The real cost of government is paid in this way. These costs produce inflation only if the burden or cost of government is ever increasing. A persistent decline in efficiency and output implies that the growth of output is reduced. Lower output growth with unchanged money growth increases inflation.

Excessive emphasis on estimates of current and future deficits diverts attention from the real value of government spending and any excess burden the economy bears as a consequence of government activity. The loss of efficiency from regulation, subsidies, and distortions is, to me, a larger cost than any burden associated with government borrowing to finance activities that reduce efficiency.

Concentration on financing shifts the policy discussion away from issues of the proper size and scope of government activity and the related issue of who receives the benefits of these activities. Elected governments in most countries tax productive effort to pay for transfers that often reduce employment and output. Deficit financing distributes the costs over time. As long as the deficits are not financed by expanding money (relative to output), the additional cost of deficit finance appears to be smaller than the distortions imposed by regulation, taxation, and resource diversion.

Deficit finance defers taxation or money increases to the future. When the deficit is large relative to current or future output, there is large uncertainty about future tax rates and inflation. After-tax real rates of return depend on the financing decision that is taken, so uncertainty about future financing affects current resource allocation, increasing consumption and reducing investment.

Tax reduction without spending reduction increases uncertainty about future taxes. Currently, no one knows how much of deficits projected for future years will be paid for by taxes or by inflation and how much will be removed by reducing spending. No one can know who will pay the taxes, or which activities will be favored and which discouraged by changes in spending, taxes, and inflation. These uncertainties create or increase distortions, delay expansion, and add to the net burden imposed by government.

CONCLUSION

Budget deficits are inflationary if continuous deficits are financed by sustained increases in money, and the increases in money are larger than the increases in the economy's capacity to produce output. Central banks or monetary authorites that try to control market interest rates often finance a large enough share of continuous budget deficits to produce inflation. Wartime inflation is a well-known example. Recent experience shows that peacetime deficits produce inflation also if continuous deficits are financed by sustained money growth.

The claim that "deficits are inflationary" means more than the statement "excessive money growth is inflationary." Do deficits financed by debt issues (public-sector borrowing) produce inflation if exchange rates are freely fluctuating? The answer seems to me to depend on the size of the deficit relative to saving or output. Deficits that are large relative to GNP, or saving, increase the *expected* rate of inflation if people believe that sooner or later the monetary authority will finance the deficit. The increase in expected inflation raises interest rates and interest payments and reduces tax payments. This increases the budget deficit.

Experience during the last decade in countries like Argentina and Chile under Allende shows the effect of relatively large budget deficits. Annual deficits of 10 to 20 percent could not be financed from private saving or capital inflow. The appearance of these deficits, and indications that public expenditure would not be restricted, generated expectations that the central bank would finance a large part, and often the largest part, of the projected deficits. People tried to reduce money balances. The rate of inflation far exceeded the rate of money growth. When the deficit fell relative to GNP or saving, the rate of inflation fell below the rate of money growth. This experience is not uncommon.

Projected deficits for the United States of 4 to 5 percent of GNP, if realized, may be followed by higher inflation. This has not

128

occurred, despite the many predictions that deficits are inflationary. Reductions in the maintained growth rate of money, if continued, will work to reduce inflation. Freely floating exchange rates remove the effect of foreign inflation. The projected deficits will not be costless, but their effect will be mainly on real activity, not on inflation, if the deficits are financed by issuing debt and money growth continues to fall in 1983 and 1984. Unfortunately, no one can be very certain about the achievement of this outcome, and monetary policy is not encouraging.

This conclusion should not be read as a defense of current or projected budget deficits. In my opinion, lower inflation would be attained at lower real cost if the reduction in the deficit could be achieved by reducing government spending and transfers. Part of the gain would come from increasing the efficiency with which resources are used. In addition, a resolution of the current fiscal stalemate would reduce uncertainty by clarifying the outlook for taxes, spending, transfer payments, and future money growth. This, too, would lower the real cost of present policies.

A more durable problem is the cost of government and the efficiency loss that society pays when that cost increases. The cost of government has risen in all western countries, as the relative size of government increased and transfer programs expanded. To limit the cost of government, we must agree, mutually, to limit demands for transfers and services financed by taxes, deficits, and inflation. A properly phrased constitutional amendment to limit the size of government spending and revenue is an agreement to abide by rules under which deficits remain manageable and efficiency increases.

CHAPTER EIGHT

BUDGET DEFICITS, FEDERAL DEBT, AND INFLATION
James Tobin

Federal budget deficits, current and prospective, are viewed these days with widespread apprehension, indeed consternation. Policymakers, politicians of all persuasions, pundits, business executives, bankers, brokers, and, yes, economists too, sound the alarm. These deficits, they say, are depressing the economy and preventing recovery. They are raising interest rates and crowding out productive investment. They are burdening our children and our children's children. They will, as in the past, cause rampant inflation. They mired the economy in the stagflationary swamp in the 1970s. So generally accepted are these evils and dangers that deficit-reducing measures are the practical agenda of the "midcourse correction" now supposedly dictated by the prolonged depressed state of the economy and mandated by the recent off-year election. A proposed constitutional amendment to require annually balanced budgets, unless deficits are authorized by extraordinary votes of Congress, commands less universal but strong support.

Consternation is, I believe, unwarranted. The truth is less simple and less alarming. In particular circumstances, fiscal policies can have, in some measure, each of the negative consequences alleged—but not all of them simultaneously. Viewed in perspective, the present fiscal outlook, while far from ideal, is not disastrous. Prudent and concerted monetary and fiscal policies can, I shall argue, bring about both economic recovery—the task of highest priority and greatest urgency—and long-run fiscal stability.

This chapter discusses the inflationary implications of budget outcomes and also the reverse effects of prices and inflation rates on those outcomes. The inflation consequences of fiscal policies cannot be understood in isolation from macroeconomic effects. Nor can talk about fiscal policy be separated from monetary policy.

Economists habitually distinguish short and long runs, and this custom is adhered to in this essay. Its short run is unabashedly Keynesian. That is, dollar wage and price trends are assumed sufficiently sticky that variation in aggregate demand for goods, services, and labor results in fluctuation in production, employment, and capacity utilization. Surely, few can doubt that the U.S. economy today exhibits Keynesian unemployment and excess capacity, capable of reduction by demand stimulus even if real wages and unit markups remain stable or decline. The long run, on the other hand, is an abstract state of full-employment equilibrium, with flexible money wages and prices, and with output constrained by willing supplies of resources. Although unrealistic, it is a useful tool for pursuing the ultimate logical consequences of actual and hypothetical trends and policies.

DEFICITS AND INFLATION IN A KEYNESIAN SHORT RUN

Primary Versus Total Deficits

I first make some preliminary conceptual and terminological distinctions to be used throughout the essay. The deficit in the federal budget can usefully be split into two parts, the *primary deficit* and *debt service*. The primary deficit is that that would occur if there were no preexisting debt. It is the difference between expenditures net of debt interest and receipts exclusive of federal taxes paid on debt interest. Debt service is interest paid to nonfederal holders; it excludes interest earned by federal trust funds and interest returned to the Treasury by the Federal Reserve System. The debt of the

Federal Government to outsiders takes two forms, *nonmonetary* interest-bearing time obligations and the unborrowed *monetary* base, currency or its equivalent in non-interest-bearing obligations to pay currency on demand, mainly deposits in Federal Reserve Banks. A deficit is financed by selling federal time obligations either indirectly to the Federal Reserve, thus enlarging the monetary base, or to banks and other nonfederal holders, thus enlarging the nonmonetary debt, or in both ways.

Programmatic Versus Passive Changes in Budget Outcomes

The Federal Government's budget program can be regarded as a complex set of schedules relating its outlays—for purchases of goods and services and for transfers to other governments and to individuals—and its revenues to the variables that determine their actual realizations. There are many such variables—demographic, sociological, and economic. For macroeconomic purposes, the most important are GNP, prices, employment, and unemployment, and interest rates. Legislation alters budget programs, especially from one fiscal year to another.

By *expansionary* fiscal policy, I mean a programmatic change that, at the prevailing values of the relevant economic variable, creates excess aggregate demand for goods and services—or, what is the same thing, creates an excess of national investment over saving. By *contractionary* fiscal policy, I mean the opposite. The two adjectives are not value laden. Expansionary fiscal policy may be a good idea sometimes and a bad idea other times. (Conceivably, a given programmatic change could be expansionary in some economic contingencies and contractionary in others, or could differ in this respect from one fiscal year to another. This is not a practical difficulty for the purposes of this chapter.)

The point of this formalism is to stress an old truth, one too often ignored these days: The change in the actual deficit realized or projected is a bad measure of programmatic change. There are two reasons.

The first is that the deficit, even if it is a refined measure of the government's own dissaving, is an imperfect measure of the budget program's impact on total national saving, for the program directly affects nonfederal saving too. Households, businesses, and state and local governments will generally save part of additional federal transfers they receive, just as they will pay extra federal taxes partly at the expense of saving and partly from spending. The Regan Treasury exaggerated these offsets to the federal dissaving stemming from the Economic Recovery Tax Act of 1981. But the Treasury officials were qualitatively correct in complaining that crowding-out alarms are crude in ignoring increases in private saving and in supplies of funds to buy securities or to replace borrowing, which are by-products of the same fiscal programs that generate higher federal borrowing requirements. Another illustration is the famous old "balanced-budget multiplier theorem," which says that a programmatic change that reduces government purchases (not transfers) and tax receipts equally, leaving the deficit unchanged, is contractionary. That is, private saving of part of the tax cut raises the national propensity to save.

An extreme view (known in the literature as the Ricardo-Barro equivalence theorem) holds that private agents completely offset governmental saving or dissaving, that the national propensity to save is unaffected by federal deficits and fiscal programs. Private agents regard debt issues as simply postponements of tax liabilities. Indifferent to such postponements, they buy the bonds, which are the perfect riskless vehicles to provide for the future tax levies. According to the theorem, deficit spending is both impotent and innocuous. Although it contains grains of truth, the theorem is not convincing enough analytically or empirically to be swallowed whole by policymakers.

The second, and more important, reason that actual deficits are bad measures of fiscal impact is that budget outcomes are extremely sensitive to macroeconomic fluctuations. Cyclical effects generally dominate programmatic changes in the short run. For example, take the unemployment rate as a cyclical indicator. Every additional point of unemployment raises the fiscal year 1983 deficit by $25 billion, 0.7 percent of GNP.[1] Every extra point of real interest rate on federal securities raises the deficit by $1.4 billion in the immediate fiscal year and by $8 billion a year after the whole outstanding debt is refinanced. In short, nonfiscal shocks to the economy and the budget—from overseas, from behavior of businesses and consumers, and, most importantly, from Federal Reserve monetary policy—are major determinants of budget outcomes. In the past three years, Fed policy has contributed to large budget deficits in both ways mentioned: unemployment and high interest rates.

The "high-employment budget deficit" concept was invented decades ago in order to provide a measure of programmatic changes in the macroeconomic impact of the budget, purged of purely passive, cyclical fluctuations in the realized deficit. Disentangling the two is important both for understanding and for policy. An increase in the high-employment deficit, best measured relative to high-employment GNP, is generally—though for reasons already given not always—indicative of expansionary fiscal policy. A passive increase in the deficit, one occurring while the budget program is constant, signals neither expansionary nor contractionary policy.

For distinguishing passive from programmatic changes in budget outcomes, any unemployment rate in the range of normal experience will do as a point of reference. It does not have to correspond to "high employment." The "high" or formerly "full" employment tag may have confused politicians and public and aroused their suspicions. The idea that the budget *should* be balanced at—and only at—some low-unemployment rate is a normative proposition quite separable from the analytical purpose of correcting for feedbacks from the economy to the budget.

Although the high-employment deficit makes this correction, it does not cope with the discrepancy between the budget deficit and the budget's impact on the balance of national saving and invest-ment. The several kinds of federal purchases, transfers, and taxes affect aggregate demand and deficits differently. That is why it is not strictly possible to summarize fiscal impact in any single indicator. A better approximation than the high-employment deficit can be obtained by weighting the various categories of outlays and receipts in proportion to the fractions of them that are directly spent on goods and services. For example, the weight of outright government purchases would be 1 and the weight of taxes half paid by reducing saving would be −0.5. The needed adjustments and the procedures for making them, although, of course, not the best numerical estimates of weights, have been known for a long time. Yet they still have not made their way into Office of Management and Budget and CBO routines, much less into official and public debate on fiscal policy.

Nevertheless, this is a matter of particular practical moment in appraising the seriousness of the present budget outlook. Consider interest payments on federal debt, which have become 10 percent of the budget and are projected to rise further. Net of offsetting receipts, interest payments will amount to some $80 billion in fiscal year 1982, for which CBO's 1982 September Update projected a deficit of $155 billion, of which about $50 billion is attributable to the forecast cyclical excess of unemployment over 7 percent. If one expected most interest receipts to be saved rather than spent, the budget would not look nearly as expansionary as the raw deficit projection, with or without cyclical correction, suggests. Likewise, there would be less concern about congestion in the capital markets.

There are, in fact, several reasons for doubting that interest outlays pack the same demand punch as, say, defense purchases. Rational bondholders will regard interest receipts that simply match price inflation, roughly $60 billion in fiscal year 1983, as return of principal rather than spendable income. The most widely accepted model of saving relates consumption to permanent wage income, other wealth, and liquidity, not to interest receipts and other cash flows from capital assets per se. Interest *rates*, not receipts, enter this model of consumption and saving decisions by affecting current wealth and as incentives to shift consumption from the present to the future. The sign and the magnitude of these effects are not clear. While some pensioners may spend whatever nominal interest flows they receive (contrary to the model), other individuals will accumulate whatever interest they earn in illiquid retirement accounts or for bequests. Supply-siders, and others who believe that the incentive effect of higher real interest rates dominates the income and wealth effects, should not regard a budget program as expansionary because higher after-tax interest rates entail higher budget outlays. Finally, in quantitative models used for macroeconomic and budgetary projections, monetary policies leading to high interest rates are expected to slow down the economy and to increase budget deficits. If those deficit projections are then taken as a signal for contractionary fiscal policy, with debt interest crowding out food stamps, school lunches, and other outlays, or triggering tax increases, the monetary policy delivers double whammy.

Dependence of Budget Outcomes on Price Levels and Inflation Rates

Budget outcomes depend on price levels and inflation rates as well as on output, real incomes, employment, and interest rates. Is the budget neutral with respect to prices? An economist's instinct is that voters and legislators seek real outcomes: quantities of weapons, purchasing power of transfer benefits, real burdens of taxes. An equiproportionate increase of all prices, including expected future prices—leaving unchanged relative prices, real interest rates, and expected inflation—would not change real budget programs: outlays, receipts, or deficits. Dollar figures would just be scaled up in proportion to the general price increase.

There surely are strong tendencies in this direction, but adjustments are imperfect and slow. Appropriations are commonly set in dollars; legislative action is required to alter them in step with dollar costs. The debt is denominated in dollars; an unexpected price jump transfers wealth to taxpayers from bondholders. Progressive tax structures, defined in nominal terms, collect more revenue from the same real tax base when prices are higher.

Experience during the age of inflation has made the federal budget more nearly price-neutral. Most entitlement programs are now formally indexed, though adjustments of nominal benefits are discrete and delayed. Entitlements for cost reimbursement, notably Medicare and Medicaid, are effectively indexed. The 1981 tax-rate reductions diminished the sensitivity of taxable business and personal incomes to nominal GNP. Personal income-tax brackets are to be indexed from 1985. CBO calculations indicate that higher prices still improve real budget outcomes, but that the budget is becoming pretty close to price-neutral if allowance is made for adjustment of discretionary appropriations.[2]

A different thought experiment is to ask what happens to budget outcomes if current output and price levels are unchanged but the expected rate of inflation is raised. Presumably, the primary deficit is the same, while debt-service outlay is increased by the rise in nominal interest rates. Under inflation-corrected accounting, as discussed above, outlays that merely maintain the real value of the debt would not be counted in the deficit. What happens to the real interest cost of the debt depends on what monetary policy is assumed. If targets for monetary base or intermediate aggregates are independent of the inflation rate, then the real interest rate will fall as wealth owners try to substitute other assets for money. Higher expected inflation is expansionary. It also improves the real budget position of the government and other debtors, even though their nominal interest outlays are increased. If, however, the central bank adjusts its targets downward so as to hold real interest rates unchanged, as would be necessary to keep aggregate demand from rising, then the budget would be unaffected except for the purely nominal increase in debt-service outlays.

Expansionary Fiscal Policy as a Source of Inflation

I must return to the main theme of the short-run half of the essay. Assume we correctly detect expansionary fiscal policy. Is it inflationary? As for any other autonomous stimulus to aggregate demand for goods and services—foreign demand for exports, investment induced by new technology, discovery of new energy resources, and so on—the answer depends on monetary policy and on the state of the economy. The first question is whether central-bank policy, given the structure of the financial system, will nullify the increase in demand or allow it to have some positive effect on output and/or prices. A nonaccommodative policy and structure—diagrammed as a vertical "LM" curve in textbooks—converts all demand shocks, fiscal or otherwise, into movements of real interest rates. In this extreme case, expansionary fiscal policy neither expands output and employment nor raises prices. It just raises interest rates and crowds out investments and other interest-sensitive outlays of private agents and state and local governments. To be sure, the crowding out could be attributed to the nonaccommodative monetary policy if labor and other productive resources would otherwise be available to meet the demands of the government and its transferees without displacing other demands; or, in other words, if the savings to finance the new public borrowing could be generated from incomes associated with expansion of production and employment. In the 1981 to 1982 recession, monetary restriction crowded out private investment by high real interest rates. The resulting recession added $60 to $75 billion to the deficit, which absorbed some of the saving that might have gone into the monetarily displaced investment. But most of that potential saving vanished, lost along with the wages and profits lost in the recession.

Generally, monetary policy and structure are not completely unaccommodative. Targeting on some monetary aggregates, operating by controlling the unborrowed monetary base, the Fed is prepared to allow, at least temporarily, a variety of outcomes—paths of output, prices, and interest rates—consistent with meeting those targets over several quarters. Partial accommodation of demand shocks occurs as households and businesses stretch their cash balances and speed up monetary velocity, and as banks economize reserves and borrow more at the discount window. In the textbook diagram, LM is not vertical but positively sloped. Given this natural partial accommodation, what are the effects of fiscal stimulus? The standard answer used to be that paths of output, prices, and interest rates will all be raised. I do not know why this is still not the right answer. It is true, however, that changes in Fed policies and operating procedures, along with deregulation of deposit interest rates, have made for less accommodation and for a steeper LM curve than in the past.

Does the LM curve actually slope the "wrong" way in a longer run? A few years ago, this proposition seemed to be implied by some economists who complained that the textbook treatment of fiscal stimulus ignored the wealth and portfolio effects of repeated additions of public debt. Over time, it was argued, these would gradually move the short-run LM curve to the left, raising interest rates and eventually overcoming the spending effects of the fiscal stimulus. The trouble with this argument is that it is hard to see why the demand for money becomes so high if income has declined while interest rates have risen. The rise of interest rates induces people to hold more wealth in the form of government bonds, but why should they demand more money too?

Standard doctrine further says that the price response to accommodated demand shocks, including fiscal stimuli, depends on the amount of slack in the economy. Expansions raise prices. They raise prices more, relative to the increase of output, when unemployment of labor and excess capacity are low. These cyclical price increases do not necessarily raise the inflation rate more than temporarily. They are not inevitably built into the economy's core wage-price inflation pattern. Changes in that pattern also depend on where the economy stands relative to full employment or to its "natural rate of unemployment," or, more neutrally, its nonaccelerating inflation rate of unemployment (NAIRU). There is no need to go further into these old Phillips Curve issues.

To summarize this review of doctrine for the Keynesian short run: Expansionary fiscal stimulus must be carefully distinguished from actual and projected increases in deficits. Passive deficits are not expansionary and not inflationary. Expansionary fiscal policies, correctly identified and measured, can raise prices and can be inflationary, just like other demand shocks of equivalent magnitude. How much demand stimuli raise output and prices, on the one hand, rather than real interest rates, on the other, depends on the degree of accommodation built into monetary policies and institutions. How much those stimuli that survive monetary nonaccommodation raise prices and inflation rates depends on the degree of slack in the economy.

Advance Effects of Expected Future Contractionary Policies

Is less more? Is more less? Today's reigning piety about budget policy seems to say so, in asserting that *contractionary* revision of the budget program will promote recovery. By the same logic, it would be somewhat inflationary, too, on the presumption that prices will be higher if the economy recovers if it stagnates. I have argued above, at least by implication, that this does not make sense.

However, there is a more subtle story that may hang together. Legislation adopted now to make contractionary revisions not of present budget programs but of future budgets, say for fiscal years subsequent to 1984, *might* help to revive aggregate demand today. I say it *might*, not that it surely would. Such budget revisions would, of course, reduce aggregate demand in those future years, and this would be read now as having several effects in those years: lowering production, employment, and profits; lowering real short-term interest rates; and lowering the price level. How do those anticipations affect demand for goods and services at present? The second effect is expansionary, because it means that real interest rates relevant to current evaluations of long-term investment projects are lower. The first and third effects are contractionary: the first because a weaker future economy is a deterrent to investment and an encouragement to precautionary saving; the third because the prospect of less inflation from now to then adds to demand for money and other liquid dollar-denominated assets. Maybe the real-interest rate effect dominates; that would justify the optimistic scenario. The countervailing income and price effects might be weak or absent if monetary policy were expected to offset the fiscal contraction in the future period. The conclusion is that a shift in the future-policy mix toward tighter fiscal policy and easier money would have favorable effects in anticipation. As for the present, recovery requires a more stimulative total package, not just a change in the mix.

DEFICITS AND DEBT IN THE LONG RUN

Preliminary Perspectives

There is one proposition on the long-run relationship of public debt to inflation that commands widespread agreement among economists. It goes something like this: Suppose the nominal debt, in dollars, grows steadily for a long, long time at a constant percentage rate per year. Suppose its composition—the relative shares of base money (currency or equivalent) and of various maturities of promise to pay currency in future—remains constant, too. Suppose the economy itself settles into a fairly steady, "natural" rate of growth of real output, determined by technological advance and increments to labor force and other productive resources. Then the economy will also experience an inflationary trend equal to the amount by which the growth rate of debt exceeds that of output. If we knew, for example, that for some reason federal deficits and debts, monetary and nonmonetary, were going to rise steadily at 8 percent per year for the rest of the century, while we expected real GNP growth to average about 2.5 percent per year, then 5.5 percent inflation would be a pretty obvious prediction. The same logic says that 2.5 percent growth of nominal debt would imply zero inflation, although common sense about the short run suggests it would be costly in time and economic pain to get there from here. Note also that budget balance, in the conventional sense of zero growth of nominal debt, is not essential to price stability unless the economy's real growth rate is zero or negative. Otherwise, budget balance spells deflation, an implication that thoughtful supporters of the constitutional amendment might wish to consider.

Arithmetic of this kind may command wide agreement, but it is not terribly illuminating. The growth rate of nominal debt, both its monetary and nonmonetary components, is not a number that central bankers and politicians just arbitrarily and capriciously choose. It is the product of fiscal and monetary decisions of more basic political and economic content. Moreover, there is no political or economic mechanism that guarantees that the two major components of debt will grow at the same pace. When they do not, steady-state arithmetic does not tell us what the upshot will be. Recently and currently, our central bank determinedly keeps the monetary growth rate below that of total debt. While this policy can be expected to pull the inflation rate down toward the rate implied by monetary growth, it also implies an upward trend in real interest rates, declining capital investment, and the short-run Keynesian difficulties so vivid today.

I present below a simple framework for discussing the long-run dynamics of deficits and debt, with particular reference to the current situation in the United Staes. I focus on the magnitudes of deficits and debt relative to GNP. Scaling to GNP gives a rough measure of their size relative to the capacity of the economy to generate saving and taxes. Moreover, as observed above, the society's total demand for nonhuman wealth is roughly proportional to its annual permanent income from work. The market for federal debt, monetary and nonmonetary, can be expected to grow with the economy, other things being equal. Those other things are numerous, including the real returns expected on federal obligations and other stores of value and the perceived variances and covariances of those returns.

A few numerical orders of magnitude will help to keep things in perspective. At the end of 1981, federal debt, monetary and nonmonetary (at book value), to nonfederal holders was 0.27 of GNP. The ratio is projected to be 0.30 by the end of fiscal year 1983. Total nonfederal net worth runs about four times GNP. Thus, federal debt is 7 to 8 percent of total nonfederal wealth, less to the extent that wealth owners (like Ricardo and Barro) discount federal securities for the future tax liabilities they presage. In a steady state that maintained these ratios, with real GNP growing at 2.5 percent, increase of federal debt would absorb at most three-quarters of 1 percent of GNP, while total nonfederal net saving would be 10 percent of GNP.

The Simple Dynamics of Deficits and Debt

Under what conditions does total debt grow faster, or slower, than the GNP. Let x be the primary deficit as a fraction of Y, the nominal GNP; let i be the nominal interest rate, after federal taxes, on the nonmonetary debt; let D be the total debt outstanding and d, equal to D/Y, its ratio to GNP; and let γ be the fraction of the debt in nonmonetary form. Then the deficit, $\dot{D}$, in dollars, is given by:

(1) $\dot{D} = xY + i\gamma D$

The proportionate rate of growth of the debt is:

(2) $\dot{D}/D = xY/D + i\gamma$

Suppose that nominal GNP is growing at rate n. Then the growth of debt/GNP ratio, d, is:

(3) $\dot{d}/d = \dot{D}/D - \dot{Y}/Y = x/d + i\gamma - n$

For example, take the situation projected for fiscal year 1984 in CBO's 1982 September Update. I calculate the primary deficit as 1.7 percent of GNP, the total previously outstanding debt as 30 percent of GNP, the nonmonetary share 86 percent, bearing an after-tax interest rate of 8 percent. The debt will be growing at 12.5 percent per year while, according to the CBO projection, nominal GNP will be rising at 9.8 percent. Equation 3 tells us that the debt/GNP ratio will be rising at 2.7 percent per year, that is, from 0.30 to about 0.31 in one year.

Formula 3 can be made more informative and more relevant by separating real and inflation effects in interest rates and growth rates. Thus, the interest rate, i, can be written as the real rate, r, plus the inflation rate, π, and the growth rate, n, can similarly be split between real growth, g, and inflation, π. The result is:

(4) $\dot{d}/d = x/d + [r\gamma - \pi(1-\gamma)] - g$

Note that the expression in brackets is the average real interest rate on the debt—call it r_D: It is the sum of the real rate on nonmonetary debt, r, weighted by its share γ, and the real rate on monetary debt $-\pi$ weighted by its share $1 - \gamma$. If, as CBO forecasts, inflation of the GNP "deflator" is running at 6.1 percent in fiscal year 1984, the real rate on the debt would be only 0.8 percent, while real GNP growth would be higher—3.7 percent.

The significance of the comparison of r_D with g can be seen as follows: Suppose the various parameters in Equation 4 remained constant, for example, at the fiscal year 1984 values assumed in the numerical illustration. Would the debt/GNP ratio ever stop changing—rising in the illustration—and, if so, at what value? By setting d/d equal to zero in Equation 4, we can calculate that hypothetical stationary value of d—call it d^*.

(5) $d^* = x/(g - r_D)$

In the example, d^* is $0.017/0.029 = 0.61$. That is, if and when the debt/GNP ratio reached 61 percent, it would stop rising. Using Equation 5, Equation 4 can be rewritten as:

(6) $\dot{d} = (g - r_D)(d^* - d)$

from which it is clear that d moves in the direction of d^* provided $(g - r_D)$ is positive, and moves away from d^* when it is negative. The former case is stable; the latter unstable. The illustrative case is stable. The indicated rise of d from 0.31 at the end of fiscal year 1984 to 0.61 would be quite slow. After ten years, d would reach 0.385.

Figure 8-1 summarizes the conceptual framework just presented. The horizontal axis measures r_D, the real interest rate on the debt. As noted, the economy's real growth rate, g, is a crucial watershed for r_D. The vertical axis measures d, the debt/GNP ratio. Its steady-state value, d^*, as shown in Equation 5, falls along the hyperbola in the northwest quadrant or on the hyperbola in the southeast quadrant. As the arrows indicate, points on the northwest hyperbola are stable and points on the southeast hyperbola are unstable. (Hyperbolas in the other two quadrants are not shown. They correspond to primary surpluses, negative values of x.)

What if r_D and g were exactly equal? The outcome would then have to fall on the vertical axis through g. Equation 4 says that in this event $\dot{d}$ is equal to x. In the example, d would rise by 1.7 percentage points a year indefinitely, reaching 0.48 in ten years. To stop the rise, x would have to be reduced to zero. Given that condition, balance in the primary budget, any point on the vertical line above g is a stable d^*.

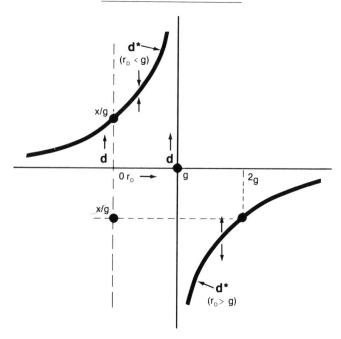

FIGURE 8-1. Steady-state Debt Ratio and Interest Rate

Which of the many possible d^*'s is the economy's long-run equilibrium? How is the steady-state value of r_D determined? This very complicated matter, cannot be treated here. The outcome depends on the economy's long-run demand for wealth and on how wealth owners wish to divide their wealth among capital, non-monetary public debt, and monetary debt. An increase in the primary deficit, x, shifts the northwest hyperbola up (and the other one down), but without specifying saving and portfolio behavior, we cannot determine whether this raises or lowers the steady-state r_D and its constituents r and π.

Calculations like those in the example above are sensitive to the assumed parameters. A real growth rate of 3.7 percent is modest for recovery from deep recession, but too high to be sustained indefinitely; 2.5 percent is a better guess for g. Although 14 percent of past deficits was monetized on average, Fed policy now implies monetization of only about 5 percent of current deficits. The inflation rate will be lower than the CBO projection, if not in 1984 then subsequently. It is not hard to construct frightening scenarios,

144

with r_D equal to or greater than g. In the next section, however, I shall argue for a more optimistic view.

Table 8-1 gives calculations, based on the framework described in this section, for five periods of the three decades 1952 to 1981. At least through 1979, fiscal policy looks pretty benign. The primary deficit was, on average, negative in the first two periods, through 1966, and the combination of fast real growth and negative r_D brought rapid reduction of the high debt/GNP ratio inherited from World War II. Even after the primary deficit turned positive, the real interest rate was very favorable. Consequently, the debt/GNP ratio remains well below its levels of the 1950s and 1960s. It is true that inflation contributed to that result in the 1970s, while policies to contain inflation worked in reverse, increasing unemployment and raising the average primary deficit.

A Recipe for Fiscal Stability and Noninflationary Prosperity

Can the U.S. economy later in this decade find a path of noninflationary growth with a stable ratio of federal debt to GNP not far from its present value? I believe it is feasible, given suitable fiscal and monetary policies. The recipe includes: reduction of the primary deficit, mainly by recovery of the economy to normal rates of utilization of labor force and plant capacity; reduction of real interest rates on federal debt to their normal historical range, around 1 percent after tax; and sufficient expansion of the monetary base, relative to GNP, to accomplish the first two goals and to satisfy the increased demand for money owing to decline in inflation and in nominal interest rates.

Frightening deficit projections, I cannot emphasize too strongly, arise from gloomy forecasts of the economy and of interest rates. Although CBO's 1982 September Update estimated a deficit of 4.2 percent of GNP in fiscal year 1984, as already noted, the projected primary deficit was only 1.7 percent of GNP, and this at an assumed 8.2 percent unemployment rate. Each point of unemployment increases with the deficit in that year by about 0.8 percent of GNP. With unemployment two points lower, there would scarcely be any primary deficit at all. Even if, as I am not ready to accept, the NAIRU is now taken to be 7 percent, at this rate the primary deficit would be only 0.75 percent of GNP. That amounts to 4 percent of federal tax revenues under existing laws. And it would be further

TABLE 8-1. U.S. Fiscal and Monetary Policy and Federal Debt Dynamics, 1952–1987

Period, fiscal years: (number of years)	1952–1957 (6)	1958–1966 (9)	1967–1974 (8)	1975–1979 (5)	1980–1981 (2)
1. Federal debt: percent of GNP, beginning and end of period	64.8–48.5	48.5–35.7	35.7–23.4	23.4–26.5	26.5–27.6
2. Federal deficit (+) or surplus (−), excluding interest: percent of GNP, average	−0.58	−0.47	+0.28	+1.38	+0.80
3. Share of debt monetized: percent range	10.5–11.3	10.7–16.6	16.6–24.0	24.0–18.1	18.1–15.7
4. Share of deficit (including interest) monetized: percent average	0	50	46	12	6
5. Growth of real GNP: percent per year average	2.8	3.4	3.8	3.5	0.9
6. Inflation of GNP deflator: percent per year average	2.2	1.9	5.2	7.2	9.1
7. Treasury 90-day bill rate: percent per year average	2.1	3.2	5.8	6.7	12.8
8. Real net interest rate on debt: percent per year, average	−0.7	−0.7	−2.8	−2.8	−0.1
9. Real GNP growth less real net interest rate	3.5	4.1	6.6	6.3	1.0

10. Hypothetical equilibrium debt/GNP ratio: percent	−16.6	−11.5	+4.2	+21.9	+80.0
Indicated trend of debt/GNP ratio:					
11. Actual, beginning of period	64.8	48.5	35.7	23.4	26.5
12. After five years	51.9	37.6	27.1	23.0	29.1
13. After ten years	41.1	28.6	20.8	22.7	31.6

Notes by lines:

1. Debt held by Federal Reserve and by nonfederal owners, par value, at end of fiscal year, relative to nominal GNP for fiscal year, from fiscal year preceding the period to final year of period.

2. Sum of National Income Accounts deficits less surpluses for period, relative to sum of nominal GNP for period. Debt interest outlays (calculated by subtracting Federal Reserve payments to Treasury from "Net Interest" line of budget) are excluded in calculating deficit or surplus, as are estimated tax receipts recouped from such outlays, estimated at 25 percent.

3. Monetized debt is the amount held by the Federal Reserve. The denominator of the ratio is, as in line 1, the monetized debt plus the debt held outside the Federal Government.

4. The increment of monetized debt from beginning to end of period, divided by the increment of total debt as defined in line 1.

8. [line 7 × 0.75 × (100 − line 4)/100] − line 6. The average Treasury bill rate for each period is taken to be the permanent cost of financing new debt and refinancing old debt, which is reckoned at par value, given the conditions and policies of the period. It is multiplied by 0.75 on the assumption that the Treasury recoups 25 percent of nominal interest outlays in taxes. The third factor reduces the net interest cost for "seignorage," the fraction of the debt monetized by the Federal Reserve. Subtracting line 6 converts the net nominal interest rate on the debt to a real rate.

9. Line 5 − line 8.

10. Line 2/line 9. A negative figure means that the hypothetical equilibrium debt/GNP ratio is negative (i.e., the government would be a net lender to the private sector).

12. 13[line 11 − line 10] × [(100 + line 9)/100]$^{-n}$ + line 10. See text.

reduced by real growth, even at sustainable rates rather than cyclical recovery rates, because growth still raises revenues faster than outlays. Modest "revenue enhancements" and slowdown of the defense buildup would do the job faster.

Given decent recovery, the major long-run fiscal problem is to keep the real interest rate on the debt below the trend growth of the economy, as it has been throughout the period since World War II. This objective coincides with the necessity to restore low real interest rates to encourage nonfederal capital formation to absorb savings the government will not be borrowing. This is at least as much a responsibility of Federal Reserve monetary policy as of fiscal policy. I stress that it is the real interest rate that matters. Reduction of nominal interest rates pari passu with disinflation does not improve either fiscal dynamics or investment incentives.

To be concrete, suppose that the after-tax real rate on non-monetary debt needs to be 1 percent, a figure not exceeded through most postwar history before 1979. Suppose that a 2 percent price trend, as in 1952 to 1966, is low enough to proclaim victory in the antiinflation crusade. It is my suspicion that any lower rate would make it difficult to obtain the adjustments in relative wages and prices needed in a dynamic economy, especially one vulnerable to external price shocks. Nominal after-tax interest rates will then have to come down to about 3 percent, a reduction of the order of 60 percent. Assuming an interest elasticity of money demand of 0.2, this will entail a one-time increase of 12 percent in the monetary base. That would raise it from 5.6 percent of GNP to 6.3 percent, still below the 8 percent ratio of the 1960s. It would require a 15 percent increase in Fed holdings of federal debt, raising them from 4.6 to 5.2 percent of GNP. (I assume that other components of the base, mainly gold and SDRs, do not change.)

I take the fiscal objective to be to stabilize the debt/GNP ratio at 30 percent. After the required monetary injection, Federal Reserve monetization of debt and future deficits would be 17 percent, a fraction much closer than current policy to earlier historical practice. The bottom line of this calculation is that the nominal interest cost of the debt will be 0.83×1 percent, while nominal GNP will be growing at 4.5 percent (2.5 percent real plus 2 percent inflation), 2 points higher than the interest cost. Recall formula 5, which says $(g - r_D)d^* = x$. Our $(g - r_D)$ is 0.02 and our desired d^* is 0.30. Consequently, x must be 0.006. The primary deficit must be held to

0.6 percent of GNP. As argued above, a primary deficit lower than 1 percent of GNP is within reach, even with conservative objectives for unemployment and without significant contractionary fiscal policy.

That is why I believe our long-run problems are manageable. But they will certainly not be solved unless the short-run crisis of stagnation is overcome. That is the immediate and urgent task. Fortunately, the monetary and fiscal measures needed for substantial and speedy recovery are the same ones that will remedy the long-run fiscal outlook. The challenge today is to take those measures rather than the counterproductive alternatives that are all too popular.

NOTES

1. Congressional Budget Office, *The Economic and Budget Outlook: An Update.* September 1982 (referred to hereafter as CBO 1982 September Update), Table B-1, p. 89.

2. CBO's 1982 September Update considered (pp. 92 to 94) a 3 percent higher price level, other things equal, in fiscal year 1985. CBO's projection of the budget deficit for that year was $152 billion. I estimate the corresponding primary deficit to be about $60 billion. Thus neutrality with respect to price means that a 3 percent higher price level would raise the deficit by $1.8 billion. Table B-4 says that automatically or indirectly indexed outlays would be higher by $7.1 billion and other outlays, still excluding debt service, would have to be higher by $10 billion to achieve the same substantive programs. Revenues, on the other hand, would be higher by $22.9 billion. Therefore, the primary deficit would be lower by $5.8 billion, a departure from neutrality by $7.6 billion. This is 6 percent of the associated 3 percent increment to nominal GNP. For comparison, a 3 percent gain in real GNP, with prices constant, would (according to the same Appendix B) diminish the primary deficit by about $40 billion, one-third of the same increment to dollar GNP. In both cases, deficit reductions in one year generate interest savings in subsequent years; I have not taken these into account, though they are estimated by CBO.

CHAPTER NINE

INFLATION, UNEMPLOYMENT, AND THE BUDGET

Robert Eisner

SOME MYTHS, PROPOSITIONS, AND PERSPECTIVE

• Federal budget deficits are not the general cause of inflation. In the last year, the rate of inflation has declined sharply while the federal deficit has soared.

• Government spending is no more a general cause of inflation than is private spending. Sharp increases in spending of any kind can, under certain circumstances, be inflationary. Some government spending can be deflationary.

• Higher tax rates to balance the budget may or may not prove deflationary. Increases in tax rates during a recession are likely to aggravate the recession and increase unemployment. Increases in some kinds of taxes can create more unemployment *and* increase inflation.

• There is no simple one-to-one relationship between inflation and unemployment. Budgetary actions that increase inflation may not reduce unemployment. Inflation itself, however, does not cause unemployment. Certain government policies to combat inflation do cause unemployment.

The propositions stated so baldly here may best be understood and evaluated in terms of those oldest of economic concepts—demand and supply. Budgetary policies that increase the total or aggregate demand for goods and services will increase output (and employment) and/or prices. Government policies that decrease the aggregate demand of goods and services will reduce output (and employment) and/or prices.

Government policies that increase the aggregate supply of goods and services to the market will increase output (and employment) and/or reduce prices. Government policies that reduce aggregate supply will reduce output (and employment) and/or raise prices.

IMPACT OF GOVERNMENT EXPENDITURES

There is no correct, simplistic conclusion to be drawn as to the impact of government expenditures on aggregate demand, inflation, and unemployment. It depends critically on what those expenditures are, how they are conditioned, and how they change. Increases in government expenditures for goods and services will generally have a direct impact upon output. If there is considerable slack in the economy, increased government spending for goods and services will generally bring about more output, less unemployment, and little or no upward pressure on prices. Particular kinds of government spending can be inflationary by directly bringing about price increases. An obvious case in point would be purchases of agricultural commodities or other materials for the express purpose of raising or holding up prices. Such action may have substantial ripple effects, as these higher prices are passed on through the process of production and as wage earners and others obtain cost-of-living adjustments in turn.

Certain kinds of government expenditures may prove inflationary because they are directed at resources in short supply. This is likely to be particularly true where the government undertakes rapid increases in expenditures for particular categories of goods, as in a rapid acceleration of military spending.

Some government expenditures for goods and services may prove deflationary. Improvement of the federal highway system may be expected to lower transportation costs, thus effecting real savings as well as lower prices. Expenditures for food stamps will clearly lower the cost of food to those who use them. Reduction in the food-stamp program will hence be directly inflationary to those affected. Similarly, government subsidies for the postal service, mass transit, and low-rent housing will hold down prices. Reductions in such government expenditures will add to inflation both directly and as the immediately higher prices feed back through the economy.

Purchases of goods and services constitute only one-third of Federal Government expenditures. Fully 42.5 percent is made up of transfer payments. These generally contribute to aggregate demand and, hence, to output and employment. How much they do so, however, depends upon the spending propensities of recipients. Increases or decreases in transfer payments are likely to have a less certain and probably more delayed effect than similar changes in expenditures for goods and services. Changes in transfer payments financed by equivalent changes in taxes will generally affect aggregate demand and production only to the extent that the marginal propensities to spend of taxpayers are different from those of the people receiving the transfers. There is therefore no prima facie reason to believe that the great recent increases in transfer payments, in social security and federal retirement benefits, in particular, have been inflationary. Similarly, there is no reason to believe that general cuts in such social benefits, along with corresponding reductions in taxes, will be antiinflationary.

Grants in aid to state and local governments constitute over 11 percent of federal expenditures and are also not readily classifiable as inflationary. Reduction in grants in aid may frequently prove both inflationary and productive of increased unemployment. They force state and local governments into some combination of layoff of employees and reduction of public services, on the one hand, and increased sales or property taxes—which directly or indirectly raise prices of final products—on the other.

Net interest paid, also currently over 11 percent of federal expenditures, is essentially akin to transfer payments in its effect upon aggregate demand and purchasing power. To the extent, however, that high interest payments reflect high interest rates, they may also, unfortunately, tend to be productive of both more inflation and less employment. High interest rates will discourage business and residential investment as well as purchase of consumer durables, thus reducing output and employment, while they will constitute a higher cost of production, thus bringing on higher prices. The latter direct, upward effect on prices may substantially counterbalance—or even outweigh—the indirect, downward effect of lesser output and greater unemployment.

Finally, the relatively small item of subsidies less current surplus of government enterprises, about 1.6 percent of Federal Government expenditures, tends to be both deflationary and productive of employment. The greater the government subsidies and the less the current surplus of government enterprises, the less will be the prices of the products affected. And the less these prices are, the greater will be demand, output, and employment.

None of these considerations should be allowed to obscure the fundamental difference between effects of federal expenditures and changes in federal expenditures under conditions of full or high employment and of substantial unemployment. All too much public and political discussion ignores this difference. Under conditions of relatively full employment, increases in aggregate demand brought on by direct government purchases of goods and services, or by transfer payments or interest payments to individuals or business, will contribute to inflation. For as such increases in expenditures swell aggregate demand, there will be little or no increase in supply available to meet that demand. Prices will rise and may set off an inflationary spiral that will be continued and reinforced if government continues to increase expenditures at a faster rate than can be accommodated by increases in supply.

These inflationary pressures may be only partly abated by higher taxes to finance the expenditures. Higher taxes to finance transfer payments or interest payments may well bring fully offsetting reductions of their effects in inflating demand. But since the depressing effect on demand of taxes is only indirect or secondary, they may well prove an uncertain and inadequate counterbalance to rapid increases in federal expenditures for goods and services. This observation proves of particular relevance to rapid military buildups. The failure to raise taxes promptly to pay for the military escalation in Vietnam has frequently been viewed as a significant contributor to the inflation of that era. It may be aptly observed, however, that even a pari passu increase in taxes might well have proved insufficient to stem inflation at that time.

The effects of government expenditures on output, employment, and prices under conditions of general unemployment and excess capacity are vastly different. Under these circumstances, increases in aggregate demand that will be generated by increases in federal expenditures can be expected to increase output and employment and have minimal effects, if any, upon raising prices. Here again, though, changes in federal expenditures for goods and services will have a more immediate and direct impact than changes in transfers or interest payments. Rapid increases in federal expenditures for particular kinds of goods and services that may be in short supply, such as those involved in rapid military buildups, may still cause inflationary movements in those areas, but their spillover effects in the general economy are likely to be damped.

It must be observed, therefore, that moves to cut federal expenditures in a time of recession, whatever the general political popularity of such, can only be expected to aggravate the recession by reducing aggregate demand and purchasing power. To the extent that reductions in federal expenditures are in purchases of goods and services, corresponding cuts in taxes are not likely to be fully offsetting in their effects upon demand, production, and employment. In this connection, it may be noted that federal expenditures for goods and services in the 1981 to 1982 recession moved down as the economy worsened, rather than in countercyclical fashion. Decreases in nondefense federal expenditures considerably exceeded increases in expenditures for national defense. Thus, from the fourth quarter of 1981 to the second quarter of 1982, total federal expenditures for goods and services declined 2.5 percent in current dollars, from $250.5 billion to $244.3 billion. The relative decline in constant dollars was 4.9 percent.

Cuts in federal expenditures to reduce demand would be indicated in order to counteract an inflation induced by excess aggregate demand. Excess aggregate demand is to be associated with high employment and an overall spending propensity that is greater than the value of output that can be produced at current prices. Since such a situation is usually, if not always, brought on by great increases in government spending to begin with, reductions in government spending are all the more the indicated remedy.

An inflation brought on by supply shocks, such as the recent bouts with tremendous oil price increases, as well as those of agricultural and other raw materials in world markets, is quite another matter. This kind of inflation may well be associated with a generally depressed state of the economy. The twin conditions of stagnation and inflation have, indeed, brought forth the descriptive term "stagflation." In the face of major price increases in some areas, the inadvertent or purposeful failure of government to provide accommodative fiscal or monetary policies results in a sharp reduction in real effective demand. Under conditions of perfect competition in all markets, one might look for downward adjustments in prices not directly affected by the supply shock, so that real demand would be maintained. It is clear that this does not occur in the real world, and cannot reasonably be expected to occur—thus, the combination of inflation and recession that hit so hard and, to some, paradoxically in 1974 to 1975.

The answer to such an inflation is not a contraction of federal budget expenditures. This is likely to have little immediate effect on either the offending prices in the initial supply shock or the general level of other prices. Its immediate effect may be expected in output and employment, both of which will be all the more reduced by a contractionary federal budget policy.

Indeed, unless the supply shocks are repeated, the initial inflationary spiral will subside. Contractionary federal budget policies (or contractionary monetary policies) will have a further effect in reducing inflation to the extent that they create a sufficiently sharp and lasting recession. The substantial reduction in inflation in the United States economy in 1982 must be attributed in part to the leveling off and decline in petroleum and agricultural prices—the ebbing of the supply shock—and in part to cuts in federal expenditures and repressive monetary policies. Many will consider the cost in lost output and employment, which has been imposed in order to achieve the marginal further reduction in inflation, excessive.

EFFECT OF TAXES

Many of the implications of changing tax rates may be inferred from our discussion of federal expenditures. Increases in income taxes, like cuts in transfer payments, will reduce disposable income and thus indirectly reduce aggregate demand. They are an appropriate remedy for an inflation owing to excess demand. As a remedy to a supply-shock or cost-push inflation, they are likely to do more to bring on recession and lost output and employment than to lower prices, unless they are pursued to extremes in magnitude and duration.

But, as with government expenditures, we must distinguish among taxes. Despite much-publicized claims of so-called "supply-side" economists to the contrary, changes in personal income-tax rates, at least in the magnitudes that have been involved, are likely to have much greater effects upon demand than upon supply. I often ask business executives whether reductions in personal income tax rates by 25 percent (say, from 50 to 37.5 percent) are likely to make them work harder, and have yet to find any with the temerity to answer in the affirmative; perhaps none wishes to assert that he or she is not already working as hard as possible. (For low-income groups, the Economic Recovery Tax Act of 1981 and changes in various programs of transfer payments do not alleviate, and in a number of areas aggravate, the serious problem of marginal effective tax rates, or loss-of-benefit rates, approaching—and in some cases in excess of—100 percent. It is in this area that the high marginal bite on current income may well be having seriously deleterious effects upon labor supply.)

But there are taxes that more greatly, if not entirely, affect supply. Payroll taxes on employment, now approaching almost 14 percent for social security (and several percent more on lower incomes for unemployment insurance), cannot but adversely affect the supply of labor. Excise and sales taxes directly reduce the supply of taxed commodities, thus contributing both to higher prices and lower output. Increases in telephone and air-travel taxes, enacted in 1982 to reduce budget deficits considered by some to be inflationary, will thus in some measure contribute to higher prices while aggravating unemployment.

Reductions in effective tax rates on capital income and saving may, other things being equal, increase saving and capital formation. Other things are generally not equal, however. In particular, the higher real interest rates that accompany the business tax reductions of 1981 have probably themselves more than offset the presumed tax stimuli to investment. And income effects may so outweigh substitution effects that lower taxes on saving may leave people with less need to provide for the future and, therefore, may reduce aggregate saving.

While cuts in income taxes will themselves increase private saving, unless they result in sufficient increases in output and income, they must reduce the total of private and public saving. With output and income unchanged, for example, each dollar reduction in taxes will reduce public saving (or increase public dissaving, the budget deficit) by a full dollar. Even if beneficiaries of the tax cut save, say, 40 cents of each of their extra dollars of disposable income, there will be a *reduction* in total saving, and hence in gross investment, of 60 cents for each dollar reduction in taxes. Ironically, beneficial effects of personal income-tax cuts on aggregate gross saving would stem not from the propensities of those with lower taxes to save but from their propensities to spend. For increases in private spending would induce greater output and income, out of which there could be more private saving as well as increases in tax revenues to offset reductions in public saving and also induce increases in investment demand for inventories and fixed capital to be used for increased production.

The effects of increases in investment demand, however, are mixed. Like any other increases in demand for goods and services, public or private, under conditions of substantial unemployment and excess capacity, they are likely to increase output and employment but to generate little or no inflation. As full capacity is reached, increases in investment demand, like other increases in demand, will tend to cause increases in prices that may initiate or accelerate inflation. It is frequently argued that more capital accumulation will increase productivity and therefore reduce costs and prices. This is at best, though, a long-run effect, and it depends both on the capital investment actually being productive—and not merely the consequence of tax advantages—and also on any gains from productivity being realized in the form of lower prices rather than higher wages and profits.

It is possible for increases in taxes to stimulate spending. Thus, the repeal of provisions of the Accelerated Cost Recovery System, which would have become effective in 1985 and 1986, could induce firms to make capital expenditures sooner because there are no longer additional tax advantages to be gained by waiting. One might add that if the Congress were to legislate now the elimination of the investment tax credit to be effective a year from now, firms would have a substantial inducement to incur capital expenditures before the credit is lost. Were this to be accompanied by cuts in business income-tax rates effective a year from now, firms would have a further incentive to make deductible expenditures sooner at the still-prevailing higher tax rates.

INFLATION AND BUDGET DEFICITS

Inflation plays all kind of tricks, and not the least on federal budgets. As was suggested earlier, budget deficits are not generally a cause of inflation. They are clearly magnified by recessions. But inflation does affect budget surpluses and deficits. Some of the effects have not been widely perceived or understood.

It is generally known that inflation tends to magnify federal revenues. Without indexing of the personal income-tax structure, the successively higher money incomes in the course of an inflation generate greater than proportionate increases in tax revenues. On the corporate side, and with regard to business income generally, inflation tends to raise Treasury revenues as taxes are levied on profits related to the higher prices of inventories and the excess of replacement cost over original cost depreciation. To the extent that capital gains are realized and subjected to tax, inflation also raises tax revenues from this source.

On the expenditure side, inflation raises outlays for a number of indexed programs, particularly social security payments, as well as general purchases of goods and services. And of considerable current significance, inflation and its concomitant of expected future inflation increase interest costs on the federal debt by raising interest rates. On balance, until now, inflation has tended to raise revenues more than expenditures, and thus has generally reduced federal deficits and pushed budgets toward surplus. The indexing of personal income-tax brackets, scheduled to begin in 1985, and the Accelerated Cost Recovery System with regard to business taxes will both contribute to reducing, if not eliminating, the excess of revenues over expenditures generated by inflation.

By focusing on an effect of inflation on the federal budget that fundamentally changes the meaning of usually measured budget deficits, it is possible to point up some of the peculiarities of federal budgeting that lead to widespread misinterpretation of the impact of budget deficits on the economy. Federal budget deficits essentially add to private holding of government debt. While the current flow of expenditures in excess of revenues is considered a short-run stimulus to aggregate demand, the theory of rational behavior would suggest that consumption and other spending may be substantially influenced by longer-run considerations of income and wealth. In this sense, federal expenditures financed by borrowing generate private claims to wealth in the form of government bonds, whereas balanced-budget expenditures leave taxpayers with only tax receipts. The increased wealth in government debt induces more consumption, which will be realized in actual production of consumer goods if there is slack in the economy, but will engender only higher prices and inflation if there is full employment.

Some have argued that the increase in public debt will not add to consumer demand, because households will view the eventual need to levy taxes to pay the interest and principal on the debt as offsetting the value of bond holdings. This argument, which would appear to demand particular assumptions about public and private discount rates, certainty, and bequest behavior, among others, would at best have limited applicability.

But if there is any impact of private holdings of government debt on consumption and aggregate demand, it must surely be the real, rather than the nominal, value of debt with which we should be concerned. And that is where the peculiar role of inflation comes in.

The basic fact, well-known but not thoroughly assimilated in the present context, is that inflation aids debtors and injures creditors by reducing the real value of obligations fixed in nominal terms. As this becomes apparent with sustained inflation, lenders demand and borrowers must pay higher nominal rates of interest to induce the holding of debt obligations. Thus, the Federal Government, with over a trillion dollars of debt (of which not much more than half, however, constitutes net obligations to the public), on the one hand, makes very large nominal interest payments, but, on the other, enjoys almost correspondingly large capital gains, year after year, as the real value of outstanding debt declines. In conventional accounting, however, we include the nominal interest payments as a government expenditure contributing to the deficit, but do not include the capital gain on existing debt, to which the interest payments are clearly coupled, as a revenue that would reduce the deficit. Hence, we measure nominal rather than real interest costs of the debt.

The Federal Government may thus run a substantial budget deficit, as conventionally measured, without increasing the public's real holdings of federal debt. But if holdings of federal debt in real terms do not increase, the public does not have any long-run reason to increase its spending as a consequence of the nominal deficit.

While inflation lowers the real value of existing debt, changes in rates of interest, whether induced by changes in expected rates of inflation or other factors, change the market value of existing debt. Thus, in periods of rising inflation and rising nominal interest rates, the real value of existing debt is reduced both by the increased interest rates, which lower market values of outstanding securities, and by the higher prices, which lower the real values of the lower nominal market values.

These effects are far from trivial. After subtracting financial assets and adapting or constructing appropriate indexes for converting values of securities from par to market, a series for the federal budget surplus and deficit, adjusted to correspond to changes in the real value of the net debt, has been developed by Paul J. Pieper[1] and the present author. For 1980, for example, when the National Income Accounts showed a federal budget *deficit* of $61.2 billion, our adjusted budget showed a *surplus* of $7.8 billion! The entire time series reveals that while, as commonly observed, the federal budget has been in deficit as conventionally measured in most years, the real value of the net debt has been declining. Per-capita adjustments indicate the reduction of debt even more sharply. At the end of 1946, the net debt per capita was $3,338 in 1972 dollars. By the end of 1980, it was less than a third of that—$1,078 in 1972 dollars.

The usual notion of a budget deficit, for good or ill, entails increasing debt. Indeed, in nominal terms, one can write the par value of existing debt at any point of time as the integral of all previous deficits minus surpluses. But unless we are to be guilty of money illusion, which economists and the rational public should be expected generally to eschew, it must be recognized that it is changes in the real market value of debt that must matter. If federal budget deficits are to have most of the economic significance attached to them, they should be measured so that their sum or integral over time equals the total debt.

It is significant to note that corresponding adjustments to measure an economically relevant federal budget surplus or deficit are in order for the high-employment budget. Such adjustments put interesting new light on the likely thrust of recent fiscal policy. Various mixtures of surprise and alarm have been expressed at the failure of alleged fiscal stimulus to prevent recessions or stagflation despite reductions in the high-employment budget surplus that have extended so far in some periods as to produce high-employment budget deficits. This has perhaps led to the inference that fiscal policy is relatively impotent, with a tight money policy clearly dominating an easy fiscal policy.

In the 1950s and early 1960s, inflation and rates of interest were generally low, so that the reported high-employment budget surplus required relatively little adjustment to correspond to changes in the real value of the debt. The increases in inflation and interest rates in recent years through 1981, however, have been another matter. The high-employment budget surplus, adjusted to reflect the resultant changes in the real value of debt, has been substantially—and, in much of the period, increasingly—in surplus. For 1981, our adjustment changes the official high-employment budget from a deficit of $2.6 billion to a surplus of $65.6 billion. Even the 1981 fourth-quarter official deficit of $38.2 billion would, with adjustment become a significant surplus. If the high-employment budget offers a first approximation of the thrust of fiscal policy, the appropriate adjusted measure of it suggests that we have not, in fact, had an expansionary fiscal policy, despite the recent tax cuts that have been so widely hailed in some quarters and deplored in others. Our adjusted measure of the high-employment budget surplus suggests that the current recession may be the consequence of an overly tight monetary policy, apparently supported by many as a necessary corrective to the *illusion* of an overstimulative fiscal policy.

There are many important improvements to be made in accounting for federal expenditures and revenues and construction of a federal budget. These should certainly include full capital budgeting and accounting for acquisition of assets, real and financial, as well as the incurring of liabilities. Appropriate measures of *net* federal debt and net worth will differ widely from the figures of budget deficits and public debt so much in the public eye. They are likely for many purposes, though, to give a much better indication of the financial situation of the Federal Government and its impact on the economy. But if the nation is to continue to be influenced by perceptions of the bottom lines in federal budgets as currently calculated, we might at least note the tricks that inflation is playing. Continuing to view as expansionary federal budgets that are not will provide a poor guide for public policy. We shall misunderstand both the causes and the potential cures of phenomena such as sharp and deep recession and high unemployment. We shall also misjudge developing trends and needs for the future. A particular case in point would be the reaction to high-employment budget deficits a few years from now if they are brought about with more modest inflation and lower, relatively stable interest rates. For in that situation, a high-employment budget deficit might truly be expansionary, and perhaps overexpansionary, from the standpoint of maintaining stable prices.

CONCLUSION

In suggesting that economically relevant measures of the federal budget may well be much less in deficit or more in surplus than has been generally perceived, we may be thought to be encouraging those who would feel free to increase government spending or reduce taxes. Increasing government spending for a number of social purposes, or at least curbing the sharp decreases that have been undertaken and are in prospect, would have important implications for the distribution of income and welfare. Increasing military spending or reducing the pressure to curb it may have quite different implications for both the distribution of income and the collective welfare. (These arguments are not meant to be used to reduce efforts to avoid further acceleration of the arms race.)

My reading of the struggle on the federal budget is that, all rhetoric aside, it really relates much more to the distribution of our nation's economic pie than to its size. The current Administration has brought about great contractions in some areas of the federal budget, while calling for very large expansions in others. While my priorities on the allocation of resources are sharply different, the main concern in this essay has been to call attention to the impact of the federal budget on the size of the economic pie, rather than on how it is cut up. Here it would appear that the grievous economic losses of the current recession may be traced in part to the active support by some—and undue tolerance by others—of an excessively tight monetary policy in the mistaken view that it was necessary to correct a federal budget incorrectly perceived as overly stimulative. It is important for current and future economic analysis and policy to avoid such misperceptions.

NOTE

1. Assistant Professor of Economics, University of Illinois, Chicago Circle Campus.

PART FOUR

IMPROVING
THE BUDGETARY
PROCESS

CHAPTER TEN

IMPROVING THE FRAMEWORK FOR DECISION MAKING

Elmer B. Staats

There have been few times in the history of the nation when budget and fiscal affairs have commanded the attention they now receive. There is recognition that the federal budget process has become the single most important tool of the Reagan Administration's efforts to put into effect vast changes in program priorities, new economic policies, and, indeed, a new philosophy of the role of government.

This has not been done without great strain on the budget process itself, both within the Congress and in the relationship between the President and the Congress. There have been ominous rumblings of discontent in the Congress that have led to many proposals to modify the process. Some would like to go back to the seemingly "good old days" when the authorizing and appropriation subcommittees went their separate ways, only to learn at the end of the year that the total was out of line with revenue and expenditure expectations; no one could really be held responsible. After roughly 40 years of concern with the federal budget process, this author finds the idea of reverting to old procedures both unrealistic and dangerous.

The Congress began operating under the 1974 Congressional Budget and Impoundment Control Act in 1975. The underlying unified budget concept and other budget principles were set forth by the President's Commission on Budget Concepts in1967. Much of today's conceptual and institutional budgeting framework, laid out in 1967 and 1974, is serving the country well. Few question—in principle, at least—the value of a unified budget in assessing its impact on the economy. Even fewer would disagree as to the need for an orderly congressional budget decision-making process that reviews total revenues and outlays in one package.

However, several developments in the wake of these changes have placed strains on the capacity of existing budget concepts and procedures to serve the budget information and control needs of the Congress, the Executive Branch, and the public. The current strains and problems present a two-pronged challenge. We must not only study them and device a variety of individual solutions to the problems, but we must also be careful to adopt measures that, taken together, do not further complicate the budget process.

It is useful to apply the following principles or concepts with respect to the data utilized in budgetary analysis, in the presentation of the budget to the Congress and the general public, and in the manner in which the Congress reviews and acts upon the budget. These principles (discussed in greater detail below) are:

- *Comprehensiveness*—the inclusion in the budget of all programs that involve budgetary receipts and outlays or other recommendations that significantly affect the economy, such as user charges, credit programs, and regulatory programs. The budget should be all-inclusive and should further the unified concept.

- *Future oriented*—It should adequately cover the multiyear implications of existing and proposed programs, and provide adequate information with respect to long-range commitments, contingencies, and the impact of alternative economic scenarios and demographic changes.

- *Credibility*—with respect to the reasonableness of economic assumptions, the realism of expected savings, and the cost implications of proposed legislation. The principle of credibility, or full disclosure, and reasonableness of expectations comprise "a first principle" in budgetary analysis.

- *Clarity*—of presentation from the standpoint of public understanding; the inclusion of cross-cutting analyses, the preparation of consolidated financial reports, and special analyses that allow the budget to be analyzed and understood as a program document.

• *Completeness*—in the sense that the analysis covers the budgetary base as well as the add-ons or increments to the budget base, including the use of tools of program planning and budgeting and zero-base budgeting.

• *Comparability*—of data for purposes of cross-cutting analyses, and program definitions that make these analyses comparable and meaningful in presentation and in understanding government-wide policies and issues.

• *Timeliness*—in providing the Congress with essential information to support the President's budget; timeliness of the Congress in acting on the budget in advance of the beginning of the new fiscal year; the timeliness in the sense of providing multiyear authority.

COMPREHENSIVENESS

Since the adoption of the unified budget in 1968, we have seen the reemergence of budget coverage as an issue—a perennial issue addressed in one form or another by major budget-reform studies. The 1967 Commission viewed the adoption of a unified budget, in which all federally owned activities would be included, as its most important recommendation. Since 1967, however, legislation has been enacted to remove certain federal programs from the budget totals or establish new organizations as off-budget entities. The off-budget activities now include such popular programs as the Rural Electrification Administration and the Federal Financing Bank (FFB), among others.

The dollar totals of these off-budget organizations are significant. The off-budget treatment of these activities reduced budget outlay totals for fiscal year 1982 by about $20 billion. This certainly lessens the meaningfulness of budget totals, including the reported budget deficit, and is contrary to sound budget policy. This off-budget matter is frequently discussed in the press in a way that adds skepticism as to the credibility of estimated budget totals.

Of particular concern is the FFB's role in converting on-budget federal loan guarantees into off-budget direct federal loans. Such

FFB direct loans totaled about $11.5 billion in 1982. This raises a most serious budget-control question, and reinforces the need to reestablish unified budget concepts and controls.

We may expect additional strains on the unified-budget approach from the increasing number of proposals for special "budgets"—namely, proposals for capital, regulatory, paperwork, and tax-expenditure budgets. The deteriorating or outmoded nature of much of the nation's physical infrastructure heightens the need for adequate budget action on capital needs or, as a minimum, the identification of governmental outlays that have a direct impact on private investment. The costs to society of the growing number of federal regulations and reporting requirements have brought about proposals for regulatory and paperwork budgets, in order to disclose their estimated costs and suggest actions to limit them. Similarly, "tax expenditures"—special tax preferences granted through legislative actions—are seen by many as appropriate for budget recognition and analysis, particularly when used as supplements to direct appropriations. Trust funds, especially the social security and the medicare trust funds, are also seen by some as deserving separate treatment.

The consequences of these and other proposed special budgets on the unity of the budget need to be studied. It is important to avoid actions that could fragment (or unnecessarily complicate) the budget and lessen overall understanding of it. This could easily happen if special budgets are used for control purposes, and not simply for the reporting of information and analysis as part of the budget process. Instead, options within the existing unified budget should be considered. For example, why should tax expenditures not be reviewed concurrently with direct outlays when both are designed to achieve a common objective, such as water pollution control?

The federal budget has grown to the point where there are now about 1,300 appropriation accounts and 2,000 "programs." But, more importantly, this growth has been accompanied by an increase in the range and complexity of federal programs as new socio-economic problems have evoked new kinds of federal responses. The dramatic increase in federal loans and loan guarantees is a notable example. Total federal direct loans outstanding have more than tripled since the time of the President's Budget Commission, going from about $47 billion in fiscal year 1967 to about $206 billion estimated for fiscal year 1982. Guaranteed loans outstanding have more than tripled over the same period, increasing from about $100 billion to an estimated $353 billion. The $1.5 billion Chrysler loan-guarantee program is a well-known case. Another example is the legislation establishing the United States Synthetic Fuels Corporation, authorizing $20 billion for Phase I loan guarantees and other activities, plus an additional $68 billion for Phase II guarantees and other forms of assistance.

The growth of federal credit activities has created budget information and control problems that need attention. Should not the budget totals, for example, include budget authority for the estimated future expenses to the government of current credit aids—such as the estimated future interest-subsidy expenses on direct loans or default expenses on guaranteed loans? If so, how should these expenses be measured and controlled? The method-ological problems are particularly acute on the Chrysler-type guarantees, where there may be relatively little basis for estimating the ultimate outlays to be borne by the Government.

The previous Administration took a step toward more sys-tematic control over federal credit activities when it included a "credit budget" package in the 1981 budget, entailing proposed appropriation-act dollar limitations on aggregate and individual direct loans and loan guarantees. The Congress, for its part, responded by including limits on total direct loans and loan guarantees in its First Concurrent Resolution on the Budget for fiscal year 1981, although it failed to prevent sales to the FFB, which tends to negate that limitation.

Comprehensive controls over credit activities have long been needed, and the credit-budget approach is a step in the right direction. However, the possible implications of budget concepts embodied in the proposed credit budget need to be studied further. The creation of a credit budget outside of the regular budget authority and outlay totals lessens comparability of credit and noncredit programs, and can add to the confusion about the meaning of budget totals. Development of the credit budget should not become a reason to delay needed reforms to bring credit activities in the unified budget as much as feasible, and to improve the treatment of such activities within the regular budget. For example, certain limitations on direct lending are now included in the credit budget but not in the regular budget. This affects net lending, but does not control the use of loan repayments into revolving funds. Thus, we need to consider such alternatives as recording limitations on direct lending as budget authority amounts and including such amounts in the regular totals of the budget. This would be a simpler and more direct way to control loan levels.

Comprehensiveness (or completeness) has another dimension—to give the same consideration to analyzing the budget "base" or the "current services budget" that we give to incremental increases and new programs. It was this concern about examining ongoing budgetary levels that gave rise to the great interest in planning, programming, and budgeting systems in the mid-1960s. Later proposals for zero-base budgeting and management by objectives had somewhat the same purpose. A similar concept had vogue in the Congress for several years in what was termed "sunset" reviews. The basic idea is to apply the test of costs and benefits to all programs systematically. When programs are reviewed thoroughly from time to time to test whether their benefits are equal to their costs, decisions can be made to discontinue, modify, or, perhaps, even expand them. A common denominator for all these approaches is the heavy emphasis on outputs, better measurement of cost inputs, and the examination of options and alternatives that might produce results at a lower cost.

A KEY TO FUTURE OUTLAYS: OBLIGATIONAL OR BUDGETARY AUTHORITY

It is most important to have meaningful, consistent, and well-understood budget-authority records, given the fact that budget authority is the key financial resource allocation controlled by the Congress and Executive Branch in their annual budget-setting actions. Unfortunately, there is confusion about budget authority because of the maze of varying applications. For example, there is no general agreement on which multiyear programs should be "fully funded" in their first years. The full-funding approach, which the Office of Management and Budget (OMB) now prescribes for several programs, can facilitate more equitable comparisons of programs and "up front" disclosure of total costs. The General Accounting Office (GAO) has taken steps to develop criteria for full funding. It is clear, however, that more work is needed to identify the programs where full funding should be applied.

Another major development that bears directly on the ability to control future outlays is the growth in the "relatively uncontrollable" portion of the budget. One of the most important changes over the last 10 to 15 years has been the increase in the part of the budget that cannot be significantly controlled by the annual appropriations process without prior changes in the authorizing legislation. OMB data indicate that the relatively uncontrollable part of budget outlays grew from about 59 percent in fiscal year 1967 to more than 77 percent in 1982. This growth largely reflects the growth of federal entitlement programs and long-term demographic trends. About 50 percent of the proposed 1982 budget was for judicially enforceable entitlement payments.

It should be added that the portion of the budget that is, from a practical point of view, relatively uncontrollable in any *one* year is even higher than 77 percent. There are numerous operations and maintenance programs for public works, defense facilities, and so on that cannot be drastically reduced without unacceptable consequences—at least in the first year. Additional (or alternative) classifications of programs to better bring out the gradations of programs between the strictly controllable and uncontrollable, in the first year and over time, should be considered.

The growth in uncontrollables (and prospects for their continued growth) points to a critical need for the Congress and the Executive Branch to take budget actions with a longer time horizon in mind. In this manner, budget priorities will increasingly reflect conscious choices made in a "strategic-planning" type of process rather than being accepted as "uncontrollable." Recent steps by the OMB and the Budget Committees to include multiyear planning amounts in the budget documents and resolutions appear to be a big step forward, although it is too early to make a definitive assessment.

This need will be magnified further if the Congress implements a schedule of oversight review and reauthorizations. The question is whether the budget processes that were largely put in place in a simpler era, when most of the budget was controllable through the appropriations process, are suitable in a more complicated and broadly participative environment.

Another problem that should be examined is whether the kinds of information considered in budgeting and reported in the relevant documents will be needed by decision makers in the 1980s and beyond. That is, more information and analyses of global and national conditions, long-term trends, and alternatives should be developed and related to the specific national needs and missions of the federal budget. An example is the kind of trend information contained in the report of the Task Force on Global Resources and the Environment.[1] Such forward-looking or "futuristic" information, along with strengthened special analyses of cross-cutting policies—for instance, research and development—would do much to enhance the analytical content of the budget.

BUDGET ANALYSIS

High on the priority list of measures to improve the analytical framework of budgetary decision making is the improvement of the process for estimating the impact of the budget changes on the economy, the savings that result from administrative or legislative actions, and the cost estimates for new program initiatives. This discussion must start with the recognition that the budget represents more than a factual analytical forecast, that is, a range of "best" estimates; it also represents the Administration's goals and objectives and the economic and other forecasts included in the budget.

Are there ways in which the President or the Congress can improve the credibility of budget forecasts and assumptions and, in doing so, improve the consistency with which elements of the budget are acted upon by the various committees of the Congress and increase the confidence in the reliability of budget estimates?

In recent years, deviations in actual economic conditions from those assumed in the President's budget have accounted for a substantial part of the change in the final budget results from the initial projections—not from actions taken by either the President or the Congress to modify the budget after it was submitted to the Congress. For example, in fiscal years 1980 and 1981, outlays were $48 billion and $45 billion above the prior January estimates, with changed economic conditions accounting for more than one-half the increase. This failure to distinguish between economic and other factors has led to confusion and uncertainty on the part of the public and congressional committees as to actions needed to bring the budget into conformity with either the President's budget or the congressional budget resolutions. Obviously, some of the changed economic conditions may have been due to factors over which the policymakers had no direct control. However, they may have been due, in part, to unrealistic initial estimates that could have been avoided.

One approach to this problem would be to achieve agreement in advance between the Administration and the Congress with respect to the economic assumptions that underlie the budget estimates. Since the President's budget reflects goals and objectives, however, this may be difficult to achieve. Therefore, other approaches must be examined. One would be to provide in the budget an analysis of the economic assumptions contained in the future budget forecasts based on the average experience of a base period, such as three or five years. Or it might be useful to base the estimates upon an average of the major current private forecasts. It would also be highly useful for the President to include in the budget—perhaps in the appendix—a "sensitivity analysis" that would simply require calculation of the impact on the estimates of a range of alternative economic assumptions. The Congressional Budget Office's update report to the House and Senate Budget Committees of September 1, 1982 contains an appendix on this subject that demonstrates the value of this type of analysis.

Whichever approach, or combination of approaches, is adopted, we need to examine estimating policies and methods in order to correct the traditional, overoptimistic bias that lessens the realism of budget authority, obligations, and outlay projections. These projections also often give the appearance that the government can accomplish things faster and at less cost than is reasonable to expect. Matters deserving further study in this regard include policy and technical impediments to making projections represent "best estimates" rather than a single optimistic "target."

It is especially important to provide fuller budget disclosure of the legislative, economic, and other assumptions underlying projections and the basis for the ranges from which the "best estimates" were selected. Such information would give the public, as well as congressional users of the budget, a greater understanding of, and confidence in, budget estimates. Many have found analysis of the impact of full employment on receipts and outlays useful. Whether used as a policy basis for formulating the budget or not, it is still a useful set of data for the Congress in acting on the President's budget proposals.

The use of offsetting business-type revenues to reduce budget totals is relevant to the credibility of the budget. This offsetting practice reduced estimated on-budget and off-budget outlays for fiscal year 1982 by about $129 billion, thus greatly understating outlay totals. Congressional control would be improved by the reporting of amounts on a gross basis.

A similar problem arises from the practice of treating sales of certificates of beneficial ownership as "asset" sales rather than borrowings. This practice (opposed by the 1967 Commission but now sanctioned by statute for some programs, the largest of which is the Farmers Home Administration) further inflates offsetting receipts and stands in the way of a full disclosure of agency borrowing.

Finally, there are inconsistencies in agency practices for recording budget authority of their borrowings. In some cases, the recordings represent authorized *net* borrowing; in other cases, the recordings are for authorized *gross* borrowing. To a certain extent, this varying practice reflects differing statutory provisions governing agency borrowings. However, action is possible to bring about more uniform treatment, as evidenced by some recent steps taken by the OMB.

IMPROVING BUDGETARY DATA—A CASE FOR CAPITAL BUDGETING

The President's budget is submitted with a breakdown among 16 functional categories, and the congressional budget resolution is then acted upon in accordance with these categories. Appropriations are made on the basis of program or agency breakdowns. Very few congressional actions are based upon an analysis of government-wide functions, programs, or activities. In many cases, these cross-cutting analyses may be more useful from the standpoint of economic and fiscal policy than the more traditional ways of presenting the budget.

A number of cross-cutting analyses is now provided in the *Special Analysis Appendix to the Federal Budget*. These include credit activities, capital-type outlays, research and development outlays, grants to state and local governments, and so on. These special analyses are "after-the-fact" summaries of recommendations included in the President's budget. They do not reflect the results of advance planning and programming or priorities based on national needs. Among the areas where improvements are needed are budget information and policy development concerning the nation's capital infrastructure, coordination in the processes by which research and development needs are developed, methodology for estimating the compliance costs of regulatory actions, and analyses of the use of tax expenditures in conjunction with, or in addition to, direct appropriations in furtherance of government programs or objectives.

A cross-cutting analysis of particular importance is that of capital outlay, by which is meant better analysis of the need for federally financing those capital programs required to support the infrastructure of the nation. Industry considers capital budgeting an essential part of conducting profitable business. It is a part of both short- and long-term strategic planning. Most states and municipalities also follow a capital-budgeting procedure. The Federal Government is an exception; it does not have a capital-budgeting program. I suspect that, in part, this results from the confusion between the concept of capital budgeting and a capital budget. A separate capital budget does violence to the concept of a unified budget and presents many additional problems, such as the definition of what constitutes a "capital" item in a federal, or national, sense. Additional concerns are expressed by those who see the capital budget as gaining priority over noncapital items by virtue of their self-liquidating character. Others see the breakout of a capital budget as a means of concealing the impact of the budget, that is, lessening the apparent size of the deficit in a given fiscal year.

In one of my last reports as Comptroller General, I recommended that the federal agencies implement a capital-investment program, audit its results, and monitor the condition of operating facilities and equipment to ensure a healthy capital plant—or at least that portion for which the Federal Government is directly responsible. No effective national capital-improvement plan exists at the present time and, consequently, we are experiencing a highly visible deterioration in physical capital across the nation. The growth of fixed costs in the budget—principally entitlements and interest costs—has apparently reduced the funds available for capital-type outlays. Moreover, since the full costs of most capital programs appear in the budget at the time they are authorized, they are at a tactical disadvantage as against programs that carry only one year's cost.

Would it be too much to ask the Congress to require the President to submit periodically a capital-improvement program for the nation, including that portion that he proposes to be financed by the Federal Government, by state governments, by local governments, and, with federal encouragement and assistance, by the private sector through user charges? Such an analysis should obviously include a breakdown of the costs and benefits accruing from the capital outlays required on a project or program basis.

An important by-product, from the standpoint of budgetary analysis flowing from the renewed dialogue and interest in the subject of capital budgeting, is that it will focus attention on those items or programs in the budget that can be repaid through special user charges, or that may even be candidates for performance in the private sector. But it is perhaps even more important that we focus on the way these programs and projects are justified from the standpoint of their costs and benefits, the use of discount rates, and similar issues that do not presently receive adequate analysis and that are not applied on a rational basis among different programs in the federal budget.

IMPROVING CENTRAL FINANCIAL REPORTING

An important step has been taken in recent years in the development of a prototype consolidated financial statement for the U.S. Government by the Department of the Treasury in cooperation with the GAO. For example, the prototype for fiscal year 1980, issued March 31, 1982, included an overall summary statement of the financial position of the Federal Government. Importantly, it also included additional supplementary schedules, which are highly valuable for analytical purposes. These included the following:

- A flow-of-funds projection, important from the standpoint of projecting Treasury borrowings.
- A restatement of the Federal Government's financial condition, adjusted for general price-level changes.

- The effect of tax benefits on federal revenues, showing revenue losses attributable to special tax exclusions, exemptions, and deductions, and special credits, tax rates, or deferrals.
- Commitments and contingencies of the U.S. Government, designed to show the maximum potential liabilities and the anticipated liabilities that are regarded as reasonably certain, based on experience and other factors.
- Federal debt maturities, reflecting information on the borrowing by the Federal Government needed to finance the government's operations by type of debt instrument, interest rate, and maturity.
- Additions to nonfederal economic resources—that is, additions to human and physical resources of the nation—without actually acquiring associated physical assets. Some of these outlays add to the assets of state and local governments and private institutions in the form of highways, hospitals, airports, and so forth.
- An analysis of the status of federal pension and retirement plans, including social security, military and civilian retirement, and similar programs.
- Estimated interest subsidies on direct loans outstanding, measuring the difference between what the government has to pay to borrow funds to support its general operations and the interest it charges to a borrower.

These highly important cross-cutting analyses are essential to an understanding of federal financial operations and should have higher visibility than they are receiving at the present time.

Finally, it would be highly desirable to have standard program entities as the basic reporting and accountable entities in both congressional authorizing and appropriations actions, as well as in Executive Branch budget actions. As more committees undertake actions that bear directly upon the budget—and this seems to be the trend—it becomes increasingly important to streamline the processes and minimize the use of competing categories for information reporting and control purposes.

Strengthening the links between authorizing legislation and appropriations categories would also provide a clearer budget focus on what the Federal Government perceives the policy needs to be and how it is allocating resources to them. This means that increasing attempts should be made to use authorizing legislation statements of needs, missions, and program objectives as the categories of appropriations actions. This will require revisions of agency budget categories to bring together activities that address common agency needs and missions. GAO's work in developing a possible mission-budget structure for the Department of Agriculture illustrates the kind of reordering that may be required.

THE IMPACT OF THE BUDGET TIMETABLE ON ANALYSIS

A matter of increasing concern, especially since 1980, is whether the workload pressures on the Congress in reviewing and analyzing the budget may be having an adverse effect on its ability to give needed attention to program oversight and the longer-range implications of the budget. The inability of the Congress to meet the timetables established in the 1974 legislation came to a dramatic conclusion in the last fiscal year. In order to avoid disruptions and provide funds for succeeding fiscal years, the Congress resorted to enacting appropriations in broad terms to cover operations in the government that were not contained in specific, completed appropriation measures. These overall appropriation measures, or "continuing resolutions," were designed to avoid discontinuance of government operations. Over the last 20 years, 85 percent of all appropriation bills was enacted *after* the start of the fiscal year to which they applied.

As fiscal years end without enactment of final appropriations, agency personnel become increasingly anxious over the prospect that the deadline will not be met, thereby slowing down or causing cessation of operations, even when congressional action was taken a day or two in advance of the end of the fiscal year.

The Congress and the Executive Branch have placed themselves under heavy budget scheduling and workload demands in recent years. The Congress, for its part, through the landmark 1974 Congressional Budget and Impoundment Control Act, increased the number of congressional participants in budgeting, and established several new scheduling and reporting requirements.

The combined effect of these mounting pressures is a reduction in the time available for needed in-depth studies and analyses. Serious attention should be given to finding ways to reduce unnecessary workloads so that better budget planning, policy analysis, monitoring, and evaluation may take place—and in a more coordinated and intensive way

These concerns with respect to inadequate oversight and the increased use of continuing resolutions have brought more and more individuals to the view that a biennial budget is worth experimentation. There are obviously many agencies whose program do not change to any significant extent from year to year with changes in the economy or other unforeseen developments. Even those programs that are sensitive to economic change can be adjusted, if necessary, in the off-year or "nonbudget" year. Many in the Congress now feel that new legislation and oversight are suffering because of preoccupation with forward budgets. A biennial budget would make it possible to provide an opportunity every other year for authorizations and oversight hearings that are currently deficient.

Action on the federal budget is without doubt the most important single action taken by the President and the Congress each year. The content of the budget and the process by which it is acted upon can do much to determine whether the result is what the taxpayer has a right to expect from the government.

NOTE

1. "Global 2000 Report to the President: Entering the Twenty-first Century." Interagency Report, Washington, D.C.: Government Printing Office, Vol. I, S/N 041011 00037-8; Vol. II, S/N 041011 00038-6; Vol. III, S/N 04100 00051-3, 1980. (Obtained from the State Department.)

CHAPTER ELEVEN

THE CAPITAL-BUDGET ALTERNATIVE

Sidney L. Jones

Budgets are not merely affairs of arithmetic, but in a thousand ways go to the root of prosperity of individuals, the relations of classes, and the strength of kingdoms.

—*Gladstone*

Government budget processes are complex and controversial because they rationalize political and economic issues to determine winners and losers. Budgets serve diverse functions: reporting past government activities and future spending and investment plans; summarizing the effects of spending and tax policies on the national economy; allocating responsibilities and resources among public organizations; serving as a management tool for setting targets and monitoring performance; providing short-term economic stabilization support; and demonstrating levels of fiscal responsibility.

Some analysts claim that the unified budget fails to achieve these goals because it ignores the differences between current expenses and capital investments, which distorts the reported outlays, deficits, current borrowing needs, accumulated public debts, and the government's apparent net worth. Others complain that current procedures exclude too much "off-budget" spending and most of the government lending and loan-guarantee programs, and that contingent liabilities requiring future outlays are arbitrarily deleted. To improve analysis and communication, proposals have been made to divide all government outlays into a current-expenses budget and a capital budget. Some analysts further recommend that capital outlays be deleted from periodic reports of budget outlays, deficits, current Treasury borrowings, and the national debt, and that a theoretical government net worth be calculated. The basic question is whether or nor the President and the Congress have the best information system for deciding budget issues.

Since adoption of the U.S Budget and Accounting Act in 1921, the rapid growth of reported federal spending, deficits, borrowing, and accumulated debts has caused sporadic debates about the propriety of budget procedures that do not distinguish between current operating expenses and outlays for those capital assets that provide a potential stream of services or income lasting beyond current accounting periods. Such investments tend to be non-recurring and often are initiated on a reimbursable, or self-liquidating, basis, in which designated taxes and user fees are earmarked to gradually retire the debts created to finance the original projects. Examples of public assets frequently recommended for capital-budget treatment include federal and federally assisted buildings, roads, dams, bridges, harbors, airports, schools, hospitals, rural electrical and telephone systems, urban renewal, subsidized housing projects, national parks, water and flood-control projects, commodity inventories, machinery and equipment, and various financial assets. A more controversial classification system would also add the share of annual defense outlays committed to physical assets such as buildings, ships, aircraft, missiles, strategic-material stockpiles, and other weapons and equipment. Some analysts would even extend the capital-budget definitions to include a variety of development programs involving education, training, health care, and the government's share of basic research outlays. It is obvious that the list of government programs eligible for the capital budget, based on positive assumptions about future benefits, is limited only by the imagination of the budget analyst.

As summarized in Table 11-1, federal outlays of an investment nature were estimated to total $171.3 billion in fiscal year 1983, divided into "on-budget" outlays of $155.3 billion, or 20 percent of total expenditures, and "off-budget" outlays of $16.0 billion. Of the on-budget total, defense outlays were projected to be $86.4 billion, representing 39 percent of the total defense budget. If only nondefense capital investments included in the budget are considered, the $84.9 billion total represents 16 percent of expected

Acquisition of physical assets: Commodity inventories	1.0	1.3	2.0	4.3	0.9	0.6
Other	2.1	2.3	2.2	2.8	2.2	1.9
Conduct of research and development	12.4	14.2	15.3	17.0	17.3	16.7
Conduct of education and training	8.9	9.4	10.6	11.7	11.5	9.8
Other	1.6	1.9	3.6	3.5	3.2	3.3
Subtotal	41.5	42.2	50.4	52.1	47.9	41.8
Off-budget investments						
Loans	11.2	13.6	14.7	21.0	16.4	12.3
Construction and acquisition of physical assets and equipment	0.3	0.4	0.4	0.5	0.5	0.9
Acquisition of commodity inventories	—	—	—	—	2.8	2.8
Subtotal	11.5	14.0	15.1	21.5	19.8	16.0
Recapitulation						
Total on-budget	104.8	120.2	136.7	146.0	148.0	155.3
Off-budget	11.5	14.0	15.1	21.5	19.8	16.0
Grand total	116.3	134.2	151.8	167.5	167.8	171.3

Source: Letter from Kenneth M. Duberstein, Assistant to the President, to the Honorable Bill Clinger, House of Representatives, February 16, 1982. Reproduced by permission.

185

nondefense spending in fiscal year 1983. Adoption of a capital budget would significantly change reported federal spending, deficits, borrowing, and accumulated debts if current unified-budget procedures were substantially modified.

BACKGROUND OF CAPITAL-BUDGET CONCEPTS

The separation of outlays by purpose and timing, gradual depreciation of tangible assets to calculate current expenses and profitability, comparison of assets to liabilities to determine net worth, and capital-budget summaries of investment plans are familiar accrual accounting procedures used by most business firms. State and local governments also make extensive use of capital budgets for planning and project-evaluation purposes. Their budget guidelines frequently prohibit deficits, but exemptions are made for capital investments financed by long-term debts with amortization schedules linked to designated taxes and user charges.

Several foreign countries also rely on formal dual-budget arrangements.[1] For example, British budgets record operating expenses "above the line," while government loans and investments are entered "below the line" and are generally ignored in budget reviews.[2]

Even more elaborate systems have been used in the Scandinavian countries. In 1937, Sweden officially abandoned the traditional principle of annual budget balance and accepted the goal of balancing the outlays and revenues over the entire business cycle.[3] To preserve "financial soundness," it was required that operating expenses be separated from government spending for revenue-producing or self-liquidating assets, and that depreciation be calculated to determine more accurately budget surpluses or deficits and the overall value of government assets (outlays for military assets were included in the current-expenses category).[4] Additional reforms in 1947 created emergency budgets for "national defense crises" and "general emergencies" involving the use of public works and grants to create public-service jobs for contracyclical purposes. Since 1947, the Swedish procedures have concentrated on near-term economic stabilization goals rather than on trying to balance the operating budget. Finally, many developing nations use capital-budget procedures for long-range economic development planning and as a tool for evaluating and monitoring investment projects.

A formal dual budget has not been adopted in the United States despite occasional positive recommendations and pragmatic compromises that increasingly isolate off-budget outlays and various lending and loan-guarantee programs. Sporadic debates about the proper budget format began in the 1930s during the trauma of the Great Depression. In 1932, authority was established to borrow funds to support the investment activities of the Reconstruction Finance Corporation[5] and President Roosevelt soon began submitting budgets that separated ordinary expenses—to be financed by current tax receipts—from extraordinary outlays included in an "emergency budget" used for fiscal stimulus.[6] In 1940, President Roosevelt asked for a more formal identification of " . . . amounts disbursed for loans, self-liquidating projects, or for other extraordinary capital outlays which increase the wealth of the Nation."[7] Concerns about fiscal policy images prevented major changes, but government budgets during World War II included a description of ordinary and "war-related" expenditures, and it was assumed that government borrowing could be used to pay for the unusual portion.[8]

In 1945, Senator Robert A. Taft proposed the exclusion from the national debt of "self-liquidating projects" and "other reimbursable expenditures," plus government loans.[9] In 1947, Senator Wayne Morse asked the Bureau of the Budget for a list of capital expenditures in the fiscal year 1948 budget, and placed the response in the *Congressional Record* as a reference source.[10] In 1949, the first Hoover Commission Report recommended that current expenses and capital investments be separately identified in the government budget. The recommendation did not result in a capital budget, but an annual review of "investment, operating, and other outlays" has been published as Special Analysis D of the budget since fiscal year 1951.[11]

The next major legislative initiative occurred in 1959 when Senator Morse and Representative Al Ullman introduced legislation to reform budget procedures by adding an analysis of capital investments to the existing budget along with other requirements for reconsidering the reporting of the national debt and development of public investment plans.[12] Despite the support of several members of Congress, including Senator Hubert Humphrey, the legislation did not gain any momentum. In 1960, the Committee of the American Institute of Certified Public Accountants issued a statement critical of proposals to create a separate capital budget, and in 1962 the Chamber of Commerce issued a negative evaluation.[13] Serious considerations of major reforms ended in 1967 when the Commission on Budget Concepts, appointed by President Johnson, recommended adoption of the unified-budget format now in use and rejected the segregation of capital investments for calculating total spending, budget surpluses and deficits, Treasury borrowing needs, and the size of the national debt, except for continued publication of Special Analysis D.[14]

Interest in the capital budget was revived in the late 1970s by the convergence of concerns about the extraordinary growth of federal spending and credit programs and recognition of the ominous magnitude of public investments required to rehabilitate and improve the national infrastructure. It is increasingly obvious that existing measures of government spending, chronic deficits, Treasury borrowing needs, and the national debt have become confusing at best, or misleading at worst. The intensity of public debate escalated on December 16, 1981, when 20 members of the House of Representatives requested that President Ronald Reagan direct the Office of Management and Budget (OMB) to explore the feasibility of converting to a capital budget that would distinguish between current expenditures and major capital investments beginning with the federal budget for fiscal year 1983.

Although the subsequent responses of the White House repeated traditional OMB objections to shifting from the unified budget to a dual presentation, interest in the concept appeared to be increasing in terms of congressional hearings, speeches, and media presentations. The apparent fusion of concerns about accounting contradictions and expectations about future public-investment requirements generated a major report from the Government Accounting Office (expressing criticism of existing practices) and led to introduction of new legislation in the House of Representatives in June 1982. Extensive hearings on H.R. 6591, "The Federal Capital Investment Act of 1982," were completed with major emphasis upon the need to increase the quality and scope of information about the status of the national infrastructure and future spending priorities.

The relatively simple concept of segregating current expenses from capital investments to create a dual presentation of the Federal Government's financial operations quickly becomes controversial when specific proposals are made. The technical term "capital budget" has a diversity of definitions, depending upon the specific goals of each analyst. At least three levels of adjustments should be considered: a cosmetic rearrangement of current outlays within the existing comprehensive framework to improve the logic and clarity of budget presentations and increase the general public's understanding and acceptance of fiscal policies; actual changes in fiscal policies used for short-term economic stabilization and long-term economic development, which might be facilitated by using a dual-budget arrangement; and fundamental changes in the budget procedures now used, resulting in the deletion of capital investments and public assets in figures reported for federal spending, deficits, borrowing, and calculations of the national debt. Advocates and critics of capital-budget proposals should carefully specify their actual goals in each category and indicate how the actual appropriations process will function if changes are made. The major advantages and disadvantages attributed to various proposals are reviewed below.

ADVANTAGES ATTRIBUTED TO THE CAPITAL BUDGET

Improved Clarity and Logic of Budget Presentations

Dividing all government outlays into current operating expenses and capital investments would make budget estimates more logical, understandable, and accurate. There is a serious timing mismatch when current spending for goods and services is simply combined with long-term investments that need not be paid for with current revenues, because potential beneficiaries should pay their share of the original costs plus operating outlays. This timing mismatch between outlays and benefits is not tolerated in accounting for other economic activities.

Intermingling federal budget outlays also creates a mismatch in evaluating the government's financial solvency and annual operating results. Ignoring the value of assets acquired creates the misleading impression that the government spends only for current consumption, causing a budget deficit in 21 of the last 22 fiscal years and an ominous increase in accumulated debt to well over $1 trillion by 1982. Standard accrual accounting rules emphasize that actual net worth is not reduced by increasing debts if an offsetting asset is required. Advocates of the capital budget argue that similar "businesslike" procedures should be used in federal budgets to avoid misrepresenting the significance of annual deficits and cumulative debts. It should be recognized, however, that accrual guidelines would also require complicated calculations of depreciation expenses to be deducted from the reported assets and added to current expenses and deficits. An even more difficult issue involves the recording of potential asset-value appreciation, particularly during intense inflation.

Critics of these timing and net-worth accounting suggestions always emphasize the importance of including asset values in evaluating government financial conditions, but there are few references to the symmetrical argument that familiar contingent liabilities should also be considered in calculating an estimated net worth.[15] Federal commitments to make future payments are analogous to the potential benefits from acquired assets. Examples of liabilities include: explicit obligations such as accounts payable, long-term contracts for purchases, unresolved claims, and commitments to international organizations; reserves for potential losses on government loans, guaranteed loans, and various insurance programs for financial institutions and physical disasters; and the overwhelming obligations created by government annuity-benefit programs for military personnel, old-age and survivors pensions, disability insurance, civil-service retirement, and railroad retirement. The potential size of these benefits swamps the relative value of other obligations and is not directly comparable with current outlays, but the issue of considering contingent liabilities as well as assets is relevant.

Increased Public Acceptance of Government Spending and Borrowing

Advocates of the capital budget claim that enlightened public understanding would create support for government spending, particularly for long-term capital projects, and increased tolerance for budget deficits, borrowing, and the size and rapid growth of the national debt. This change in public attitudes would make federal spending and borrowing more politically acceptable by demonstrating that some tax revenues are spent for long-term assets rather than current consumption. This point is particularly important to analysts who support increased public-works spending and expanded antirecession programs.

Removing capital expenditures from current budgets would also have a major psychological effect in providing a different perspective on fiscal responsibility by reducing the chronic budget deficits (or increasing any surpluses). Demands for a balanced federal budget would become more realistic by assuming that only current expenses would have to be matched by current tax revenues. Outlays that add to national assets and create future benefits would not be considered deficits, although accounting symmetry should require calculation of current depreciation charges to be added to budget expenses and reported deficits.

Capital budgets could also be used to justify government borrowing to finance durable assets that yield future benefits or operating revenues. While debt financing of capital investments need not be automatic, there is inherent logic in matching debt and interest obligations against potential operating revenues, user fees, and designated tax revenues. Cumulative debt burdens would become more acceptable to the general public if it were explicitly recognized that the net financial position of the Federal Government is not eroded if additional borrowing is matched by acquired assets. Switching to capital budgets would reduce the apparent burden of the national debt, but it should be emphasized that unfunded contingent liabilities as well as assets should be considered in evaluating the Federal Government's financial status.

Critics of capital budgets argue that the information necessary for making these analytical adjustments is already available in budget publications, such as Special Analysis D, so that no additional psychological support for increased spending and borrowing would occur. While this argument is technically correct, it fails to recognize that current procedures provide only historical reports; that the information provided in the special analysis is relatively obscure and used by only a few technicians; and that there is no effort to revise the reported amounts of government spending, deficits, borrowing, and accumulated debts.

Improved Budget Control and Project Evaluation

A third advantage claimed for the capital budget involves improved spending controls and project evaluations. Chronic budget deficits have occurred despite a series of supposedly tight guidelines: budget balance each year; budget balance over the entire business cycle; budget balance at high or full levels of employment; zero-based budgets; and proposals for a constitutional amendment requiring an annual budget balance unless Congress approves a deficit. Some analysts argue that separating expenditures into operating expenses and capital investments would make it easier to require the current outlays to be balanced each year by taxes and user fees. It is further claimed that this new rule would be a more effective restraint over increased entitlement programs and other spending, and would avoid erosion of the government's financial position.[16]

Deleting capital investments, which tend to have a "lumpy" pattern, would also make the operating budgets more predictable, enabling the government to stabilize its long-term tax revenues because the irregular capital investments would be financed by borrowing. It is questionable that this new "balanced-budget" rule would actually be enforced when previous guidelines have failed, but both liberal and conservative analysts apparently agree that this accounting change would create improved spending controls.

A related claim is that separating capital investments would lead to better project evaluation and asset-management procedures. Determining the present value of a discounted stream of future benefits for ranking competing investment proposals is a familiar process in business decisions. Although the Federal Government does not use profit-maximization guidelines, there should be comparable efforts to evaluate competing spending programs that create claims against future public resources. Advocates argue that separate capital budgets would encourage a more analytical framework instead of the "pork barrel" approach to approving public capital investments, which tends to be buried in the total budget when all types of spending are combined.

It is also claimed that formal capital budgets would provide better project management and maintenance results. Regular accrual accounting procedures, including net worth and asset-depreciation calculations, have long been required for government corporations under the Government Corporation Control Act of 1945. Prior to the unified budget, the federal highway program and the social security plans were operated outside the regular budget, using special trust funds. Critics of existing appropriation processes believe that public works would become relatively more important, using a separate budget, because the time frame of budget planning would shift from short-term spending priorities to a long-term master plan for economic development. Developing nations typically use the capital budget as a model for developing natural resources, export promotion, domestic industrialization, and creation of a national infrastructure. Critics of the existing unified-budget procedures claim that the short-term orientation makes it difficult to establish and sustain priorities, so that capital investments become erratic and poorly coordinated. Creating a comprehensive master plan for public investments would increase efficiency and reduce redundant spending. Formalizing the capital-budget procedures would also help shield investment projects from irregular budget cutbacks, particularly across-the-board reductions, and specific interest-group pressures. In general, advocates of the capital budget believe that long-term planning, project evaluations and controls, property management, and program accountability would all be improved.

Promote Increased Investments in the Public Infrastructure

A fourth advantage claimed for the capital budget involves support for increased investments in roads, bridges, transportation terminals, schools, health-care centers, and other public facilities. Considerable media attention has recently been focused on the deteriorating physical condition and inadequate capacity of public facilities. The 1981 report of the National Governors Association described the situation as "America in ruins" and decried the major erosion of public-works spending relative to other budget priorities. Other analysts now refer to the "rebuilding of America" as the most expensive budget challenge for the 1980s. As the national unemployment rate has increased sharply to unprecedented postwar levels, critics have increasingly stressed the unfortunate juxtaposition of growing public infrastructure needs and extraordinary levels of unemployment. The views of organized labor were summarized in congressional testimony on capital-budget legislation during 1960 hearings: "Therefore the AFL-CIO regards the capital budget principle as a necessary foundation for what will be urgently required in the immediate years to come—a greatly expanded investment role in a wide range of public improvements by the Federal Government."[17]

In developing the public infrastructure needed for future national welfare and economic development, it is generally agreed that the Federal Government will be responsible for comprehensive planning, evaluation, coordination, and monitoring of public investment projects, even though most of the actual work is completed by state and local governments. This approach implies larger federal capital-investment authorizations and continued grants and aid programs. It is also apparently assumed that capital-budget procedures would reduce resistance to expanded public-works spending—despite current efforts to gradually restrict expenditures, deficits, and borrowing—by simply deleting capital investments from the reported figures. Advocates hope that changing the information given to Congress and the general public might enable increased capital investments to be added to other government spending programs. This "add-on" approach to government budgets is more responsive to perceived needs, but it tends to ignore the realities of competing claims against available public resources. Whatever accounting system is used, the fundamental requirement is to establish and enforce priorities, and the capital budget must be judged against this standard.

Improved Short-Term Economic Stabilization Programs

A fifth argument for capital budgets is that the Federal Government would improve short-term economic stabilization efforts by planning and managing public-investment programs to smooth business-cycle swings. Since the 1930s, government spending has been used to moderate economic recessions, but unfortunate timing lags have delayed and reduced the anticipated benefits. Capital-budget procedures would create a backlog of investment projects for more immediate use when overall economic activity declines. It is also claimed that the planning and coordination advantages provided by capital budgets would help prevent excessive investment outlays during periods of strong economic expansion. Giving capital investments a higher priority in countercyclical programs would reduce the current reliance on transfer payments and fine-tuning of other spending and taxes, resulting in improved budget continuity, more stable revenues, and more jobs. The goal would be to plan an inventory of potential projects to avoid the usual legislative and bureaucratic delays. A planned investment strategy could also be coordinated with state and local government investment programs.

Several European nations have relied on contracyclical spending and tax programs that emphasize public investments to moderate cyclical unemployment. Sweden has planned formal emergency budgets, including government investments and public-service employment grants. High-priority capital-investment projects are systematically moved into the regular budget from the emergency plans during periods of economic growth. Early Swedish budget reforms emphasized balancing government budgets over the life of the business cycle, but since 1947, the emphasis appears to have shifted to economic stabilization goals of avoiding declining output and rising unemployment: " . . . the question of the balancing of the working budget over the long range must be examined from a broader viewpoint than that which inspired the 1937 budget reform."[18] Despite the historical experiences of having contracyclical spending lag behind the declines and then continue after the expansion phrase begins, it is widely assumed that government spending for public facilities can help neutralize cyclical swings.

DISADVANTAGES ATTRIBUTED TO THE CAPITAL BUDGET

Reduced Scope of Fiscal-Policy Analysis

The unified budget attempts to provide a comprehensive summary of the impact of current federal spending on the national economy and financial markets in accordance with the recommendations of the 1967 Presidential Commission on Budget Concepts. Dividing the budget into separate categories based on the anticipated timing of benefits, rather than the actual timing of outlays, reduces the scope of analysis and understates the stimulative or restrictive effects of current spending and borrowing decisions. Critics argue that deleting capital investments from reported spending and borrowing evades the real necessity of determining relative priorities among all competing claims for government financial resources. Even though specific capital investments may be beneficial in an absolute sense, it is still necessary to rank them individually relative to all other budget claims. The rapid growth of off-budget and government lending and loan-guarantee programs has already seriously distorted the meaning of the unified budget as a measure of fiscal policies.

The capital-budget approach would not change the total effect of current spending or government borrowing required by chronic deficits. Even though long-term assets may be acquired, total federal borrowing competes with the growing credit needs of consumers, business firms, foreign borrowers, and state and local governments. Current interest rates, maturities, terms, security requirements, and the relative availability of financing are influenced by this competition. The more comprehensive format now used attempts to measure the overall economic effects of current outlays as distinguished from the accrual accounting procedures used by private business firms to estimate operating profitability and net-worth values. The spending and borrowing capacity of the Federal Government is based on its authority to levy taxes and sell debt obligations, rather than on the traditional measures of profitability, liquidity, and solvency used to evaluate private credit needs.

Capital Budgets Would Encourage More Government Spending and Borrowing

Critics of the capital-budget process assume that deleting long-term investments from the budget results would lead to increased total spending, reduced tax revenues, larger combined deficits, increased government borrowing, and a larger national debt (not adjusted to reflect the value of assets acquired). The proliferation of off-budget outlays and hundreds of government lending and loan-guarantee programs is cited as an example of what happens when the discipline of the comprehensive unified budget is evaded. Existing budget guidelines have obviously not prevented the rapid growth of federal spending and borrowing, plus chronic budget deficits, but there has been some pragmatic value to using the balanced-budget dogma as a timid restraint on increased spending. Most analysts now assume that the growth of spending and borrowing will continue and that large deficits will be reported for the forseeable future, but critics still contend that switching to a capital-budget accounting format would remove a useful restraint.

Advocates of capital budgets generally assume that the changed reporting standards would provide added flexibility to increase capital investments, particularly to expand and rehabilitate the national infrastructure. Because it is very unlikely that current spending patterns for defense, income security, health care, and interest on the national debt will be reduced in future budgets, even if outlays for other government programs are not restricted, it is probable that increased capital investments would be added to the existing budget projections rather than substituted for existing priorities. This approach may be a desirable allocation of resources, but it should be explicitly recognized that the budget figures will be larger, the government will be assuming a larger role in the economy, and there is an inherent risk of accelerating inflation if the increased capital investments occur when human and material resources are already fully employed. Congress and the general public should evaluate these potential results by combining all spending and borrowing categories, including the off-budget and government credit programs. It is the combined impact of total spending that affects how fiscal and monetary policies are played out in the real world of consumption and investment and in the financial markets.

Capital-Budget Procedures Reduce Fiscal-Policy Flexibility

Critics argue that capital budgets would reduce the government's ability to fine-tune fiscal policies to achieve short-term stabilization goals. This argument assumes that investment projects are typically too slow to respond to deteriorating economic conditions when stimulus is desired, and continue too far into the expansion phrase when budgetary restraint may become preferable. A large and sustained increase of capital investments may be generally desirable, but synchronization problems can occasionally frustrate the stabilization goals of the Employment Act of 1946.

Advocates of capital-budgeting procedures argue that these timing problems can be overcome by better budget planning and project management, and that formalized capital-investment programs would actually contribute to stabilization efforts by identifying and approving a backlog of projects for rapid activation whenever economic recessions appear to be developing. This lively debate demonstrates that comprehensive fiscal policies cannot be determined by focusing on only one goal—such as increasing investments in the national infrastructure—because they involve broader issues of overall economic performance; the distribution of functions between the public and private sectors; the desired mix of immediate consumption and investments for the future; the significance of current deficits, borrowing, and accumulated national debts; and relations with state and local governments.

Spending Bias Toward Government Investment Priorities

A fourth criticism of capital budgets is that they would tilt spending toward long-term projects and away from other current priorities. The tangible nature of capital investments often makes them easier to justify to skeptical members of Congress and the general public, and the traditional use of debt financing to pay for the acquired assets adds to their competitive advantage by easing the immediate pain of deficit financing. In fact, critics of the capital-budget principle suspect that this cosmetic adjustment is its major goal. Special-interest groups in favor of large investment projects are typically powerful and skilled in congressional liaison efforts, whereas beneficiaries of current spending programs tend to be less effective. The cumulative effects of these factors may be to emphasize capital investments, particularly for contracyclical programs, where the lagged impact of accelerated outlays may actually disrupt the total economy.

These concerns caused the Commission on Budget Concepts to issue a negative appraisal of the capital-budget process in 1967. This debate has heated up considerably as fundamental questions about the value of many entitlement programs have escalated at the same time as unemployment has moved above 10 percent—and analysts have become increasingly concerned about the capacity and quality of the national infrastructure.

Capital-Budget Information is Already Available

It is sometimes argued that a formal capital budget is unnecessary because the information has been available in the regular government budgets (historically referred to as Special Analysis D). Outlays have been divided into three categories—investment, operating, and other—with considerable departmental functional detail, and government corporations have prepared operating and balance-sheet reports using familiar accrual accounting procedures.

It is also significant that many of the arguments cited for segregating government capital investments from current operating expenses have already been partially accommodated by creating many off-budget and credit-program categories. Added emphasis on the distinctions between different government expenditures and an estimate of asset values relative to the national debt could be achieved without changing the fundamental format now used by including supplementary statistical tables and explanations in the familiar budget summary materials used by officials and the media to explain the detailed information to the general public. The logic and clarity of unified budgets could be significantly improved by highlighting this information.

Traditional Accounting Problems in Analyzing Capital Investments

A sixth criticism of capital-budget proposals involves the difficulty of preparing meaningful appraisals of government asset values and depreciation rates as a basis for adjusting the spending, deficit, borrowing, and national debt figures now used. Accrual accounting estimates are always difficult, but at least business firms have competitive market values and official tax guidelines to follow.

There are no comparable benchmarks for evaluating national roads, monuments, dams, bridges, and various buildings, since government assets are rarely sold and do not have alternative private uses for calculating market values. Defense expenditures comprise a large proportion of federal capital investments, and there is a particular problem in assigning a value to weapons and facilities that obviously cannot be used for other purposes. Similar difficulties occur when analysts try to estimate depreciation rates for government assets. If depreciation rates are not identified, the capital-budget process would not provide information beyond what is now available in Special Analysis D. Whatever decisions are made will necessarily be arbitrary and may even deteriorate into accounting games that state and local governments sometimes use to shift current expenditures "below the line" into the capital-investment accounts to avoid tight legal restrictions against budget deficits. The difficulty of making such accounting decisions is not a conclusive reason for rejecting the capital budget, but the crudeness of the procedures should be recognized.

SUMMARY

Capital-budget proposals lead to debates about technical accounting and financing procedures that tend to conceal more fundamental fiscal-policy issues. Individual preferences depend upon assumptions about political and economic developments and personal priorities, value judgments, and professional experiences. Advocates of segregating operating expenses from capital investments criticize the unified budget as a "horse and rabbit stew," which defies logic and misleads Congress and the general public about the status of government finances and the proper allocation of resources, which, they argue, should be tilted toward capital investments. Critics respond that simply rearranging the accounting format would not change the realities of total government spending, combined deficits, borrowing needs, and accumulated debts. Switching to a capital-budget format might contribute to more meaningful financial analysis and expanded capital-investment efforts, or it might become a subterfuge to conceal increased overall spending, higher deficits, and more borrowing. Whatever budget-reporting procedures are used, the fundamental issues will remain the same; the distribution of functions between the private and public sectors; the mix of consumption and investment; the capacity of financial markets to fill total federal credit needs plus the claims of individuals, business firms, foreign borrowers, and state and local governments; and the relative priorities assigned to controlling inflation and unemployment. Achievement of fiscal-policy goals does not depend upon any specific reporting process, because the appropriations procedures and financing techniques remain the same. Therefore, governments cannot be dominated by a single goal—such as maximizing capital investments—without considering the total array of political, social, economic, and national security needs.

In reviewing the advantages and disadvantages attributed to the capital budget, there is a serious mismatch between the timing of current spending and actual benefits and in comparisons of accumulated government assets and liabilities. It is not necessary, however, to replace the unified-budget format to achieve desired improvements in logic and clarity. Adding detailed statistical tables and text materials to the unified budget to emphasize capital investments and estimated values for government assets would help correct the disparities without disrupting the more comprehensive coverage provided by current procedures. The explanation of capital-budget information could be provided to Congress and the general public in the same way that off-budget spending and federal lending and loan-guarantee programs have been emphasized in recent years. Simply deleting information from the comprehensive budget totals would not increase the relative priority of capital investments or the public's tolerance of deficits, government borrowing, and the national debt. These issues should be approached directly rather than by isolating the information.

The arguments that there is a need for improved planning and longer time frames, better project evaluations and management, and increased emphasis on the importance of at least paying for current operating expenses with current revenues, while relying on debt financing for long-term commitments, are obviously correct. But these desirable planning and control goals can also be achieved through better fiscal management practices in the Executive Branch and Congress while continuing to use unified-budget procedures. The quality of capital-investment project planning, evaluation, and management does not depend upon the specific budget format used or how the information is communicated.

Similar recommendations that capital investments in the national infrastructure should be sharply increased and better coordinated with other federal spending and with state and local government programs are also persuasive, particularly during a period of extraordinary unemployment. Extensive empirical and anecdotal evidence can be presented in support of increased investments. These arguments would be even more appealing if governments would demonstrate the ability and willingness to shift future priorities away from current consumption toward the necessary investment projects, rather than merely adding the new proposals to existing budget commitments. The comparative value of a "rebuild America" program should be recognized on its own merits without creative accounting adjustments. Isolating capital-investment proposals would, unfortunately, erode the process of establishing priorities among total spending claims. Despite the considerable appeal of increasing investments in the national infrastructure, the outlook for federal spending and tax policies requires more discipline and comprehensive analysis, rather than additional fragmentation, unless the real goal is simply to perpetuate the fiscal policies that have prevailed for two decades under a variety of political arrangements.

Finally, the argument that improved planning and management of capital investments would contribute to improved short-term economic stabilization efforts is another example of a desirable goal that can be achieved within the existing unified-budget framework by strengthening internal procedures. Once again, the quality of project planning and management does not depend upon the accounting procedures used to communicate goals and results.

In summary, the important timing mismatch and failure to consider government assets in evaluating fiscal-policy results should be corrected by adding detailed statistical and explanatory information to the unified budget, comparable with the recent emphasis given to off-budget outlays and federal-credit and loan-guarantee programs. Improved planning and management of capital investment projects, particularly in preparing short-term stabilization programs, are obviously desirable. It is also apparent that investments in the national infrastructure are needed, either as a replacement priority for existing government spending, or as an additional claim against national resources. This let's-put-a-man-on-the-moon approach can be accommodated within the existing budget processes by shifting priorities and tightening management controls.

Existing budget information provides the building blocks necessary to emphasize whatever planning goals are selected without destroying the major advantage of comprehensive analysis of the economic and financial results of current budget decisions. Forcing all government spending programs, including off-budget outlays and commitments that are now being cleverly concealed in some of the credit program arrangements with the Federal Financing Bank, to be considered together is a desirable rationing and control procedure. Increased government spending and borrowing may turn out to be the correct goal for the United States, but the decision should be based on more, not less, comprehensive information. Deleting a large part of potential outlays, or isolating them in separate categories, would dilute the managerial control of spending and borrowing, creating additional skepticism about fiscal-policy prospects. While I favor many of the goals recommended in the current capital-budget proposals, the current unified budget remains the best approach to evaluating the total economic and financial consequences of fiscal decisions if it can be modified to include increased emphasis upon the importance of public investments.

NOTES

1. Richard Goode and Eugene A. Birnbaum, "Government Capital Budgets," *International Monetary Fund Staff Papers*, February 1956, pp. 23–46.

2. U.S. Congress, House Committee on Government Operations Hearing, *Establishing Federal Budget Policies on Capital Investments*, June 8, 1960, p. 57.

3. Jesse Burkhead, *Government Budgeting*. New York: John Wiley and Sons, Inc., 1965, pp. 194–201.

4. United Nations, *Budgetary Structure and Classification of Government Accounts*. New York, 1951, pp. 68–69.

5. Maynard S. Comiez, *A Capital Budget Statement for the U.S. Government*. Washington, D.C.: The Brookings Institution, 1966, p. 12.

6. J. Wilmer Sundelson, "The Emergency Budget of the Federal Government," *American Economic Review*, Vol. 24, March 1934, pp. 53–66.

7. U.S. Bureau of the Budget, *The Budget of the United States Government for the Fiscal Year Ending June 30, 1940*, pp. ix–x.

8. Lillian Rymarowicz, *The Capital Budget Process Contrasted to the Unified Budget; A Review of Selected References*. Congressional Research Service, The Library of Congress, February 2, 1981, p. 2.

9. U.S. Congress, House Hearings, June 1960, p. 27.

10. *Congressional Record*, 1947, Volume 93, Part 7, pp. 8596–8601.

11. U.S. Congress, House Hearings, June 1960, p. 28.

12. U.S. Congress, House Hearings, June 1960, pp. 1–70.

13. Comiez, p. 15.

14. President's Commission on Budget Concepts, *Staff Papers and Other Materials Reviewed by the President's Commission*. Washington, D.C.: Government Printing Office, October 1967, p. 55.

15. Rudolph G. Penner, "How Much Is Owed by the Federal Government?," *Carnegie-Rochester Conference Series on Public Policy*, Spring 1982, pp. 233–256; David R. Ranson, "Toward a Broader Picture of the Budget Deficit," *Policy Review*, Winter 1978, pp. 35–54.

16. Albert T. Sommers, "The Federal Budget Should Be Rebuilt from the Ground Up," *Across the Board*, May 1982, p. 19.

17. Statement of George H.R. Taylor, Department of Research, AFL-CIO; *Establishing Federal Budget Policies on Capital Investments*, in U.S. Congress, House Hearings, June 8, 1960, p. 13.

18. United Nations, 1951, p. 69.

CHAPTER TWELVE

CONTROL OF FEDERAL CREDIT

Alice M. Rivlin and Robert W. Hartman

The enormous growth in federal credit activities in the past four years is in large part a by-product of the increasing control exerted over other federal spending programs under the congressional budget process. By the same token, any hope of improving control over the growth of federal credit in the future will require that these activities be integrated successfully in the ongoing budgetary process.

HOW THE BUDGET PROCESS WORKS

Congressional procedures for developing a budget have been evolving since enactment of the Congressional Budget Act of 1974. For the most part, the evolution has been in the direction of strengthening the control of the budget procedures over federal spending and revenues.[1] As the process now stands, the control mechanism contains both goal-setting and enforcement procedures.

The authors thank the following for comments and assistance on previous drafts: Andrew Carron, Richard Emery, Robert Reischauer, Elisabeth Rhyne, and John Shillingburg.

Goal Setting

The budget resolution specifies an aggregate ceiling on budget authority and outlays for the budget year and two subsequent "out years," as well as a floor for revenues over the same period. These aggregates are simply goals or plans. The only aggregate restraint on legislative action in the Budget Act is at the end of the budget cycle. The Congress can, at the late stage, revise legislation already passed and/or amend its original budget resolution. Once a resolution becomes "binding," the rules embodied in the Budget Act permit any member to raise a "point of order," preventing consideration on the floor of the Congress of a tax or spending bill that would breach the spending ceiling or the revenue floor. Thus, the ultimate control in the budget process is a roadblock against any legislation that violates the limits specified in a budget resolution.[2] However, this last-ditch control has never been the real enforcement mechanism in congressional budget procedures.

Enforcement

Fortunately, the budget process imposes restraints at a much earlier stage than at the end of the budget cycle when the aggregates are about to be breached. These restraints are part of the follow-up to the budget resolution passed in the spring of each year. That resolution not only sets goals for total budget authority and outlays, it also specifies budget authority and outlay limits for each budget function (national defense, agriculture, etc.) over a three-year period. These are implemented along two tracks.

The first, known as "reconciliation," consists of instructions requiring committees in each House to file legislation that would achieve specific dollar savings (spending cuts or tax increases) for the multiyear period. This is followed by a reconciliation act or acts, which are a compilation of the responses to the instructions, according to a tight schedule.[3] As the budget process has evolved, reconciliation has become the prime vehicle for control over entitlement spending and changes in the tax code.

Second, for the remainder of the budget, control is exerted by a process of allocation supplemented by moral suasion and benign obfuscation. Once the budget resolution has passed, the Budget Committees (under section 302a of the Budget Act) allocate the aggregate budget authority and outlays to the committees of their respective Houses. (In so doing, they are guided by the functional limits that are also part of the resolution, and by the legislative history of the budget resolution; nevertheless, the Budget Committees must make certain "assumptions" to allocate the totals.) The largest block allocation is made to the Appropriations Committee in each House. Once these allocations are made, the committees suballocate their allowance to specific programs or subcommittees under their jurisdiction, acting under the requirements of section 302b of the Budget Act. Once these allocations are reported, it becomes possible for the Budget Committees, with the assistance of the Congressional Budget Office, to "keep score" on legislative activity as it proceeds during the months after the spring budget resolution is passed.

Scorekeeping becomes control in various ways. When a committee reports a bill—for example the appropriations bill for military construction—the Budget Committee can compare the fiscal implications of the bill with the section 302 allocation and determine whether it is "over or under budget." The Budget Act provides no automatic sanction if it is over budget, but several control devices have come into play. The Chairperson of the Budget Committee can, and sometimes does, take the floor of Congress and oppose the bill on the ground that it is a "budget buster." Or the Budget Committee can exert its influence, particularly over appropriations bills, to ensure, for example, that if military construction is over budget, then the labor, health and human services, and education appropriation will be under budget by an equivalent amount.[4] Finally, under a procedure set out (but not used) for appropriations and other spending bills in 1982, the Congress may "delay enrollment"—that is, not send to the President for signature—any bill that goes over budget until all spending legislation has moved through the Congress. In principle, this would give the Congress a second chance to revise such bills before they become law.

This process of control over legislation is, to say the least, not without problems. Since the committees in each House are given separate allocations, and in each House the committees may suballocate without coordinating with the other House, bills may emerge that comply with budget requirements, but do not jibe with one another. (It is left to the Senate-House Conference Committee to resolve the differences as best it can; no questions are asked when the conference report on the bill returns to the floor, sometimes accompanied by ritual language about consistency with the budget resolution.) Another ambiguity, also solved by benign obfuscation, arises from the fact that the initial committee allocations of budget authority and outlays may not be consistent with what the Budget Committees intended or with what the committees themselves decide to do. In practice, the outlay targets are more strictly watched, and deviations from plan in budget authority are overlooked.[5]

In sum, the congressional budget process has developed institutions and mechanisms for setting aggregate fiscal and major allocative goals (primarily the budget resolution) and for ensuring that legislative action is consistent with enforcing these goals (primarily through reconciliation and through the monitoring of appropriations and other legislation). Without the essentially self-imposed curbs on committee action, the aggregate goals standing alone would not constitute a working budget.

Importance of Common Accounting Measures

The congressional budget process could not work at all unless aggregate budget outlays and revenues were agreed upon as significant measures of the budget's economic impact, and unless each dollar's worth of outlays in various programs was treated as the same. Thus, when an Agriculture Committee is directed by a reconciliation instruction to draft legislation that reduces the deficit by $1 billion—with the composition of the package left to the committee's expertise—all parties to the compact must agree that $900 million in outlay reductions for food stamps can be added to $100 million in reduced outlays for farm-price supports to produce a package that legitimately complies with the instruction. Moreover, there must be confidence that when all these microadjustments are made and the results aggregated, the total outlay, revenue, and deficit numbers will meaningfully represent the Congress's intent. Otherwise, a strong measure like the point-of-order restraint on budget aggregates would be untenable.

Economists know that every dollar of outlays is not exactly equal in its impact on macroeconomic behavior. Most have qualified their statements on fiscal policy for a long time by noting that the spending propensities of different recipients of government-generated incomes may differ, resulting in a variety of possible multipliers.[6] Many economists also would view tax code changes with equal revenue losses as having different economic impacts, depending on who is affected and how marginal tax rates are changed.[7] Perhaps only those who view the stimulative effect of government as resulting from the creation of public debt, treated by the private sector as net worth, would have no trouble in just adding up outlays under different programs or revenues from all sources. Notwithstanding these differences in perspective, economists who advise the Executive and the Congress tacitly treat a dollar in outlays as roughly comparable in different programs and a dollar in deficit as a meaningful measure no matter what the sources.[8] Differences in the economic effects of different outlays are treated as of second-order importance for broad budgetary planning.

HOW CREDIT ENTERS THE BUDGET

The tacit consensus that allows budget outlays and revenues to be traded off, added up, and subtracted breaks down when it comes to federal credit programs. It is this fact that has spurred the quest for a credit budget and an alternative mechanism for controlling federal credit.

Credit Items in the Unified Budget

The unified budget was set up to produce a bottom line that represents the cash needs of the Federal Government. This basis of organization dictates a treatment of credit items that makes control impossible under the unified budget alone.

Direct loans (where the government supplies the capital) enter the unified budget in a manner bound to obscure what is going on and to understate activity levels. For the large number of direct loans operated out of revolving funds, unified-budget practice is to record "net loan outlays"—the difference between the face amount of gross loans disbursed and the repayment of principal on past loans. Programs with high activity levels may therefore appear negligible because of high repayment flows. Moreover, since repayments are not controllable, strict limits on net loan outlays would be impossible to enforce. Finally, the treatment of interest paid or received by federal agencies makes it next to impossible to estimate the size of interest subsidies that would provide an alternative measure of the cost of credit to the budget.[9]

Guaranteed loans (where the government insures a private lender against default) are even more intractable under the unified budget. The credit advanced under guaranteed loans does not enter the budget at the time the loans are made, because such loans do not involve any need for federal cash. Thus, at decision time, loan guarantees are free goods as far as unified-budget accounting is concerned. If and when loans default, the federal payment to the lender is recorded as an outlay. But because the budget entry is not recorded at the time decisions are being made, default costs cannot be used as an instrument for control of federal lending.

Off-Budget Federal Entities

In addition to the basic problem of treatment of credit items in the budget, the Congress has created a loophole for budget control in the form of "off-budget federal entities." These are federal agencies whose activities are not recorded in the unified budget because the laws creating such entities specified their exclusion. Almost all the activity of the off-budget agencies is credit, most of it attributable to the Federal Financing Bank (FFB).[10]

The FFB was created in 1974 to reduce the government's borrowing costs in financing the lending activities of federal agencies.[11] Before that time, individual agencies would raise funds in capital markets by issuing their own notes of indebtedness. Now the FFB raises the funds for the agencies, but in so doing causes direct loans to disappear from the budget. When credit is advanced as a direct loan, the unified budget records an outlay. A typical arrangement is for the agency to package its direct loans together as backing for securities (called certificates of beneficial ownership) that the agency sells to the FFB. Current budget-accounting practice treats the sale of a certificate of beneficial ownership by the agency to the FFB as a negative outlay. Agency direct loans that are financed by the FFB are thus entirely off budget and do not contribute to the unified-budget deficit.[12]

The FFB also plays a role in federally guaranteed loans. It is allowed to lend directly to a private borrower if a federal agency guarantees the loan. In effect, such an arrangement converts a guaranteed loan into a direct loan from the government (FFB), but the loan is not recorded on budget and the Treasury has to borrow on behalf of the FFB.

In short, the existence of the FFB and its treatment in the unified budget mean that direct lending can take place without affecting unified-budget outlays or the federal deficit, which are the control aggregates for the congressional budget process. Even in the absence of the FFB, credit-program entities in the unified budget do not represent program levels, and their timing does not coincide with decisions. Taken together, the existence of the off-budget FFB and the understatement of new program activity of credit programs under the unified budget made credit an attractive vehicle for fulfilling federal functions in the 1970s. Credit became even more attractive as control of the ordinary budget tightened.

GROWTH OF FEDERAL CREDIT

Federal direct and guaranteed loans grew in the 1970s at about the same rate as unified-budget outlays (see Table 12-1).[13] Up to 1977, credit activity grew quite moderately, but in 1978 to 1980, credit advanced rapidly—both because the budget process became stronger and because high interest rates in private-credit markets made federal credit even more attractive to borrowers. The treatment of different types of credit in the budget led to different rates of expansion in the components of federal credit. From 1972 to 1981, on-budget direct loans expanded by only $2 billion, while guaranteed loans rose by $9 billion and off-budget direct loans by $21 billion. Between 1978 and 1981, both off-budget and guaranteed loan flows doubled, suggesting to some that as the conventional budget process was tightened, federal spending found outlet through the uncontrolled expansion of federal credit.(No one really knows the relative importance of the many causes of federal credit expansion, but the perception that credit is the escape valve for tightening spending control is widespread.)

TABLE 12-1. Net Federal Direct and Guaranteed Loans, Fiscal Years 1972–1981 (dollars in billions)

	1972	1973	1974	1975	1976	1977	1978	1979	1980	1981	Change 1972–1981
Direct loans											
On-budget	3.0	0.9	3.3	5.8	4.2	2.6	8.6	6.0	9.5	5.2	2.2
Off-budget	—	0.1	0.8	7.0	6.7	9.0	11.2	13.6	14.7	20.9	20.9
Guaranteed loans	18.9	16.6	10.3	8.6	11.1	13.5	13.4	25.2	31.6	28.0	9.1
Total direct and guaranteed loans	21.9	17.6	14.4	21.4	22.0	25.1	33.2	44.8	55.8	54.1	32.2
Direct and guaranteed loans as a percentage of unified-budget outlays	9.5%	7.2%	5.4%	6.6%	6.9%	6.3%	7.4%	9.1%	9.7%	8.2%	—

Source: *Budget of the U.S. Government, Fiscal Year 1983*, Table 22, and *Special Analysis F*, Table F-1.

DEVELOPMENT OF A CREDIT BUDGET

The growth in federal credit volume spurred the government into action in 1980. Beginning in that year, the President's budget included estimates of obligations for direct loans and commitments for federal guarantees and estimates of planned FFB activity levels. The Congress has begun to integrate these concepts into its budget process, making some progress each year.

By 1982, the credit-control process in the Congress had come to mean the following for the fiscal year 1983 budget: All credit programs (guaranteed and direct loans) are measured on a gross obligations or commitments basis. That is, the measure of the activity level in any program is the dollar volume of binding agreements to lend that an agency may incur in the fiscal year.[14] Budget resolutions now incorporate separate "credit-budget" aggregate limits on direct-loan obligations and primary guarantee-loan commitments for the budget year (but not for the out years).[15] Each of these aggregates is allocated by budget function in the budget resolution (see Table 12-2). Finally, the amounts subject to annual appropriations limits are allocated to the Appropriations Committees, while the Budget Committees allocate the remaining amounts to authorizing committees. In fiscal year 1983, $42.5 billion in direct loans (about 71 percent of the credit-budget aggregate) and $77.7 billion in guarantees (76 percent of the credit-budget limit) were subject to appropriations limits. The amounts allocated to the Appropriations Committees are suballocated to their subcommittees (see Table 12-3). Programs that are not subject to appropriations limits are, for the most part, like entitlements—for example, farm-price supports and Veterans Administration mortgage guarantees.

ATTAINING CONTROL UNDER THE CREDIT BUDGET

In large part, these accounting and procedural steps are simply an imitation of what has already been done on the ordinary unified budget. But there are crucial differences. First, in practice the numbers in the credit budget have represented forecasts (not goals) of lending activity, and these have even been padded to ensure that the credit budget would not prove too restraining.[16] Second, the

TABLE 12-2. Credit Budget by Function, Fiscal Year 1983 (in millions of dollars)

Budget function		Direct loan obligations	Primary guarantee commitments
050	National defense	50	50
150	International affairs	10,200	9,300
250	General science, space, and technology	200	—
270	Energy	12,000	500
300	Natural resources	30	—
350	Agriculture	18,100	2,600
370	Commerce and housing credit	12,100	41,000
400	Transportation	500	800
450	Community and regional development	2,200	600
500	Education, training, employment, and social services	800	7,200
550	Health	100	100
600	Income security	2,000	18,700
700	Veterans' benefits and services	1,000	20,900
750	Administration of justice	—	—
800	General government	50	—
850	General-purpose fiscal assistance	200	—
	Total	59,700	101,900

Source: First Concurrent Resolution on the Budget—Fiscal Year 1983, S. Con. Res. 92, Section 1(b).

only implementation technique so far introduced in the credit budget is that the Senate (but not the House) has accepted the credit-budget aggregates for fiscal year 1983 as "binding," and thus subject to a point of order if breached. No mechanism for reconciliation or for adjusting excessive individual appropriations bills for credit overruns has been instituted. Disputes over whether appropriations limitations on particular programs are too severe have been resolved by raising the appropriation or by not imposing appropriations limits at all. Third, the Congress has not addressed

TABLE 12-3. 1982 Appropriations Limitations on Credit Programs, by Appropriations Subcommittee (in millions of dollars)

Subcommittee	Direct loans		Loan guarantees	
	1st resolution assumptions	Appropriation action	1st resolution assumptions	Appropriation action
Agriculture	22,083	22,275	1,592	1,142
Commerce, justice, state, judiciary	1,764	1,686	3,002	2,366
Defense	50	—	50	—
District of Columbia	145	126	—	—
Energy and water development	67	—	67	—
Foreign operations	9,449	9,359	9,349	9,130
HUD-independent agencies	7,000	2,617	56,889	59,688
Interior	692	692	-636[a]	-636[a]
Labor, health and human services, and education	768	692	7,389	7,389
Transportation	468	468	101	-118[a]
Treasury	35	—	—	—
Total	42,520	37,982	77,736	78,961

[a] Primary guarantee amounts are negative because the sum of new loan-guarantee commitments is less than the sum of adjustments for loan-asset sales and guarantees held as direct loans by the FFB.

Source: Congressional Budget Office, Credit Budget Scorekeeping System as reported to the Senate Budget Committee on October 15, 1982.

215

the problem that the credit budget treats loan dollars as if each one were the same—a controversial proposition when the loans are made on such a wide variety of terms (see below). Thus, the features that have made the regular budget process effective—serious binding constraints, detailed implementation procedures, and an understanding of what the aggregates mean—have not yet been applied to the credit budget.

As the credit budget approaches the point where it can become an effective constraint, there appear to be two broad strategies available to guide its implementation. One would be to follow up on what has already been done and develop an independent credit budget with its own implementation mechanism. The other would be to integrate credit decisions with spending decisions. While these approaches are not incompatible, each has a different focus for policymakers and requires different informational resources. The remainder of the essay highlights these differences, discussing the strengths and weaknesses of each approach.

A Free-Standing Credit Budget

One way to put teeth into the credit budget would be to set credit limits in the budget resolution that would, in fact, constrain credit behavior—and then stick to them. Procedurally, this would require treating the credit-budget figures in the budget resolution as binding, extending them to the out years, increasing the visibility of the credit-budget scorekeeping, and, in general, having some central coordinating unit to police the credit estimates to keep them from being padded or overrun. Reconciliation could be applied to credit programs—authorizing committees would be instructed to save $X billion in loan commitments by tightening eligibility or loan terms in their entitlement-type programs. Finally, the problem of off-budget deficits could be ignored because the off-budget credit activity would be "on" the credit budget. (Indeed, it might make sense if all credit items such as net loan outlays were purged from the spending budget to avoid duplication with the credit budget.)

The development of a free-standing credit budget is the track the Congress is currently on. It is a route that implicitly gives considerable emphasis to the importance of controlling the total volume of federal credit. By using some measure of participation of the Federal Government in credit markets—such as funds advanced under federal auspices to total funds advanced—credit-budget decision makers could decide on a maximum level and set direct-loan obligations and guarantee-loan commitments accordingly.[17] Under this approach, the allocation of a fixed amount of total credit to specific government functions or congressional committees would probably be guided by perceptions of the need for intervention in credit submarkets (are small businesses getting crowded out?). Because of the emphasis on controlling aggregates, it would probably make sense to continue having separate, enforceable levels for direct loans and guaranteed loans, since that would make keeping track of legislative activity somewhat easier.

A free-standing credit budget would raise two major research and data needs. First, since the credit budget would exert control through obligations and commitments, it would be necessary to forecast actual lending from commitments. To do this would require a much better understanding of the "lend-out rates" (corresponding to "spend-out rates" from budget authority to outlays) in different programs than exists today. A solution to this problem would take time and resources.

A solution of the other major problem would be harder to achieve. Very little is understood about the effect of federal credit on capital markets in general, and there is wide disagreement among experts about the effects of particular programs on particular submarkets. Some analysts contend that many federal loan programs are irrelevant to economic activity or to capital markets, because exactly the same transactions would take place at virtually the same terms without government lending. Others treat all federal loans as totally additive to other claims on savings.[18] Moreover, at a time when financial institutions are being deregulated, conclusions based on past experience—even if we had them—would not be of much help. With the time drawing close for congressional leaders to turn to their economic advisers for assistance as to "appropriate levels of federal credit," the empty black box we have to consult is embarrassing. Pursuit of the free-standing credit budget requires a good deal more agreement about the impact of federal credit on capital markets than now seems available.[19] Moreover, until the Congress is comfortable that the aggregates being controlled have significant economic impacts, it is not likely to put into effect at the program level credit limits that have real bite.

Integrating Credit with the Congressional Budget Process

The starting point for an alternative approach to controlling federal credit is the notion that the major problem is not so much the extent of intrusion into capital markets, but rather the government's overuse of credit in meeting its objectives—in large part because of the misstatement of credit costs in the regular budget process. For example, the growth of the guaranteed student-loan program would be viewed as troublesome, mainly because its expansion did not result from a rational evaluation of the pros and cons of various forms of college-student aid, but rather because the cost of student loans was understated in the budget.

If control over federal credit were to emphasize improvement of this general problem of allocating resources by the government, the credit-budget process would have to be implemented along different lines from the free-standing budget. Rather than stressing the development of two independent budgets—one for spending and one for lending—this approach would encourage trade-offs between noncredit items and credit programs. Decisions on credit would have to be integrated with budget decisions in the existing budget process. For example, if a committee were instructed under reconciliation to save $X billion, it would be given some incentive to meet all or part of that goal by reducing credit-program activity. Similarly, an appropriations subcommittee that wished to contract the volume of guaranteed loans rather than limit direct spending would have to be rewarded in the regular budget process for doing so.

Integrating credit decisions with the ordinary budget process is difficult in that the accounting system does not have a way of comparing credit with direct spending. No one would argue that one dollar in new loan commitments is the economic, or programmatic, equivalent of one dollar in ordinary (goods and services or transfer payment) spending. These differences are thought to be much greater than those between different types of spending in the unified budget. It would certainly not do simply to trade off a dollar's worth of loans against a dollar's worth of other spending.

Economists would agree, we think, that credit oranges can be turned into noncredit apples by measuring credit-program levels by the present value of the interest subsidy. The difference between the rate of interest the borrower would pay in the absence of government intervention and the rate actually paid measures the income transferred to the borrower in a way that is conceptually equal to outlays on most spending programs. That is, if a credit program offers loans at 3.6 percent interest for a period of 37.2 years when the private market rate of interest is 15.1 percent (these are Office of Management and Budget estimates for rural housing loans in 1981), each $100 loan represents the equivalent of a $68 grant (present value of the interest subsidy).[20] The variation in the present value of the interest subsidy in several different federal programs in fiscal year 1981 is illustrated in Table 12-4. Because of its highly subsidized nature, a dollar's worth of lending for rural housing represents a lot more economic activity than a dollar's worth of lending for veterans' housing, where only about 3 cents on each dollar lent represents a subsidy.

Under an approach emphasizing integration of credit into the ordinary budget process, one might envision a congressional committee being instructed to bring forward legislation to reduce spending by $1 billion, with the added proviso that a food-stamp dollar saved counts as a dollar; a rural housing-loan dollar saved counts 68 cents; and a veterans' housing-loan dollar saved counts as 3 cents.[21]

This method of making credit and noncredit programs comparable is most suitable for direct-loan programs in which the interest charge is controlled by the government. For guarantee programs, the same methodology could be used—that is, basing the "shadow cost" of a program on the difference between the interest rate the borrower would have had to pay in the absence of a government guarantee and the interest rate actually paid. In many guarantee programs, estimating the market rate would be difficult because of program complexity and the difficulty of assessing the characteristics of borrowers. In other cases, where the loan is so highly risky that a private lender might not be found without a guarantee (Chrysler), the estimation of an interest subsidy might be impossible. Some have suggested that for loan guarantees, the discounted value of expected defaults be treated as the program's cost for budgetary purposes.[22] Aside from the fact that such an approach would show the eventual budgetary cost of guarantee programs, it does not seem to have any conceptual advantage over the interest-rate comparison.[23] Others have compared the actual interest rate charged with the government's borrowing rate, which

TABLE 12-4. Interest Subsidy Values for Selected Federal Credit Assistance, Fiscal Year 1981

| | Average terms | | | | |
	Interest rate (percent)	Years to maturity	Annual market rate (percent)	Obligations ($ millions)	Present value of subsidy ($ millions)
VA housing loans	14.6	29.0	15.1	739	22
Rural housing loans	3.6	37.2	15.1	6,079	4,126
Export-Import Bank	10.5	11.0	20.6	5,431	1,808

Source: *The Budget of the U.S. Government, Fiscal Year 1983, Special Analysis F,* Table F-11a.

makes the computation simple, but hides the subsidy that derives from the fact that federal-credit recipients are not risk-free entities with taxing power.

To sum up, an integrated budget-control strategy would imply that at key enforcement points in the current budget process—namely, in reconciliation and in the evaluation of whether appropriations bills were consistent with the budget resolution—credit-program savings could be substituted for noncredit program savings by placing a weight on each dollar of federal credit. The weight would be based on the interest-subsidy content of the loan. (There is no need to change the definitions of spending and lending in the unified and credit budgets themselves—present values of interest subsidies would be used merely to guide decisions. Once the decisions were made, they could be carried out by changes in underlying laws or by appropriations limits as in the current credit-budget process. There is merit in retaining a unified budget whose bottom line is directly related to borrowing requirements.)

The integrated strategy has a number of problems. First, it would make the aggregates under both the unified and credit budgets somewhat less firm predictors of budget outcomes. This arises because if one leaves a congressional committee free to cut direct spending programs by, say, $100 million or to cut guarantee obligations by, say, $220 million (assuming these are equivalent), the decision will affect the unified-budget outlays and credit-budget obligations aggregates in different ways that cannot be set out in advance. (For example, if all cuts were made in guarantee programs, unified-budget outlays would not be cut at all.) As long as the integrated strategy is implemented faithfully at the enforcement stage of the budget process, this new ambiguity in the aggregates will be worth it. (As noted above, there are already some ambiguities in the budget process, and this one should not be any more difficult to live with.)

A second problem: Because of the considerable number of federal credit programs, all with different lending terms, the Congressional Budget Office would have to compute outlay equivalents for a host of programs, and the result would be greater complexity and confusion.[24] Moreover, for purposes of comparison to noncredit programs in which outlays greatly understate program activity (as in some housing-subsidy programs), it might be more appropriate to trade off the present value of the interest subsidy against budget authority. It is fair to say that CBO's technical inexperience with estimating interest subsidies, and congressional unfamiliarity with the concept of present value of interest subsidies, would make it very difficult to implement an integrated approach in comprehensive fashion in the immediate future.

Once the integrated approach was adopted, off-budget lending activity would fall into its proper place automatically. If congressional scrutiny of the interest subsidies in rural housing led to a revision of its loan terms and a reduction loan volume, the major public-policy problem would have been corrected. Even though net loan outlays would continue to be the entry in the unified budget, the decision on program level would have been based on a measure comparable with that used in spending programs. The only remaining question would be whether the FHA should borrow directly from the public or through a central FFB. This is clearly a matter of means of financing; it implies that if the FFB continues to be a source of funds, sales of CBO to the FFB should not be offset against agency outlays.[25]

CONCLUSION

The major element missing in the current federal credit system is a systematic evaluation of credit programs in comparison to other means of accomplishing federal goals. This kind of comparison will probably not be made in the Congress until appropriate equivalence scales between credit and spending (and taxing, for that matter) programs are developed. But it will not be enough to develop equivalence measures, such as the present value-of-interest subsidies, unless something is done to motivate behavioral change based on the new measures. Every effort should therefore be made to work the trade-offs between federal credit and other programs into the ongoing budget process.

Unfortunately, the conceptual and technical bases for a fully integrated approach to federal credit have barely been established. As an experiment, it should be possible to try the present value-of-interest subsidy approach in some areas of the budget to see how well it would work. This is feasible because interest subsides are fairly well concentrated in a few areas of the budget—agriculture, housing, the Export-Import Bank, small business, and student loans.

Meanwhile, the free-standing credit budget that Congress has been gradually developing ought to be perfected. It has already given exposure to programs that would otherwise have escaped attention. It has spurred better accounting for federal credit than ever before, and this pressure should be kept up. Finally, as the integrated evaluation of credit takes place, the current credit-budget setup will probably be useful in carrying out the decisions made. One danger in pushing forward with the credit budget as it is now constituted is that people will become frustrated if progress is not made in curbing federal credit. This is, in fact, all too likely until an effort is made to integrate credit-program decisions into the budget process.

NOTES

1. For a discussion of this history, see Allen Schick, *Congress and Money*. Washington, D.C.: Urban Institute, 1980; Alice M. Rivlin, "The Political Economy of Budget Choices: A View from the Congress," *American Economic Review*, May 1982, pp. 351–355; Robert W. Hartman and Robert D. Reischauer, "A Defense of Current Federal Budgetary Procedures," in Alvin Rabushka and Craig Stubblebine, eds., *Constraining Federal Taxing and Spending*. Palo Alto: The Hoover Institution, 1982.

2. The budget process is, in large measure, simply a codification of congressional rules. As such, the rules can generally be overturned by a vote to waive them. In other words, budget procedures are not set in concrete but in semi-hard putty.

3. In 1980, committees were given ten weeks to file legislation to be reconciled. In 1981 and 1982, four to six weeks was given.

4. This kind of trade-off is particularly important in omnibus continuing appropriations acts, covering several agencies, where the Budget Committees try to police the aggregates rather than the parts of the bill.

5. This practice is not without program implications: In national defense, a given outlay reduction in the budget year would involve much larger cuts in budget authority if procurement lines were reduced than if operations lines were cut because of slower spending rates in the former. As a result, outlay cuts in defense in the short run invariably reduce operations.

6. Edward M. Gramlich, "Measures of the Aggregate Demand Impact of the Federal Budget," in Wilfred Lewis, Jr., ed., *Budget Concepts for Economic Analysis*. Washington, D.C.: Brookings Institution, 1968, pp. 110–126.

7. Congressional Budget Office, *Understanding Fiscal Policy*. Washington, D.C.: Government Printing Office, April 1978.

8. Most economists do distinguish outlays and revenue changes that are induced by changes in the economy from those undertaken in discretionary fashion. The concept of the high-employment surplus still has its day, although it is getting shorter all the time. See Frank deLeeuw, Thomas Holloway, Darwin Johnson, David McClain, and Charles A. Waite, "The High-Employment Budget: New Estimates, 1959–80," *Survey of Current Business*, November 1980; and Congressional Budget Office, *The Economic and Budget Outlook: An Update*. Washington, D.C.: Government Printing Office, September 1982.

9. Interest received by federal agencies is generally recorded as a negative outlay (but is aggregated separately so "net loan outlays" represent only principal). If an agency borrows directly from the Treasury, its payment of interest is recorded as an agency outlay, but is offset by a receipt at Treasury. All interest payments and receipts are recorded on a cash basis, thus making budget flows represent mainly past, not current, decisions.

10. In fiscal year 1982, the total (net) outlay of off-budget entities was $17.3 billion, of which $14.1 billion was by the FFB.

11. Most of the information in this section is from Congressional Budget Office, *The Federal Financing Bank and the Budgetary Treatment of Credit Activities*. Washington, D.C.: Government Printing Office, January 1982.

12. The FFB, in turn, receives its funds by borrowing from the U.S. Treasury. Under present budget circumstances, however, the Treasury would have to borrow from the public to finance the loan to the FFB. This borrowing is referred to as the off-budget deficit.

13. In fact, it can be said that federal credit grew more rapidly than the budget in the 1970s. If one adds credit extensions by government-sponsored enterprises to direct and guaranteed loans, the resulting aggregate (funds advanced under federal auspices) does grow faster than budget outlays. A good discussion of the recent growth of federal credit can be found in Herman B. Leonard and Elizabeth Rhyne, "Federal Credit and the 'Shadow Budget.'" *Public Interest*, No. 65, Fall 1981, pp. 40–58.

14. The obligations level is analogous to an appropriation, in that it would generally exceed the level of loans actually made or disbursed. Congress cannot really control the latter in the same sense that it does not have full control over outlays.

15. "Primary" means simply that double counting has been eliminated by removing from gross guarantees those guaranteed loans that are counted as direct loans because they are financed by the FFB.

16. The credit-budget estimate for Farmers' Home Administration (FHA) mortgage assistance for both fiscal years 1982 and 1983 was $40 billion, the amount specified in the appropriation. This "limit" is double the estimated actual obligations level for 1982.

17. The participation rate is given in *Budget of the U.S. Government, Fiscal Year 1983, Special Analysis F*, Table F-1. It usually also includes federally sponsored (but private) enterprises (such as Fannie Mae) whose activities are beyond the scope of the budget and this chapter.

18. See the overview and discussion of papers in Congressional Budget Office, *Conference on the Economics of Federal Credit Activity*, Part 1, *Proceedings*, December

1980, and Part 2, *Papers*, September 1981. Washington, D.C.: Government Printing Office.

19. This is not to say that everyone agrees about the impact of federal spending on the economy, but in that area there is at least a wide body of (unfortunately divergent) research that can be evaluated. This is not true for federal credit activity.

20. Annual repayments on a 15.1 percent loan for 37.2 years would be $15.18 per $100 borrowed. For a 3.6 percent loan, repayments drop to $4.92 per $100 borrowed. The annual difference between these repayments, $10.26, is the subsidy in the program. Discounted at 15.1 percent, 37.2 annual payments of $10.26 have a present value of $67.58.

21. One of the problems of the budget process today is that some programs that should be directly compared are under the jurisdiction of different committees. This problem is especially acute when tax expenditures are considered. For a discussion of inventive ways to force trade-offs between tax and spending programs, see Congressional Budget Office, *Tax Expenditures: Budget Control Options and Five-Year Projections for Fiscal Years 1983–1987*. Washington, D.C.: Government Printing Office, November 1982, Chapter III.

22. See statement of Barry Bosworth in Hearings before U.S. House of Representatives, Committee on Banking, Currency, and Housing, 94th Congress, *Loan Guarantees and Off-Budget Financing*, Nov. 10, 1976, pp. 39–42.

23. The present value of the interest subsidy and the present value of expected defaults will be equivalent when lenders' evaluation of default risk is the same as the government's and when lenders are free to lend all they want under the guarantee program.

24. CBO has computed interest subsidies, limited to a five-year horizon, for its cost estimates of pending legislation.

25. Congressional Budget Office, *Rural Housing Programs: Long-Term Costs and Their Treatment in the Federal Budget*. Washington, D.C.: Government Printing Office, June 1982.

CHAPTER THIRTEEN

CONSTITUTIONAL AND STATUTORY APPROACHES

Rudolph G. Penner

Polls consistently indicate that about 70 percent of those questioned favor a constitutional amendment to balance the federal budget. Polls also indicate that the opposition to the specific program cuts and tax increases necessary to obtain a balanced budget is almost as intense as the desire to have one.

It is not surprising that this same ambivalence is reflected in Congress. Not long after voting for a budget resolution to ensure a long string of deficits of well over $100 billion, the Senate passed a constitutional amendment requiring a balanced budget by a vote of 69 to 31. Prior to the 1982 election recess, the House fell short of the necessary two-thirds majority by about 50 votes. Nevertheless, a bare, simple majority approved the amendment.

Clearly, a considerable number of citizens and legislators feel that a constitutional approach is needed to help to save us from

---

This paper benefited greatly from the analysis in Congressional Budget Office, *Balancing the Federal Budget and Limiting Federal Spending: Constitutional and Statutory Approaches*. Washington, D.C.: Government Printing Office, 1982.

ourselves. While at first sight the situation seems paradoxical, if not slightly absurd, public-choice theorists have shown that there is no a priori reason for collective decision-making procedures to reflect the tastes of individual voters. Even a series of honest majority votes can lead to paradoxical results.[1] But when the voting is modified to allow for complex voting strategies and a role is given to special-interest groups, the likelihood of biased, or even perverse, results rises greatly.[2]

Those who draft constitutions hope to set down rules that minimize biases and perverse results to the greatest extent possible. Believing that the drafters of the Senate Joint Resolution (S.J.R.) 58, which passed the Senate, failed in their effort to offset biases in the current system, I also believe that those who argue that fiscal-policy formulation should be left out of the Constitution are quite wrong. If there were a way of amending the Constitution to make budgeting more rational, I would support it. But the practical difficulties are enormous, and the proposal in S.J.R. 58 is more likely to worsen than to ameliorate the situation.

S.J.R. 58 does attempt to address a real problem. I agree that our system of representative government is very likely to produce biased results. Special-interest groups that feel intensely that a program should be expanded can exert disproportionate pressures on the legislature. Because the costs of such a program can be diffused widely across the electorate, the resulting pain imposed on individual voters is not sufficient to motivate them in organizing any effective opposition. Consequently, the aggregate level of spending is likely to be higher than that desired by the median voter, even though that same voter might mount a vigorous fight to save his or her own favorite programs.

The problem has been exacerbated by the Keynesian Revolution. Wagner and Buchanan argue that, before Keynes, it was presumed that the budget should be balanced year after year.[3] Keynes argued that deficits could be used to counter recessions.

Keynesian theory has been much criticized by the monetarist and rationalist expectations schools of economics; but whatever its economic merits and deficiencies, it is extremely convenient for politicians. They can rationalize expanding programs without levying the taxes to pay for them by forecasting that private demand will be weak in the near future. The incentive for making such forecasts is very strong, for, as Wagner and Buchanan point out, expanding government by selling debt represents a voluntary exchange and is much less painful than levying taxes.

Put another way, Keynes took away the fiscal norm that budgets should be balanced year after year. That norm exerted considerable discipline over spending, and nothing has been created to take its place. Many have argued that there should be a new rule that the budget should be balanced over the business cycle, and President Nixon attempted to argue that the high-employment budget should be balanced, but no substitute rule has even gained the force of the old budget-balancing rule.

It is hard to review the history of the last 20 years without concluding that a strong bias toward deficits exists. The last balanced budget was in fiscal 1969; since then, the deficit has been on an upward trend relative to GNP. In the ten years prior to 1969, the budget was balanced only once.

While it has long been recognized that narrow special-interest groups and the lack of a fiscal norm can result in upwardly biased spending, a new—and perhaps more dangerous—phenomenon has arisen in recent years. The social-security program has expanded to the point where there are 36 million persons directly dependent upon its benefits. Together with those nearing retirement and relatives who would otherwise be responsible for the beneficiaries, it is possible that those with an intense interest in the system constitute a near majority of the electorate. (Roughly 85 million voted in the 1980 presidential election). While those who are concerned about special-interest groups worry about minorities exploiting majorities in our system, we also face the more worrisome problem of a majority exploiting a minority of the electorate. This is a much more difficult problem to deal with outside of the Constitution, and it is not surprising that many supporters of S.J.R. 58 see the amendment as the only way to control the social-security problem.

In fact, much of the Bill of Rights is concerned with just this problem—preventing the majority of the electorate from exploiting minorities. Thus, though many people wish that S.J.R. 58 and other variants on the theme would disappear without a trace, it cannot be denied that the debate over budget-limiting amendments goes to the core of some very real problems in our society. To argue that it is not appropriate to seek constitutional remedies to such problems is as foolish as to believe that the Constitution can provide a perfect cure.

PROPOSED REMEDIES

There are many who agree that there are severe biases inherent in current decision processes, but feel that it is extremely difficult—and perhaps dangerous—to attempt constitutional remedies. Many advocate statutory remedies that would seek the same goals, but would be easier to alter if unintended consequences emerged. Some see statutory remedies as a substitute for a constitutional amendment, while others feel that we should first experiment with a variety of statutory rules in order to identify the best approach to amending the constitution at some later date.[4]

Any statutory approach that places definite quantitative limits on total outlays, tax burdens, and/or deficits involves all of the same practical difficulties as a constitutional amendment. Much of the following discussion of practical difficulties does not differentiate between the two approaches on the basis of their practicality. The main differences involve flexibility and enforceability.

The very rigidity deplored by opponents of the constitutional approach is seen as an advantage by its proponents. They argue that statutory limits would have very little force. Indeed, it might be argued that any set of appropriations and tax legislation that violates statutory limits automatically supersedes them. Something like this seems to have happened to the much-ignored Byrd Amendment, which legislated a balanced budget. Originally passed in the late 1970s and reaffirmed more recently, it has had no noticeable effect on deficits.

An enormous number of statutes and constitutional amendments have been offered to place quantitative limits on one or more budget aggregates. All of the major proposals that impose definite quantitative limits also allow escape routes. Most would not be binding if war were declared, and most can be overriden by a "super majority"—usually a 60 percent vote. In some proposals, an override requires a super majority of those voting; in others, a super majority of the entire membership of each house of Congress is required.

The various approaches fall into three categories. Some would just require a balanced budget without explicitly limiting the size of government. Most proponents of this approach do believe, however, that a restoration of the balanced-budget norm would automatically provide the discipline to limit spending growth. A variant on this theme would, as a complement, limit the public debt constitutionally. This reduces the danger that a balanced budget would be achieved by redefining outlays and receipts. Even off-budget outlays must be financed. And while many constitutionally limited state and local governments have shown that debt can also be redefined, a constitutional debt limit would create at least one more hurdle to be overcome.

Another approach limits outlays without requiring a balanced budget. It allows receipts to fluctuate countercyclically, and permits a little Keynesianism without losing control of outlays.

Yet another approach combines outlay restraint with a balanced budget approach. S.J.R. 58 achieves this by combining a limit on tax burdens with a balanced-budget requirement. The variant passed by the Senate also contains a constitutional debt limit.

There are various approaches to limiting outlays and receipts. The rate of growth of nominal outlays can be limited to a set amount, such as 7 percent per year. The intent is to provide an incentive for fighting inflation, since the real growth of outlays would vary inversely with the inflation rate in such a system. Some proposals go further and lower the nominal growth of outlays by an amount depending on the extent to which inflation exceeds some limit, say 3 percent.

Other approaches limit outlays and/or tax receipts to a certain percentage of GNP, while still others prohibit outlays and/or receipts from growing faster than some other economic indicator. In S.J.R. 58, tax receipts are not allowed to grow faster than "the rate of increase of national income in the year or years ending not less than six months nor more than twelve months before such fiscal year, unless a majority of the whole number of both Houses of Congress shall have passed a bill" approving the increase in receipts. The intent is to prevent the Congress from profiting from "bracket creep." Some seem to believe that the indexing provisions passed in 1981 (effective in 1985) satisfy this rule, but the indexing is only for inflation, and considerable bracket creep can result from real growth. Tax burdens can also rise because of problems in defining capital income during periods of inflation, and it is impractical to resolve this problem through indexing. Consequently, indexing does not satisfy the rule, and the Senate Judiciary Committee report on S.J.R. 58, which implies that it does, is in error.

IMPLEMENTATION PROBLEMS

Advocates of constitutional or statutory limits on actual outlays, receipts, and/or deficits must face up to the problem that neither the Congress nor the President exerts any direct control over actual outcomes. Outlays, receipts, and deficits are controlled indirectly and somewhat loosely by the creation of budget authority, by laws governing eligibility for entitlement programs, and by tax, user fee, and other legislation governing receipts. Once the relevant laws are passed, it is extremely difficult to predict actual budget outcome. To provide a budget forecast, it is necessary to forecast the effects of changing inflation rates, interest rates, and unemployment rates—all of which have profound effects on outlays and receipts. For example, an unexpected rise in the unemployment rate of one percentage point can raise outlays on income-maintenance pro-grams by an amount equivalent to about 1 percent of total budget outlays, while the associated fall in receipts can be between 2 and 3 percent. At fiscal year 1983 budget levels, this implies a shift in the deficit of almost $30 billion.

In addition to being sensitive to the economy, actual outcomes are affected by unpredictable noneconomic variables. For example, outlays on agricultural programs are sensitive to crop yields. Payments for natural disasters depend upon the number of earthquakes, volcanic eruptions, hurricanes, and tornadoes. Bud-geteers must also guess the value of various property rights—for example, offshore oil leases—that will be sold over the year. And, where outlays are dependent on multiyear appropriations, it is necessary to guess how much the bureaucrats will spend in any one year. This is particularly difficult in the defense budget, where forecast errors can often be as large as $5 billion to $10 billion.

It would be difficult to forecast all of the relevant economic and noneconomic variables under the best of conditions, but given the immense uncertainties, it is hard to say that one forecast is definitely better than any other. This opens the door to game playing by politicians. The incentives to resort to overly optimistic forecasts are very strong and would be intensified by the enactment of consti-tutional and legislative restraints on budget outcomes.

For example, assume S.J.R. 58 were in place. It requires that a planned budget balance be enacted prior to the beginning of the fiscal year. That is not usually hard with a very little bit of manipulation of the assumptions. President Carter *planned* a balanced budget for fiscal 1981. The actual deficit turned out to be $58 billion. At current budget levels, a planned balanced budget could be consistent with an actual deficit of $100 billion.

S.J.R. 58 does, however, require that actual outlays not exceed planned outlays. The original version did not require that actual receipts equal or exceed planned receipts, and this allowed considerable room for actual deficits to emerge. But the more stringent constraint on outlays is problematic. Who decides whether actual outlays are on the forecast path, and when is it decided? The true value of actual outlays is not known until a month *after* the fiscal year ends.

The incentive to play games is enormous. One can imagine the Congress passing an overly optimistic budget forecast and maintaining the fiction until the fiscal year is half over. Suppose a new forecast, six months into the fiscal year, shows that outlays are running 2 percent above the plan. To adhere to the plan will then require a 4 percent cut in outlays for the six months remaining in the year. But by that time any bureaucrats worth their salt will have tied up as much of their budgets as possible in legal contracts. Cuts far greater than 4 percent will be required in the few areas in which some flexibility remains. It is in the interest of prospending legislators to delay the necessary decisions as long as possible, because the necessary corrective action becomes more and more drastic as time goes on. Under these circumstances, an impasse is highly likely. That is to say, it will be impossible to get a majority to vote to enact the necessary cuts in outlays, or the 60 percent vote necessary to sanction a budget plan containing the deficit—which would be the situation very likely to arise in such circumstances. Later the perverse incentives that emerge in such circumstances will be analyzed. It suffices here to say that the likely result is a delay that lasts long enough to give 60 percent of the legislators little choice but to approve a deficit.

As already noted, in the original version of S.J.R. 58, there was no requirement that receipts equal or exceed actual receipts. This greatly increases the incentive to make overly optimistic receipts forecasts. However, an amendment was added during the Senate floor debate that requires a 60 percent vote to raise the debt limit. In effect, this places a more stringent floor on actual receipts. But, again, this creates a strong incentive for delaying action. Once the constitutional debt limit is approached, the alternative to raising the debt limit will involve such dramatic changes in tax and/or spending laws that a 60 percent vote will probably emerge, but perhaps, as shown later, at great cost.

If a constitutional or legislative limit on actual outlays and receipts were to be made at all workable, two reforms would become essential. First, it would be necessary to change the approach to arriving at the appropriate economic and noneconomic assumptions. At a minimum, the House and Senate would have to agree to a single set of assumptions before the debate on the budget plan occurred. The incentives for unwarranted optimism would remain, but, at least, the debate over assumptions would allow some opportunity to hear from countervailing political forces. It would be desirable, but not essential, for the Administration to agree to the same assumptions, so that public debate could clearly differentiate disagreements among the main participants—the President, House, and Senate—stemming from the use of differing assumptions from disagreements stemming from different policy proposals.

An alternative would be for all participants to adopt a forecast formulated by an independent, bipartisan board of experts. This approach is taken in some states that have constitutions requiring a balanced budget.

Even if institutional reforms increase the openness and honesty of forecasting, it must be recognized that even honest forecasts can be quite wrong. To make rigid restraints on actual outlays workable, it would be essential for the budget plan to contain a sizable allowance for contingencies. Something equal to about 2 percent of total outlays should suffice in most years if forecasting could be made more honest. It must be recognized that if this is done correctly, any balanced-budget requirement becomes a requirement for having a surplus, on average. With actual deficits likely to be far in excess of $150 billion through 1985, given current policies, moving toward an actual surplus may be more than most readers can imagine.

ENFORCEMENT

It is not at all clear who pays the penalty, or even if there is a penalty, if a budget-constraining constitutional amendment or a legislative requirement is violated. The original version of S.J.R. 58 was interpreted by many to require the President to use impoundment to ensure that actual outlays would not exceed planned outlays. Since there is no inclination in Congress to give the President such power, the resolution was amended on the Senate floor to make it clear that impoundment could not be used.

It is easy to understand the feeling of unease about impoundment. Just as the Congress could use overly optimistic assumptions to rationalize almost any budget plan, a President could use overly pessimistic assumptions to rationalize slashing programs found undesirable.

The big unknown is whether the courts would become involved in enforcing the amendment. Some experts believe that the courts would regard enforcement as a "political issue" and, therefore, would stay out of the fray in order to maintain the separation of powers among the three branches of government.

There are a number of reasons why the courts might wish to avoid the issue. They would have to face two different uncertainties. The first is the issue of forecasting. A court would have to be willing to declare during a fiscal year that the forecast used by the Congress was wrong—something that cannot be proved beyond any doubt until after the fiscal year is over. There is also the problem of the escape clause that exists in almost all constitutional amendments. Theoretically, under S.J.R. 58, 60 percent of the Congress can revise the budget plan to recognize a fait accompli until the last day of the fiscal year. Would any court be willing to order the Congress to hold such a vote?

On the other side, the courts seem to be enjoying activism more and more. Whatever the final judgment of the Supreme Court, it would probably be possible to find a judge somewhere who would enjoin the Congress to do or not to do something or other. While such action was proceeding, enormous policy uncertainty could be created. And we cannot be certain that the Supreme Court would not become heavily involved in enforcement.

In conclusion, it is possible to envision anything from a hands-off attitude by the courts to an intensely activist judiciary that would soon have to form its own budget committees. The fact that the likely outcome is so unpredictable is, in my view, sufficient cause by itself for caution in passing any amendment.

EFFECTS OF FISCAL STABILIZATION POLICY

Many believe that the Federal Government has the duty to vary spending and tax laws in an attempt to use surpluses and deficits to offset cyclical fluctuations in the economy. The Keynesian theory upon which this belief rests has come under intense criticism in recent years, but even if one accepts Keynesian theory, it is hard to use this argument against constitutional amendments or legislation requiring a balanced budget.

The main intent of the proponents of such restraints is to reduce the bias that now exists to rationalize deficits on the grounds that stimulus is almost always needed. Under all of the important proposals, stimulative policies can still be enacted if 60 percent of the legislature can be convinced that they are appropriate. The original S.J.R. 58 even allows for built-in stabilizing forces to work on the tax side without a super majority, although the later version makes this impossible because of the new constitutional debt limit.

Moreover, nothing in pure Keynesian stabilization theory requires varying the deficit. Varying a surplus will do just as well, and the expected response that this is totally impractical simply reveals the strong bias toward deficits that exists in our current system.

There might be transition problems if the constitutional amendment became effective at a time when deficits were running to 4 to 5 percent of GNP, and that is quite possible given the current budget outlook. Even a non-Keynesian would have some concern about the adjustment costs of eliminating such a deficit overnight.

However, the political constraints upon reducing the deficit are so severe that reducing the deficit too fast should be the least of our worries, regardless of the constitutional or legislative restraints in effect at the time. It just will not happen. Political constraints will become binding far earlier than economic restraints.

POSSIBILITY OF PERVERSE RESULTS

It is, in my view, highly probable that the passage of a constitutional amendment would do more harm than good. The same cannot be said about legislative approaches, primarily because they are so easy to change. The potential for harm stems from the fact that the most important constitutional approaches are too flexible in some respects and too rigid in others.

Curious incentives stem from the fact that the restraint can be overridden by a super majority. This makes the proposed constitutional amendments very different from the typical state restraint from which there is no escape. (Only two states allow a super majority to approve a deficit.)

The curiosity results because the amendments typically require 60 percent, or some other super majority, to approve a deficit, whether that deficit is large or small. In other words, it is as hard to approve a $1.00 as a $300 billion deficit. Similarly, where a constitutional debt limit is included, a given super majority is required whether the limit is increased by a large or a small amount.

Past experience with the Congressional Budget Act indicates that it is frequently impossible at first to get a simple majority to approve any budget. Faced with such impasses, the President and congressional leadership have engaged in logrolling, promising this or that member of Congress a bit extra for his or her favorite program in order to get a vote for the overall budget.

Suppose that under a constitutional amendment like S.J.R. 58, we approach the beginning of a fiscal year with laws in place that essentially ensure a deficit. The leadership can attempt to get a majority behind outlay reductions or tax increases that lead to a balanced budget, or to get 60 percent to sanction a deficit. Given past experience, the first attempts to achieve either solution are likely to fail. Logrolling to break the impasse is very difficult if a balanced budget is to be pursued, because the requirement of a balanced budget limits the amount that can be spent to purchase votes. On the other hand, it is as cheap to buy a vote for a big deficit as for a small deficit if a super majority is to be pursued. In other words, a new bias favoring a deficit is introduced. The main effect of a 60 percent vote requirement is to allow legislators to raise their price above that that would be required if only a simple majority were needed.

The price would probably be even higher if a vote were required to sanction a deficit that emerged during the year because the original assumptions were too optimistic. Indeed, as already explained, the incentive to delay the vote as long as possible would be particularly strong for prospending factions. This would create a lot of policy uncertainty among investors; and the bureaucracy could not make spending plans with any certainty.

In other words, the possibility cannot be ruled out that a constitutional amendment would lead to higher spending and deficit levels and that government policy would become even more erratic. One might conclude that an amendment without escape clauses would be preferable, but greater rigidity raises a completely different set of problems. Even those with an escape clause are probably rigid enough to do great harm.

The basic problem is that constitutional amendments restraining the budget are very easy to evade. The budget represents only one set of tools through which the government affects the economy. Government regulation is often almost a perfect substitute for taxing and spending. For example, an immensely costly national health-insurance scheme could be established with little impact on the budget. The government could simply require that firms buy health insurance, meeting certain government-designed standards, for their employees. President Nixon once proposed such a scheme, but it was not passed.

Similarly, loan guarantees, government-sponsored corporations, and a host of other tools can be used to manipulate the allocation of economic resources. This would not be of much concern if the worst that could be said of such off-budget activities was that they made a constitutional amendment less effective. But the problem is more serious than that. However badly we may control budget totals, we clearly do a worse job controlling the costs of regulation and other off-budget activities. Increasing the incentive to engage in such activities—and it is already very powerful—would make government less efficient.

One could go on and on regarding the perverse incentives created by a constitutional amendment. The nature of the perversity varies considerably with the nature of the amendment. For example, an amendment limiting only outlays encourages the use of programs having negative outlays and tax expenditures to manipulate resources. Balanced-budget amendments encourage the redefinition of outlays, receipts, and deficits. There is no end to the mischief that can be done.

EXPERIENCE AT THE STATE LEVEL[6]

All but two states—Vermont and Connecticut—have some sort of constitutional or legislative restraint on their budget totals. Thirty-nine have constitutional restraints on spending, receipts, or deficits.[5]

It is therefore not reassuring to note that the growth of state spending and debt has far exceeded the growth of federal spending and debt since World War II. However, it should be noted that over the long run, most state constitutional restraints have attempted solely to control debt issues and not to limit the growth of spending or tax burdens. Efforts to limit the total size of state governments or particular tax burdens, as with Proposition 13 in California, have a fairly limited history. I doubt that they will be at all effective, but it will take a while before the evidence accumulates.

Nevertheless, no restraint is in place very long before efforts to evade it begin.[6] A common practice is to establish independent agencies outside of the budget. The debt issued by such agencies typically bears a "moral" rather than a legal guarantee. Nine states only issue debt that is not legally guaranteed. The number of independent agencies authorized to issue nonguaranteed debt range from 27 in Alabama to none in Oregon. New York has 20 and Louisiana 19.

If such agencies were constrained, little harm would be done, but usually they escape normal budget controls. New York has all sorts of constitutional constraints on its budget, but almost went bankrupt in the middle 1970s. Its Urban Development Corporation expanded irresponsibly and eventually collapsed financially. Its so-called "moral obligation bonds" turned out not to be very moral as investors suffered severe capital losses.

CONCLUSIONS

This analysis provides little encouragement that constitutional constraints can effectively counter the biases in the current system toward higher spending levels and deficits than the typical voter desires. It is not only that such amendments would not work perfectly; nothing ever does. The problem is that such amendments are likely to do more harm than good.

That is because perverse incentives are created, and evasion is so easy and so likely to be destructive to economic efficiency. If the electorate were strongly behind the goals of such amendments, evasion would be less likely. But the empirical record of ever-growing deficits indicates that while the public may desire balanced budgets, it opposes deficits less strongly than the policies necessary for their elimination. A budget-restraining amendment is therefore likely to go the way of the prohibition amendment.

A major part of the problem is that the public remains woefully uneducated regarding the true nature of budget trends. If one believes public-opinion polls, the public strongly desires a balanced budget, higher defense spending, no cuts in social security, and lower tax burdens. A casual glance at budget trends indicates that they cannot have all of those things. But there is no reason that the public should be informed on such issues. Politicians are promising the people they can have all that they want, while fostering the notion that it can be obtained by cutting welfare and waste and fraud out of the budget. There is little recognition that by 1985, defense, social security, health, and interest on the debt will constitute almost 80 percent of outlays, or that one year's increase in social security will be enough to pay for almost an entire food-stamp program plus the entire Aid to Families of Dependent Children program.

Opponents of the budget-limiting amendments are often challenged to come up with their own cures for the budget dilemma. Proponents argue as though an unworkable cure is better than no cure at all.

One could go on at great length regarding possible amendments to the Budget Act that would convey better information to decision makers and the public. I think that a slight increase in the impoundment power of the President would also be useful, if carefully constrained still to require the tacit consent of the Congress.

However, I cannot claim to have any very satisfactory answers to the dilemma. The sort of reforms that I have in mind would have a marginal impact at best. One ultimately comes back to the fundamental constraint on the formulation of budget policies: that the public is abysmally uninformed, and that only the public that can eventually constrain the politicians. It is the lack of public information that allows special-interest groups to act their will so often, and it is the lack of public information that will allow—and does allow at the state level—politicians to run roughshod over any constitutional constraints.

Recent events do show, however, that the situation is not without hope. When the pain intensifies, the public tends to become better informed. I do not remember when more attention has been devoted to budget issues in the media, and it has had a major, though still far from adequate, impact on congressional decision making. Certainly, the quantity of budget information available to the public has greatly increased in recent years. Now it is necessary to start to work on the quality of that information.

NOTES

1. Kenneth Arrow, *Social Choice and Individual Values*. New York: John Wiley and Sons, Inc., 1951.

2. Mancur Olsen, *The Logic of Collective Action*. Cambridge: Harvard University Press, 1965.

3. Richard E. Wagner and James M. Buchanan, *Democracy in Deficit: The Political Legacy of Lord Keynes*. New York: Academic Press, 1977.

4. Arthur F. Burns, "Prudent Steps Toward a Balanced Budget," in W.S. Moore and Rudolph G. Penner, eds., *The Constitution and the Budget*. Washington, D.C.: American Enterprise Institute, 1980, pp. 46–49.

5. Allen Schick, "Negative Evidence: The Effect of Constitutional Restrictions on State Debt," in *Balancing the Federal Budget and Limiting Federal Spending: Constitutional and Statutory Approaches*. Washington, D.C.: The Congressional Budget Office, 1982, pp. 121–128.

6. B.U. Ratchford, *American State Debts*. Durham: Duke University Press, 1971.

GLOSSARY

Balanced budget: a budget position in which expenditures equal revenues

Bracket creep: increasing tax burdens, owing largely to inflation, which push taxpayers into higher brackets with higher marginal tax rates

Bretton Woods: the system of fixed exchange rates and convertibility of currencies that characterized the international monetary system from the end of World War II to the early 1970s, as opposed to the present system of floating exchange rates; a system in which the dollar was convertible into gold at $35 per ounce

Budget authority: legal permission from Congress for government agencies to enter into obligations requiring financial expenditures; normally takes the form of appropriations that allow the obligations and expenditures; obligations usually liquidated by "outlays"— payments in cash or checks

Capital budgeting: a budget-operating procedure that distinguishes programs involving capital assets that yield services beyond the current accounting period, such as roads and bridges, from current operating expenses

CBO: Congressional Budget Office

CED: Committee for Economic Development

The Congressional Budget and Impoundment Control Act of 1974: established the Congressional Budget Office (CBO), and was intended to enhance the role of Congress in budgetary decisions and to establish greater control over budget totals

Crowding-out: the idea that the financing of unusually large federal deficits in credit markets will take place at the expense of private borrowers, who will be priced out by rising interest rates

Economic Recovery Tax Act of 1981: a program of broadly based tax cuts intended to promote incentives to save and invest; included a reduction in marginal income-tax rates of 25 percent over three years, faster depreciation, and indexation of personal tax brackets for inflation starting in 1985

Employment Act of 1946: set a national goal of full employment (all those willing to work can find work at existing wages); established a formal governmental responsibility for economic growth and job creation

FFB: Federal Financing Bank

FHA: Federal Housing Administration

Fiscal policy: the use of budget expenditures, taxes, and deficits (or surpluses) as tools to achieve objectives for the total economy

Fisher, Irving: an American economist whose name is often associated with the quantity theory of money and the distinction between real and nominal interest rates

Full-employment budget: a restatement of the actual budget based on the assumption that the economy is at full employment

GAO: General Accounting Office

Gross national product (GNP): the total output of a nation's goods and services in current dollars (nominal GNP) or in constant dollars (real GNP)

Impoundment: Presidential withholding of authorized funds from use

Keynesian Economics: a theory of the forces that determine changes in total output and employment based on John Maynard Keynes' *The General Theory of Employment, Interest, and Money*; in general, sought active use of fiscal policy to stimulate the total economy

LM: a function that provides combinations of income and interest rates at which the demand for money (L) equals the supply of money (M)

Monetarism: a body of reasoning that stresses the primary importance of controlling the rate of growth of money and a direct link between money, growth, and prospective inflation

Monetary policy: the use of central-bank actions (open-market operations, changes in the discount rate, and reserve requirements) to influence economic activity through money, credit, and interest rates; in the United States, the Federal Reserve System functions as the central bank

Monetizing deficits: central-bank provision of additional reserves to the banking system to promote the purchase of U.S. government securities at appropriate rates of interest, and actual acquisition of government securities by the Federal Reserve itself

Money supply: refers to narrow and broad measures of money: for example, M_1 is the sum of currency, demand deposits, travelers' checks, and other checkable deposits; M_2 includes M_1 plus (non-institutional) money-market mutual fund balances, money-market deposit accounts, savings and small time deposits, and other items; M_3 includes M_2 plus large time deposits and several other items

NAIRU: the nonaccelerating inflation rate of unemployment, or the unemployment rate below which inflation will accelerate

National income (and product) accounts: a statistical statement of the size and composition of national output and its relative income flows

OECD: Organization for Economic Cooperation and Development

Off-budget activities: federal and federally related transactions that are excluded from the budget totals

OMB: Office of Management and Budget

Phillips Curve: a description of the relation between changes in money wages (or inflation) and unemployment; in its simplest form, expresses the proposition that higher inflation is associated with low unemployment and vice versa

PSBR: public-sector borrowing requirement

Rational expectations: a system of thought that emphasizes that in a market-clearing system, individuals draw expectations from informed appraisal of the state of the economy and the probable course of economic policy; in contrast to "adaptive expectations," which are drawn simply from recent past experience

SDR: Special drawing rights. A form of internationally agreed currency created by the International Monetary Fund

S.J.R. 58: a constitutional amendment requiring a balanced budget; passed the Senate during the 97th Congress, but fell short of the two-thirds majority required in the House of Representatives

Special Analysis D: Investment, Operating, and Other Federal Outlays—an analysis accompanying the budget document that separates both "on-budget" and "off-budget" items into those of an operating nature and those of a longer-term, or investment, nature.

Stagflation: the condition in which an economy experiences a low rate of growth of real GNP and an unsatisfactorily high rate of inflation

Steady state: a theoretical device to describe the passage of an economy or an economic process, without change in level or composition, from one time period to another; for example, an economy whose components are stable or are all growing at the same rate

Structural change: a fundamental change that is independent of particular phases of the business cycle, as opposed to a "cyclical" change that is related to specific phases of the business cycle

Supply-side economics: a policy approach that emphasizes the importance of increasing the rewards for productive activity on the part of labor and capital (for example, through reduced tax rates) as contrasted with the emphasis on demand management in Keynesian economics

Transfer payment: the channeling of purchasing power by the Federal Government without any specific productive service in return; for example, social-security payments, unemployment compensation, aid to families of dependent children, food stamps

Uncontrollable budget items: outlays determined by already existing statutes or by other factors that place them beyond administrative control at the start of the fiscal year (for example, veterans' benefits and beneficiaries eligible under social security)

Unified budget: a statement of the receipts and expenditures of the Federal Government and its trust funds, excluding off-budget transactions

U.S. Budget and Accounting Act of 1921: an attempt to reform budget procedures; established the Bureau of the Budget and ceded congressional coordination of federal spending and revenue estimates to the Executive Branch

Zero-base budgeting: a budgeting process intended to improve efficiency by examining alternatives and eliminating unnecessary activities; requires managers to examine programs at various funding levels, and then to rank these programs in order of importance

CONGRESSIONAL BUDGET TIMETABLE

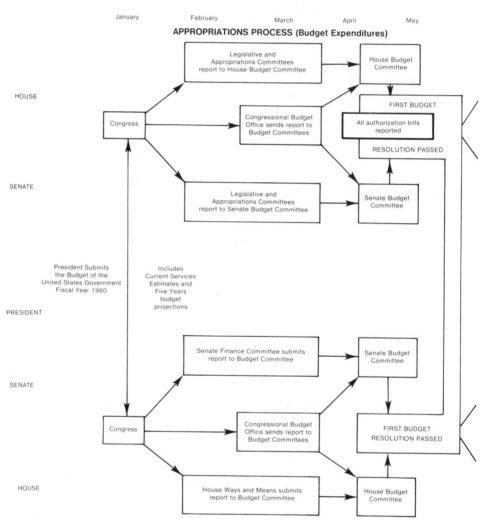

Source: Adapted from Michael E. Levy (assisted by Delos R. Smith and Steven Malin), *The Federal Budget: Its Impact on the Economy.* The Conference Board, April 1975 through June 1979.

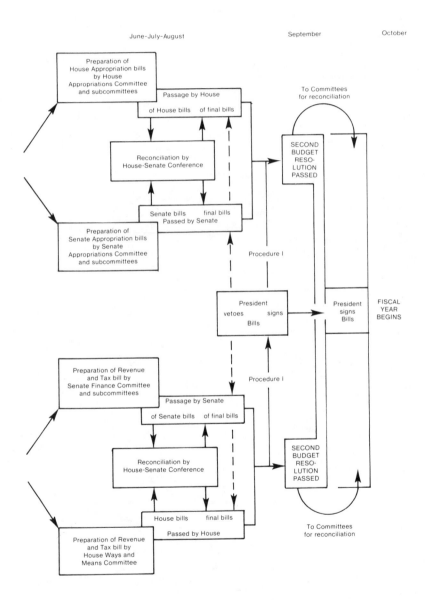

June–July–August   September   October

Preparation of
House Appropriation bills
by House
Appropriations Committee
and subcommittees

Passage by House

of House bills   of final bills

To Committees
for reconciliation

Reconciliation by
House-Senate Conference

SECOND
BUDGET
RESO-
LUTION
PASSED

Senate bills   final bills
Passed by Senate

Preparation of
Senate Appropriation bills
by Senate
Appropriations Committee
and subcommittees

Procedure I

President
vetoes   signs
Bills

President
signs
Bills

FISCAL
YEAR
BEGINS

Preparation of Revenue
and Tax bill by
Senate Finance Committee
and subcommittees

Procedure I

Passage by Senate

of Senate bills   of final bills

Reconciliation by
House-Senate Conference

SECOND
BUDGET
RESO-
LUTION
PASSED

House bills   final bills
Passed by House

Preparation of Revenue
and Tax bill by
House Ways and
Means Committee

To Committees
for reconciliation

INDEX

ABOUT THE EDITOR
AND CONTRIBUTORS

Albert T. Sommers is Senior Vice President and Chief Economist of The Conference Board since 1972. He is a Fellow of the National Association of Business Economists, and past winner of the Butler Prize of the New York Association of Business Economists. Mr. Sommers was chairperson of the Price Advisory Committee to the Council on Wage and Price Stability in 1980. He was a lecturer in economics at Columbia University, and is economic adviser to the Ford Foundation. He is a Director of the National Bureau of Economic Research and a number of private corporations.

Robert Eisner is William R. Kenan Professor of Economics at Northwestern University (1974–   ). He joined Northwestern in 1952 as an Assistant Professor of Economics. In 1954, he was made Associate Professor of Economics, and was Professor of Economics from 1960 to 1974.

Benjamin M. Friedman is Professor of Economics at Harvard University (1980–   ), where he has taught since 1972. Before that, he was an Assistant to the Director, Division of Research and Statistics, Board of Governors of the Federal Reserve System. Mr. Friedman also serves as Director of Financial Markets and Monetary Economic Research at the National Bureau of Economic Research.

Robert W. Hartman is Senior Analyst for Budget Process at the Congressional Budget Office (1982–   ). From 1971 to 1982, Dr. Hartman was a Senior Fellow at The Brookings Institution. He has taught economics at Brandeis University and the University of California-Berkeley Graduate School of Public Policy. Dr. Hartman is the author of numerous books and articles, including *Pay and Pensions for Federal Workers*.

Sidney L. Jones is Resident Scholar at the American Enterprise Institute (1979–   ). He has also been a Lecturer at Georgetown University since 1979. Dr. Jones has been Assistant to the Board of Governors of the Federal Reserve System; Counsellor to the Secretary and Assistant Secretary of the Treasury for Economic Policy; and Deputy Assistant to the President, Deputy to the Counsellor to the President for Economic Policy, and Assistant Secretary of Commerce for Economic Affairs.

Allan H. Meltzer is John M. Olin Professor of Political Economy and Public Policy at Carnegie-Mellon University. Dr. Meltzer has been Cochairperson of the Shadow Open Market Committee; cochairperson of the Shadow European Economic Policy Committee; coeditor of the Carnegie-Mellon Conference Series on Political Economy; and Visiting Professor at Getullo Vargas Foundation, Harvard University, the University of Chicago, the Hoover Institution, and Stanford University.

Rudolph G. Penner is Director of Tax Policy Studies at the American Enterprise Institute (1977–   ). He was Assistant Director for Economic Policy at the Office of Management and Budget from 1975 to 1977. He has also served as Deputy Assistant Secretary for Economic Affairs, Department of Housing and Urban Development, and as Senior Staff Economist at the Council of Economic Advisers. Prior to 1975, Mr. Penner was Professor of Economics at the University of Rochester, and held teaching positions at Princeton University and at the University College, Dar-es-Salaam, Tanzania.

Alice M. Rivlin is Director of the Congressional Budget Office (1975–   ). She is the author of *Systematic Thinking for Social Action* (1971), and a coauthor of three volumes on the federal budget, *Setting National Priorities* (1971–1973). Before becoming Director of the CBO, Mrs. Rivlin was a Senior Fellow at The Brookings Institution. She also served as Assistant Secretary for Planning and Evaluation in the U.S. Department of Health, Education, and Welfare.

Paul A. Samuelson is Institute Professor at the Massachusetts Institute of Technology (1966–   ). He received the Nobel

Memorial Prize in Economics in 1970. Dr. Samuelson was an adviser to Presidents Kennedy and Johnson, and has been a consultant to government, foundations, and private businesses. He is the author of the well-known text *Economics: An Introductory Analysis*.

Leonard J. Santow is Principal at Griggs & Santow Incorporated (1982–   ) and Advisor to the Board of the J. Henry Schroder Bank & Trust Company. Dr. Santow is a coauthor of the Griggs and Santow Report. He has held previous positions with the Federal Reserve Bank of Dallas, Aubrey G. Lanston & Co., Lehman Brothers, and the Schroeder Organizations. Dr. Santow is active in senior management of several major corporations, and serves on the Board of Directors of a number of firms.

Elmer B. Staats completed his 15-year term as Comptroller General of the United States in 1981. He previously served as Deputy Director of the Budget under Presidents Truman, Eisenhower, Kennedy, and Johnson. Mr. Staats currently serves on the Board of Directors of several corporations and nonprofit organizations. He is President of the Harry S Truman Scholarship Foundation, and is a Councillor of The Conference Board.

Herbert Stein is A. Willis Robertson Professor of Economics at the University of Virginia (1974–   ) and Senior Fellow of the American Enterprise Institute (1975–   ). Mr. Stein served as a member of the President's Council of Economic Advisers from 1969 to 1971, and as Chairperson of the Council from 1972 to 1974. He is now a member of President Reagan's Economic Policy Advisory Board.

James Tobin is Sterling Professor of Economics at Yale University (1957–   ). He was a member of the President's Council of Economic Advisers from 1961 to 1962. Dr. Tobin served as Chairperson of Yale's Department of Economics from 1974 to 1978. He is a recipient of the Nobel Memorial Prize in Economics.

Henry C. Wallich is a member of the Board of Governors of the Federal Reserve System (1974–   ). Formerly Professor of Eco-

D